To Sharon
Make Joy to ♡ W9-DGG-454

Ay Bak

Adult Children of
Parental Alienation Syndrome

Adult Children
of Parental
Alienation Syndrome

Breaking the Ties that Bind

Amy J. L. Baker

W. W. Norton & Company
New York • London

For information about permission to
reproduce selections from this book, write to
Permissions, W. W. Norton & Company, Inc.,
500 Fifth Avenue, New York, NY 10110

Production Manager: Leeann Graham
Manufacturing by R. R. Donnelley–Harrisonburg

Library of Congress Cataloging-in-Publication Data

Baker, Amy J. L.
   Adult children of parental alienation syndrome: breaking the ties
that bind / Amy J.L. Baker.
       p.   cm.
   "A Norton professional book."
   Includes bibliographical references and index.
   ISBN-13: 978-0-393-70519-5
   ISBN-10: 0-393-70519-6
      1. Parent and adult child.   2. Parental alienation syndrome.
   3. Psychological child abuse.   4. Adult children—Interviews
   I. Title.
HQ755.86.B33   2007
362.76—dc22   2006047155

W. W. Norton & Company, Inc., 500 Fifth Avenue, New York, N.Y. 10110
www.wwnorton.com

W. W. Norton & Company, Ltd., Castle House, 75/76 Wells St., London
W1T 3QT

1   3   5   7   9   0   8   6   4   2

This book is dedicated to the adult children of parental alienation syndrome and their targeted parents, may they find their way back to each other.

> We must never forget that we may also find meaning in life even when confronted with a hopeless situation, when facing a fate that cannot be changed. For what then matters is to bear witness to the uniquely human potential at its best, which is to transform a personal tragedy into a triumph, to turn one's predicament into a human achievement—Victor Frankl, *Man's Search for Meaning*

Contents

Author's Note

THIS BOOK IS BASED ON INTERVIEWS WITH 40 INDIVIDUALS (SEE APpendix) who believed that they had been turned against one parent by the other parent. Their stories are described in this book, along with clinical and developmental theory that places these experiences in context. For ease of reading and interpretation, statements are made throughout the book about the parents of these individuals. It is important, however, for the reader to bear in mind that everything that is written about these parents is based on what the interviewees described about their experience and my interpretation of these descriptions. At no time did I interview the parents or have access to documentation regarding their behavior.

Consistent with standards of research in psychology (American Psychological Association, 2001), the participants were offered confidentiality for the interviews. It was deemed likely that in general they would not want others to know about their participation in the study and this was confirmed during the interviews. All names, with the exception of Robin, are pseudonyms.

Acknowledgments

THERE ARE SEVERAL PEOPLE TO WHOM I OWE THANKS, WITHOUT whom this project would not have been possible. First I owe a debt of gratitude to my old friend Sam Stoloff, who lent his literary agent skills to me on an ad hoc basis, especially in providing a much needed critique of early drafts of the proposal. Dr. Richard Warshak generously offered detailed suggestions for improving the proposal as well as enthusiastic encouragement for the project. I also wish to thank Lorna Goldberg for providing me with ongoing insight and understanding, especially on the issue of cults. She was generous and supportive, sharing books and ideas, as well as professional contacts. Dr. Deirdre Rand has also been a supporter of this project, referencing it in her work and encouraging others to do the same. I am immensely grateful to Dr. S. Richard Sauber who has been a champion of this project, publishing two chapters as journal articles and helping me forge professional collaborations. My team at Norton has been a dream to work with, including Deborah Malmud who believed in this project, Michael McGandy who shepherded it through the process, and my copyeditor Patricia Connolly, whose meticulous editing vastly improved the text. My husband Paul provided several critical line edits and conceptual reconsiderations that added depth and nuance to the material in several places. His fingerprints and heart are all over this project. I also want to thank my daughter Alianna, who taught me what it means to love a child. And, finally, I owe everything to the individuals who participated in the interviews. They shared their stories, their lives, their pain, and their feelings with honesty, openness, and a sense of desire to help others that was nothing short of remarkable. I hope that when they read this book they feel that they have achieved their goal.

Four of the chapters in this book first appeared as articles: Chapter 1 appeared in *American Journal of Family Therapy, 34,* (2005) 63–78 and Chapter 7 appeared in *American Journal of Family Therapy, 33,* (2005) 289–302. Both are reproduced (with changes) by permission of Taylor & Francis Group, LLC., http://www.taylorandfrancis.com. Chapter 2 appeared in *Cultic Studies Review, 4,* (2005), and is reprinted with changes courtesy of the International Cultic Studies Association. Chapter 3 appeared in *American Journal of Forensic Psychology, 23,* (2005) 43–62 and is reprinted with changes courtesy of the *American Journal of Forensic Psychology.*

Adult Children of
Parental Alienation Syndrome

Introduction

Ask a question and you're a fool for three minutes; do not ask a question and you're a fool for the rest of your life.
—Chinese Proverb

THE THREE FOLLOWING INDIVIDUALS ARE VICTIMS OF PARENTAL alienation: the attempt on the part of one parent to disrupt the relationship between the child and the other parent. In its extreme form parental alienation can evolve into what is known as parental alienation syndrome (PAS).

Kate's Story

Kate, 21, was born in California. Her mother was 30 when she met Kate's father. He was younger but had been married before. Kate was the only child of her parents' marriage. Kate recalled a stormy marriage, which ended when she was a young child: "My mother changed the locks on my dad while he was at work; I remember because she asked me to get her a screwdriver. And then I remember a few nights later my dad knocking on the window. He tried a few more times to come over but my mom was pretty adamant that he not come in."

Following the separation Kate had visitation with her father every other weekend. "And it was supposed to be every

Wednesday night for dinner but my mom kind of started to go off it." Additional alienation strategies used by Kate's mother included not passing on letters and gifts sent to Kate by her father and vehement disparagement. "Growing up I got the idea that my dad was everything she had ever hated and that he was a horrible monster." Her mother also instigated conflict between Kate and her father, which spoiled whatever time they did spend together. These alienation strategies created confusion in Kate's mind about her father. "Overall it made me very doubtful of what he would say and why he was doing what he was doing, whatever it was. Every action he ever did, everything he ever did for me I would question, was there some reason why he was doing this? I was very into the ulterior motive idea because my mother kept saying there were reasons why, that he didn't do things because he loved me."

Kate did not recall having a close relationship with her mother, who nonetheless threatened to abandon her if she went to live with her father: "If I went there I wouldn't be able to talk to her anymore so living with her and being able to see him meant I was able to see both of them. Whereas choosing him meant I might lose her." However, when Kate turned 18 years old she moved out of her mother's home and at the time of the interview she was living with her father. Over time she had come to believe that her mother's behavior was manipulative and spiteful. Kate appreciated her father's ability to maintain a relationship with her and that he kept his equanimity throughout the stormy times. "He understood that if the ugliness touched me it would hurt and these are things a child should not have to deal with. You should be honest and tell the child but don't force your opinion so much. He understood that if you are honest with your own opinions, they'll figure it out," which in the end, is what happened with Kate.

Larissa's Story

Larissa experienced parental alienation from her father despite the fact that her parents remained married and lived together for her entire childhood. The alienation began when Larissa was about 12 years old. "My mother always made both my brother and me feel that our father was somehow to blame for everything." Larissa recalled that her mother created negative feelings and distance in Larissa toward her father by telling outright lies or grossly exaggerating the negative aspects of his character. "Every day there'd be some attempt by her, some tale she'd tell me to turn me against my father." Larissa felt that her mother resented Larissa's ability to relate positively with her father and would convey disapproval at any sign of camaraderie between them. "If I so much as spoke to him in a civilized way. . . . This disapproval was in the form of throwing sour looks my way, and then turning her back and ignoring me." In addition, Larissa's mother repeatedly told her things that, if true—some were and some were not—were guaranteed to make her dislike her father. For example, Larissa was told that her father could not stand her; that he told her mother that he did not find the mother attractive, which made Larissa feel furious at her father and sorry for her mother; that he was a homosexual; and that he was having an affair.

As a result of this ongoing denigration Larissa began to hate her father. "Eventually, I grew to detest him with a truly visceral hate. I couldn't stand to be in the same room with him, or even talk to him or have him talk to me. I became my mother's puppet, her ally against my father." Larissa did not reevaluate her relationship with either of her parents until she was an adult, after going through a very difficult adolescence filled with low achievement, self-loathing, and depression.

From being alienated from my father and hating him while being in thrall to my mother, I went to wondering about my father, not trusting my mother, and hating myself. I began to think I was capable only of hating people. It seemed as if perhaps I always needed someone to dislike, and I felt a very hateful person for this.

As an adult Larissa had tried to maintain some connection with her father until his death, but had not spoken to her mother for several years. Although she was happily married, she chose not to have children, which she attributed to a fear of them hating her as she had hated her father.

Jonah's Story

Jonah was 8 years old when his parents divorced. His father, a man unafraid to use physical violence against his family, threatened Jonah's mother in order to obtain joint custody. Initially Jonah lived half of each week with his mother and the other half with his father. During this period Jonah was exposed to an intense campaign of denigration of his mother by his father, and Jonah came to believe that, "Everyone else was wrong and my father was right and my father was the only person who actually cared about me and everyone else wanted to do me harm." Although Jonah spent half of each week with his mother, their relationship was conflict-ridden. Jonah's father had successfully created a system to interfere with the time that Jonah spent with her: Jonah would have to wait for his father's call at four o'clock every afternoon after school and eight o'clock each evening. During these calls his father would induce intense feelings of resentment in Jonah toward his mother for making him spend time with her. He was also trained to spy on her and report back to his father on her socializing and spending habits. Jonah, at his father's behest, became physically and verbally abusive toward his mother. Eventually visitation became untenable and Jonah moved in with his father full time. All contact between Jonah and his mother ceased for several years, and Jonah lived completely in his father's world. Jonah was not allowed to speak to his siblings, who remained with his mother; he was taught to despise them; he was not even allowed to accept gifts from them. Jonah now understands that he lived in fear of his father's disapproval.

> My father was an alcoholic and basically when he would come home drunk . . . . It was the fear that he instilled in me if I didn't comply with his demands that harm was going to come to either himself or the rest of my family. My father—when he would come home drunk at night—would make me confess, espouse my faith and allegiance to him, and if I didn't do it he would kill himself and during the rages when he came home drunk—this continued for about three or four years—he would get his gun out and say he would kill himself if I didn't do that.

It was not until many years later that Jonah came to realize that his father's control over him was outside the bounds of normal parent–child relationships, and that in order to appease his father he had made many personal sacrifices, including forgoing a relationship with his mother.

THE PARENTAL ALIENATION SYNDROME

According to noted psychiatrist, researcher, and child advocate Richard Gardner (1998), PAS occurs when one parent in a post-divorce custody arrangement successfully manipulates the children to turn against the other parent. In its most extreme form, children report that they despise or are frightened of their parent and steadfastly refuse to have any relationship whatsoever with him or her. PAS, Gardner noted, is a disturbance in which children are preoccupied with unjustified deprecation and criticism of a parent. Although the debate regarding the existence of PAS as a formal psychological syndrome continues to be waged in the professional and legal communities (e.g., Johnston & Kelly, 2004; Warshak, 2001b), few deny that some children placed in the middle of intense postdivorce conflict align with one parent against the other. When this occurs in the absence of a rational and legitimate cause (such as abuse or neglect), parental alienation syndrome has occurred.

According to psychologist Douglas Darnall (1998) there are three types of parents who undertake to alienate their children from the other parent: naïve, active, and obsessed. In his experience most, if not all, parents occasionally will behave as naïve alienators, making negative comments about the other parent such as, "Your father better be on time. He has no idea how wrong it is to be late picking you up." Despite momentary lapses, naïve alienators usually support the child's relationship with the other parent.

It is with the more determined and intense alienation (active and obsessed) that problems arise. Active alienators understand that they should try to support the child's relationship with the other parent but sometimes let their intense hurt or anger cause them to lose control over their behavior or over what they say. Later, they may regret how they behaved. It is not their objective to destroy the child's relationship with the other parent, but they cannot always control their anger and frustration, especially during prolonged court battles over custody and visitation.

In contrast, obsessed alienators intentionally aim to destroy the relationship between the child and the other parent. They cannot separate their own negative feelings toward the other parent from the child's independent relationship. They convince themselves that the other parent is harmful and it is their duty to save the children from this parent. According to Darnall (1998), a typical statement would be, "I love my children. If the court cannot protect them from their abusive father, I will. Even though he has never abused the children, I know it is just a matter of time. The children are frightened of their father. If they do not want to see him, I am not going to force them. They are old enough to make up their own minds." The obsessed alienator has a mission to align the children wholly to his or her side to the exclusion of a relationship with the targeted parent, and aims to have the children feel and think about the targeted parent exactly the way he or she does. Characteristics of obsessed alienators include trying to destroy the children's relationship with the targeted parent, enmeshing the children's personalities and beliefs about the targeted parent with their own, complete conviction in the badness of the targeted parent, and willingness to repeatedly go to court to "save the child" regardless of the financial and emotional costs.

When obsessed alienating parents are successful, they can induce the parental alienation syndrome in their children, which according to Gardner (1998) has eight primary manifestations in child victims:

1. There is a campaign of denigration against the targeted parent, the child becoming obsessed with hatred of him or her. Parents who were once loved and valued seemingly overnight become hated and feared. This often happens so quickly that the targeted parent cannot believe that a loving child has turned into a hateful, spiteful person who refuses to so much as share a meal. The campaign of denigration is all-inclusive.

All of a sudden there is nothing of value in the targeted parent and the child behaves as if there was never a meaningful relationship and no history of positive experiences. It is important to note that when there is a legitimate reason for the child's fear and hostility toward the targeted parent, such as abuse or neglect, the negative reaction to the parent is not considered PAS. It is only when there is no legitimate cause and yet the child behaves as if the targeted parent is to be feared and despised that the most likely explanation is PAS. Gardner also highlighted the fact that the hatred expressed by a PAS child reflects much of what the alienating parent has encouraged the child to believe about the targeted parent but also includes a unique contribution made by the child. That is, "the child's contributions will piggyback on the parent's indoctrinations and provide elaborations not even mentioned by the programming parent" (1998, p. 77). It was this that led Gardner to conclude that more than programming was at work.

2. There are weak, frivolous, and absurd rationalizations for the depreciation of the targeted parent. The objections made in the campaign of denigration are often not of the magnitude that would lead a child to hate a parent, such as slurping soup or serving spicy food.

3. There is a lack of ambivalence about the alienating parent on the child's part. It is a truism of development that children are ambivalent about both of their parents. Even the best of parents are imperfect or set limits for their children that cause resentment and frustration. A hallmark of PAS, however, is that the child expresses no ambivalence about the alienating parent, demonstrating an automatic, reflexive, idealized support. The child acts as if she or he has no mixed feelings or never has negative reactions to the alienating parent. One parent becomes all good while the other becomes all bad. Even much older children who typically express mixed feelings about all sorts of people in their lives (teachers, friends, coaches, and so forth) claim to have no mixed feelings whatsoever for their alienating parent. As one PAS child proudly proclaimed, "I love my father to death."

4. Children strongly assert that the decision to reject the other parent is their own. This is what Gardner (1998) called the "In-

dependent Thinker" phenomenon in which children adamantly claim that the negative feelings are wholly their own and the alienating parents defend the children's right to make their own decisions regarding visitation. This independent thinker phenomenon contributes to the difficulty in countering PAS. An observer might conclude that such children have been brainwashed or unduly influenced but their experience is authentic to themselves. The more one tries to talk PAS children out of their beliefs, the more attached to those beliefs they become. The ownership children take of the alienation through the independent thinker phenomenon is one of the strongest weapons alienating parents have at their disposal. Such children no longer require the alienating parent to tell them what to believe because they have adopted those beliefs themselves.

5. There is an absence of guilt about the treatment of the targeted parent. PAS children will make statements such as, "He doesn't deserve to see me." Gratitude for gifts, favors, or financial support provided by the targeted parent is nonexistent. PAS children will try to get whatever they can from the targeted parent, believing that it is owed to them and that the parent is a despicable person who does not deserve to be treated with respect or gratitude. Psychologist Richard Warshak (2001a) has noted the particularly negative effect of this aspect of PAS on the character of the children, who are encouraged to be selfish, manipulative, and exploitive.

6. These children show reflexive support for the alienating parent in the parental conflict, with no willingness or attempt to be impartial when faced with interparental conflicts, and no interest in hearing the targeted parent's point of view. As Gardner noted, PAS children often make the case for the alienating parent better than the parent does. Nothing the targeted parent could do or say would make any difference to the PAS child. Their mind has been made up (for them) and the book is closed.

7. Using borrowed scenarios, PAS children often make accusations about the targeted parent that utilize phrases and ideas adopted wholesale from the alienating parent. One clue that a scenario is borrowed from an alienating parent is the child's use of language and ideas that he or she does not seem to understand, such as making accusations that cannot be supported

with detail or using words that cannot be defined. This is what lends PAS its feel of programming. Children will adamantly claim things to be true when they do not even understand the words they are saying.

8. Not only is the targeted parent denigrated, despised, and avoided but so too is the parent's entire family. Formerly beloved grandparents, aunts, uncles, and cousins are suddenly avoided and rejected.

According to Gardner (1998), PAS can be experienced at three levels: mild, moderate, and severe. These levels may or may not coincide with the naïve, active, and obsessed alienating behaviors on the part of the parent. Mild cases are characterized by some parental programming against the targeted parent but visitation is not seriously affected and the child manages to negotiate the transitions to be with the targeted parent without too much difficulty. The child has a reasonably healthy relationship with both parents. In cases of moderate PAS there is significant parental programming against the targeted parent and considerable struggle around visitation. The child often has difficulty during the transition but eventually adjusts to the visits. The relationship between the child and the alienating parent is reasonably healthy, despite the shared negative beliefs about the targeted parent. The child with severe PAS is adamant about his or her hatred of the targeted parent, refusing visitation and threatening to run away if forced. The alienating parent and the child have an unhealthy alliance often based on shared paranoid fantasies about the targeted parent. In these cases the relationship between the child and the targeted parent is completely destroyed.

The number of cases of severe parental alienation is unknown, in part because the concept is relatively new and there is no formal mechanism for measuring or tracking it (Turkat, 2002). What is known is that the number of children involved in divorce increased from 6 in 1,000 in 1950 to 17 in 1,000 by the 1980s. Maccoby, Mnookin, Depner, and Peters (1992) found that one quarter of all divorces in their sample met the criterion of being high-conflict more than one year after the separation, while Garrity and Baris (1994) contend that one third of all children of divorce are caught in the middle of animosity between their parents. Opperman (2004) estimated that approximately 20 million U.S. children are already victims of mild, moderate, or severe alienating behavior, and another 25 million children will likely face some form of alienating behavior between the time of the divorce and attaining adulthood.

When PAS meets the criteria for the severe level, and the relationship between the child and the targeted parent is destroyed, Gardner (1998) believed that the most appropriate response was a court-ordered therapeutic intervention to create an opportunity for the child to experience the targeted parent outside the confines of the alienation. (For example, Weitzman (2004) developed a procedure for reunifying alienated children and targeted parents that utilized a one-way mirror and drew on systematic desensitization theory.) Gardner contended that in the absence of a combined legal and therapeutic approach, PAS would remain intact and the child and targeted parent would be lost to each other. While this may be the case, only now are researchers beginning to look at the long-term development and impact of the parental alienation syndrome on children. That was the primary impetus for this book, to learn what happened to children who had PAS, both in terms of the progress of PAS and in terms of the impact of the PAS on their development.

In the research literature on the effects of divorce on children there are areas of disagreement and even controversy, but there is universal consensus that children who suffer the most are those who have been exposed to intense and chronic parental conflict such as parental alienation. For example, research has consistently shown that children whose parents divorce suffer emotionally and psychologically, especially when the divorce is contentious and the children are exposed to ongoing conflict between their parents (e.g., Amato, 1994; Johnston, 1994; Wallerstein, Lewis, & Blakeslee, 2001; Wallerstein & Blakeslee, 1996.)

To date no empirical investigation has been conducted to document the effects of parental alienation syndrome, although Rand, Rand, and Kopestski (2005) did conduct a follow-up study to determine the course of PAS in cases with various legal interventions. It has been argued that the effect of PAS is

likely to be profound because children are exposed to malevo-
lent and intense emotions between parents. For example, Waldron and Joanis (1996) speculated that the severity of the effects
depends on several factors such as the extent of the brainwashing the child was subjected to, the amount of time the child
spent enmeshed with the alienating parent, the age of the child,
the number of healthy support people in the child's life, and
the degree to which the child "believes" the delusion. However,
to date the actual experience of the alienated individuals once
they reach adulthood is notably absent from the literature. That
was the motivation for this book—to give a voice to individuals
who had been at the center of intense conflict between their
parents. These are people whom so many others have spoken
for but who have not yet had a chance to speak for themselves.

OVERVIEW OF THE RESEARCH STUDY

This book is based on a series of confidential voluntary research
interviews. When designing the study, it was unknown how
difficult it would be to find people who identified themselves
as having been alienated from a parent due to the influence of
the other parent. It quickly became apparent that many people
were willing and interested in being interviewed. In all, 40 interviews were conducted. People were recruited from the Internet and by word of mouth. Those who responded to the call
for participants were asked to briefly describe their situation in
order to ensure that the alienation was at least in part due to
the behaviors and attitudes of the other parent as opposed to
realistic estrangement (Cartwright, 1993; Kelly & Johnson,
2001). Interviews were scheduled with people who met the criterion for the study. These were emotionally intense discussions
for these individuals who, nonetheless, appreciated that someone recognized their particular experience and wanted to hear
what it meant to them. Some of the interviewees were still actively involved in working through the alienation, while others
for the most part had put it behind them. Regardless of where
they were on the recovery timeline, they all felt that it was a
formative albeit traumatic aspect of their childhood.

The Interview Schedule

Interviews followed a semistructured protocol which ensured that comparable information was obtained from all participants while allowing each person to tell his or her story in full. The interview schedule was developed in order to capture the 12 aspects of the qualitative research interview outlined by Kvale (1996): the interview aimed to understand in a *focused* way the *subject's everyday life world* as it related to parental alienation and the *meaning* of the alienation for them, in a *qualitative* rather than quantitative form, with an emphasis on *description of specific* experiences. This information was obtained through a *sensitively* conducted *interpersonal* exchange that because of the *deliberate naiveté* of the interviewer allowed the subject to express *ambiguous* statements and come to new or *changed understandings*. The interview was conducted in such as manner as to produce a *positive experience* for the participant.

The interview had five major sections. The first section obtained basic demographic information including age, gender, place of birth, and so forth. The second section focused on memories of the interviewee's parents' marriage, the relationship to each parent up until the time of the separation or divorce, how he or she was told about the separation, which parent moved out of the home, and a description of the custody/visitation schedule through the age of 18 (this section was eliminated for individuals whose parents were not divorced). In the third section of the interview, the discussion centered on the alienation, beginning with which parent was the alienating and which the targeted parent. Each interviewee was asked to catalog all of the different strategies used by the alienating parent and to provide examples of each. Each was asked to describe the relationship to the targeted parent and how that changed over time, as well as the relationship with the alienating parent during this period. This section ended with a discussion of how the targeted parent tried to counter the alienation, whether the interviewee knew about these attempts at the time, and the perceived motivation of the alienating parent. In the fourth section of the interview, the focus was on the process by which relationships with each parent were reevaluated, when the realization occurred that the negative feelings and thoughts about the targeted parent had been induced by the alienating parent rather than based wholly in reality. Whether or not the alienating parent was ever confronted, whether the targeted parent was told about the realization, and what, if anything, the targeted parent could have done to mitigate the alienation were discussed. Any reunification with the targeted parent was described in full including who initiated it and what the outcome was. The final section of the interview entailed a conversation about the person's life at the present, including what kind of relationship he or she had with each parent and what the impact of the alienation had been. At the end of the interview a checklist was reviewed in order to ensure consistency of data.

Sample

Forty-two adults participated in the interview process. Two were subsequently removed from data analysis because of faulty tapes. Thus, data for 40 participants are presented. The interviewees were between 19 and 67 years of age (with a mean age of about 40); 15 were male and 25 were female. For the most part the interviewees were born and raised in the United States, although a few were Canadian or British, and 1 was born in Brazil. Their ethnicity was not assessed. Three fourths of the participants' parents were divorced and in all but six cases the alienating parent was the mother. Appendix A presents a description of the sample, alphabetically by the pseudonym used throughout the book. In only one case did a participant not want a pseudonym used (Robin).

Analysis

Audiotapes were transcribed verbatim. Transcripts were then submitted to a content analysis in which each unique unit of thought was separated from the transcript and placed on an index card. The analysis was guided by an inductive grounded theory approach outlined by Berg (2003) and Straus (1987) in which the texts were read in order to identify the major themes. Each card was coded according to its essential idea (i.e., relationship with targeted parent prior to the alienation, strategies utilized by the alienating parent, impact of the alienation). In all, there were 11 major categories. Cards within each category were examined as a set in order to identify common themes among the participants within each of the topics.

OVERVIEW OF FINDINGS AND OUTLINE OF BOOK

Based on the content analysis of the interviews, the following conclusions have been developed, each of which is explored in this book.

There Are Three Different Familial Patterns of Parental Alienation Syndrome

The way in which parental alienation unfolded within each family varied—there was more than one parental alienation syndrome "story." In fact, there appeared to be three primary patterns of parental alienation syndrome: (1) narcissistic mothers in divorced families alienating children from the father; (2) narcissistic mothers in intact families alienating the children from the father; and (3) cold, rejecting, or abusive alienating parents of either gender—in intact or divorced families—alienating the children from the targeted parent. Each of these patterns represents a dysfunction in the structure of the family system (despite most of the families being divorced, the two parents and child still represent a system in that they continue to interact with and influence one another in significant ways [Goldsmith, 1982]). That is, the three patterns reflect a significant breach in the "parental unit," typically involving triangulation in which the child is asked to take on the parental role, making decisions or providing the parent with emotional support or involving cross-generational alliances in which parents compete for the child's attention and support (Minuchin, 1974). Thus, PAS can be thought of as a specific type of structural family disorder. Case vignettes are presented and the motivating forces underlying the alienation in these three patterns are explored in Chapter 1.

Many Alienating Parents Seemed to Have Personality Disorders

Based on the descriptions of the alienating parents provided, it can be inferred that many met the diagnostic criteria for a personality disorder, a pervasive and distorted relational style, including narcissism, borderline, and antisocial personality. The ways in which personality disorders provided the psychic foundation for parental alienation are also discussed in Chapter 1.

Parental Alienation Co-Occurs with Other Forms of Child Maltreatment

Many of the adult children of PAS experienced physical or sexual abuse by the alienating parent. This finding is consistent with epidemiological research on the co-occurrence of different forms of abuse, demonstrating that parents who abuse their children in one way tend to abuse them in other ways as well. The role of other forms of maltreatment is also discussed in Chapter 1.

Alienating Parents Function Like Cult Leaders

The parents who perpetrated parental alienation utilized techniques similar to those employed by cult leaders. Alienating parents were described by their adult children as using emotional manipulation strategies such as withdrawal of love, creation of loyalty binds, and cultivation of dependency. They were also described as using brainwashing techniques such as repetition of negative statements about the targeted parents and black–white thinking. Chapter 2 compares alienating parents to cult leaders and describes "the cult of parenthood."

Parental Alienation Strategies Disrupt the Attachment Between Child and Targeted Parent

The adult children of PAS described 32 different parental alienation strategies their parents used. These are described in Chapter 3, and examined through the lens of attachment theory as developed by John Bowlby (1969). Within this framework, the strategies are viewed as effective tools for interfering with the developing or existing attachment relationship between the child and the targeted parent.

Parental Alienation is a Form of Emotional Abuse

Parental alienation can be considered a form of emotional abuse for at least two reasons. First, the strategies that the alienating parents used to effectuate the alienation were emotionally abusive in and of themselves. That is, the alienating parents verbally assaulted, isolated, corrupted, rejected, terrorized, ignored, and overpressured the children in order to alienate them from the targeted parent. These behaviors are part and parcel of what constitutes emotional abuse of children. In addition, it is proposed that separation of a child from a parent also constitutes emotional abuse. Chapter 4 explores the similarities between emotional abuse and parental alienation syndrome.

Realization of Parental Alienation is a Process Not an Event

It was usually a slow and painful process for the interviewees to realize that they had been turned against a parent by the other parent. For most of the adult children of PAS, the realization did not occur in a single transformative event. The defense mechanisms constructed to support the alienation take time to be broken through: they involve denying that the alienating parent is selfish and manipulative; denying that the targeted parent has positive qualities; denying that the child wants a relationship with the targeted parent; and denying that the child is afraid of losing the love of the alienating parent. Although all of the adult children had come to realize that they had been alienated from one parent by the other, the length of time they had been alienated and the age of awareness varied. Length of time alienated ranged from 7 to 47 years, with an average of about 20 years. Chapters 5 and 6 present a description and analysis of this realization process. Specifically, 11 different catalysts for the realization process are identified and case vignettes describing each are presented.

The Impact of Parental Alienation is Life
Long and May be Intergenerational

The long-term effects of parental alienation on the adult children are presented in Chapter 7. A significant portion experienced depression, divorce, and substance abuse problems as adults. They had difficulty trusting others as well as trusting themselves. In addition, several reported becoming alienated from their own children. Three different patterns of the intergenerational transmission of PAS are presented.

How the Targeted Parent Responded
Made a Difference

What did the targeted parents do that helped their children to eventually realize that they had been manipulated? What more could they have done to prevent or mitigate the alienation? These issues are explored in Chapter 8 with the presentation of brief vignettes about what the targeted parents did and should have done from the perspective of the adult children.

The final three chapters of the book present clinical implications and suggestions for therapists and other mental health professionals. Chapter 9 discusses clinical implications for working with adults who were alienated from a parent as a child due to PAS. This chapter describes ways that the adult client and therapist can work together to determine whether and how to reunite with the targeted parent and to confront the alienating parent. In all cases, the adult client can be helped to reunite with those parts of him- or herself that were cut off, denied, or buried in order to appease the alienating parent.

Chapter 10 presents implications for working with children who currently are alienated from a parent due to PAS. Mechanisms for identifying PAS (outside the context of court-ordered custody evaluations) are offered and suggestions for helping children develop a more balanced and realistic view of both parents are provided.

Chapter 11 discusses clinical implications for working with parents who are currently targeted for alienation. Those who might have a tendency to dismiss and minimize the alienation can be encouraged to recognize the gravity of the situation. Professionals can provide parents with specific advice about how to respond to and counter attempts at alienation.

MYTHS ABOUT PARENTAL ALIENATION SYNDROME

The findings from this study refute three common myths about parental alienation syndrome. The first myth is that parental alienation is only perpetrated by mothers against fathers. Although this was the case for many of the adult children, it was not true of all of them. In 6 of the 40 interviews, fathers were the alienating parent. Because the sample was neither random nor representative it is not possible to calculate the actual proportion of fathers in the general population of alienating parents. But it can be concluded definitively that some fathers do practice parental alienation. The reason there may have been gender bias in the phenomenon to date is that mothers experienced a shift from being the presumptive custodial parent (under the tender years doctrine) to needing to prove that they should be the custodial parent (under the best interests of the child doctrine). Thus, they have had more to lose in the custody battles and may have been more likely to resort to parental alienation as a tool to preserve what they were once granted automatically: custody of their children. Now that gender roles have shifted sufficiently for men to experience the loss of custody after years of devoted parenting, they may be just as likely to exploit whatever tactics they can in order to maintain custody of their children. The fact that in considerably less than half the sample for this study fathers were the alienators may indicate that time has not yet evened out the use of this strategy. It might mean, however, that the child victims of alienating fathers are less likely to become aware of the alienation and thus would not have volunteered to participate in the study.

This book can only give voice to those individuals who were aware of the fact that they had been victims of PAS.

The second myth is that parental alienation syndrome only occurs in divorced families. Gardner (1998) identified the phenomenon of PAS in the context of postdivorce custody litigation and evaluations, but he did not rule out the possibility that parental alienation syndrome can take place in intact families. That was certainly the case in this study.

The third myth is that parental alienation syndrome is only effectuated by custodial parents. Again, Gardner's (1998) prototypical case was of a custodial mother alienating the children from their father following a divorce. Although this may have been the norm, it is not the only scenario. The custodial parent has a far greater degree of access to the child in order to effectuate the alienation, but this does not preclude the possibility of alienation being perpetrated during visitation with a noncustodial parent, especially if visitation is frequent and the parent is especially effective at thought control and emotional manipulation techniques.

Debunking these myths highlights the more complex nature of parental alienation syndrome than was previously recognized. It is not solely the province of bitter ex-wives exacting retribution on the men who abandoned them, although that is one pattern. A more nuanced understanding of parental alienation syndrome is clearly called for, and this book will take a first step in that direction.

Part I

UNDERSTANDING PARENTAL ALIENATION SYNDROME

Chapter 1

Patterns of Parental Alienation

Domination becomes anchored in the hearts of those who
submit to it.

—Jessica Benjamin, *The bonds of love*

EVERY STORY OF PARENTAL ALIENATION IS SOMEWHAT DIFFERENT.
Each person has his or her own individual voice and unique
tale to tell. However, even among these disparate experiences,
patterns can be detected. As noted in the introduction, the patterns of PAS represent structural dysfunction in the family system, reflected by profound triangulation and cross-generational
alliances (Minuchin, 1974). Three patterns of PAS are described
below followed by a discussion of several notable issues.

PATTERN 1: NARCISSISTIC MOTHER IN
DIVORCED FAMILY (14 families)

In Pattern 1 families the parents were divorced; the mother was
the custodial alienating parent, and the father was the noncustodial targeted parent. The most distinguishing feature of these
families was that the alienating mother appeared to have a narcissistic personality disorder. That is, she had a pervasive relational style that was selfish and grandiose with an inability to

truly comprehend the needs and feelings of others. For example, Mitch described his mother as ". . . definitely totally conceited. She thought of herself as always wanting the best in things. She was very insistent about her skills and if somebody didn't recognize that, that was their problem not hers. Her actions were self-centered. She really did see herself as the center of the universe." Likewise, Nicole believed about her mother, "Mainly I think she always wants to be your everything. She wants to be your center of attention." While the term *narcissism* was not uniformly used, all of the Pattern 1 mothers were portrayed as self-centered, demanding a high degree of attention and admiration, and not able to see their children as separate individuals—the very essence of narcissism. According to psychologist James Masterson (1981) the main clinical characteristics of the narcissistic personality are, "grandiosity, extreme self-involvement, and lack of interest in and empathy for others, in spite of the pursuit of others to obtain admiration and approval" (p. 7). The alienating mothers in these families were portrayed as charming, dynamic, and preoccupied with having their own needs met rather than meeting the needs of their children. These narcissistic mothers cultivated an emotionally enmeshed relationship with the adult children of PAS when they were young children, which appeared to serve the mothers need for love and admiration, rather than promoting the emotional health and growth of the children. They were able to instill in their children a sense of awe and admiration. The following comments made by Hannah, Alix, and Veronica, respectively, convey the intensity of their feelings for their mothers, "It was fabulous. I was her daughter. I didn't individuate from her. I did everything for her to make her life better" (Hannah). "I was in my mom's world not my own" (Alix). "We were really good friends. It was brilliant. I used to be called her shadow because we'd do everything together" (Veronica). In a similar vein Walter said, "I'm a mama's boy."

Maternal narcissism may have fueled the alienation in at least three ways. First, despite the powerful personality presented to the world, narcissists tend to feel empty inside and easily become enraged at the first sign of humiliation or abandonment. Therefore, it is likely that the end of the marriage triggered in these women feelings of shame and rage that became directed toward the husband. As Masterson noted, once individuals with narcissistic personality feel belittled or psychologically abandoned they, "avoid, deny, and/or devalue the offending stimulus or perception, thereby restoring the balance of his narcissistic equilibrium" (1981, p. 16). Thus, once the father had left the marriage he became an object of intense devaluation and hatred. This is consistent with the steady stream of negative statements made about the absent father following the divorce. These men were referred to as cheaters, gamblers, rapists, alcoholics, and abusers. Carrie said of her mother, "She would constantly bad-mouth my dad saying that he didn't love us. He wanted to move on with his life with my stepmom and she would make us feel bad for wanting to go there." And Mitch recalled that his mother, "said all these terrible things about him my whole life." Amelia's mother, too, denigrated the father, saying, "That he did not want nothing to do with us and that basically he was a very bad person." Thus, the alienation may have been partly motivated by revenge, as if the mothers were saying to their ex-husbands, "If you don't want me you cannot have the children either." Such a desire for revenge has long been recognized as a motivating factor in parental alienation (Clawar & Rivlin, 1991; Gardner, 1998). Further, the father's interest in having an ongoing relationship with the children (he was not rejecting the children) may also have been experienced as a narcissistic injury. The mothers seemed to wish that if the fathers left them that they should abandon the children as well. Statements such as "Daddy doesn't love us anymore," which conflated the rejection of the mother with the rejection of the children, might be seen as a wish rather than a statement of fact or a criticism of the father. Such comments were common occurrences.

A second underlying motivation of the alienation fueled by the mothers' narcissism may have been anger toward the children for wanting to have a relationship with the father despite the fact that he had rejected the mother. This too might have triggered a feeling of abandonment in these mothers. They seemed to feel that because they were hurt and angry with the father, the children should be as well. This is consistent with the fact that narcissists generally have difficulty comprehending that others (including, if not especially, their children) have separate feelings and experiences of the world (Kernberg, 1975). If they are displeased with someone, the children should be as well. Julia experienced this: "If she was angry with him then I was supposed to be angry." For this reason, the children's interest in having a relationship with their father following the divorce was experienced as a betrayal and contributed to the mothers' desire to alienate them from their fathers.

Third, the narcissistic mothers might have felt especially alone and fragile following the divorce and might have relied on their children for comfort, companionship, and reassurance. Seen in this light, the time the children spent visiting with the father would have been experienced as a profound loss. To be alone in the house while the children were with the father might have been unbearably lonely and threatening. Many narcissists do not know how to be alone and require an audience to feel real and to reassure them of their value. Serita's mother would ask the children where they'd been and would say, "Oh. I was left on my own and nobody really thinks of me." The children's visitation with their father may have triggered the mother's feelings of loss and anger, which was an underlying motivation to alienate the children from their father.

For all these reasons, the relationship between the children and their fathers following the divorce would have been experienced by the mothers as abandonment, loss, and humiliation. To ward off these threatening and noxious feelings (and perhaps to punish the divorced ex-husband) the mother created a loyalty conflict. Serita felt, "We were made to choose"; and if Maria showed any positive feelings for her father her mother would say, "How could you do this to me? You are betraying me." In having the child choose them over the father, these mothers' emotional needs for revenge, for comfort, for reassurance were satisfied.

Thus, the narcissistic mothers convinced their children to reject the targeted parent. In Chapter 3 the full range of strategies used by the alienating parents is described. Particularly relevant for the discussion of Pattern 1 narcissistic mothers are two strategies, described briefly below: cultivation of dependency/

threat of rejection and creation of a sense of obligation/guilt. These strategies correspond to the FOG (fear, obligation, and guilt) of emotional blackmail described by popular psychologist Susan Forward (1997).

First, as noted above, the mothers were able to cultivate in their children an unhealthy reliance on their acceptance and approval, much the way cult leaders encourage cult members to become dependent on them (see Chapter 2 for a full discussion of the similarities between alienating parents and cult leaders). To be out of their mother's favor represented an unimaginable loss for the children. Disapproval was to be avoided at all costs; and this was achieved through compliance with the alienation. Thus, alienation from the father was the price for the mother's approval, a price they were willing to pay in order to avoid her rejection. Such excessive reliance on parental approval has been described by psychologist Jessica Benjamin (1998) as a subjugation of the self, "If the child does not want to do without approval, she must give up her will" (p. 36). Similarly, family systems theorist Salvatore Minuchin (1974) described the trade-off between parental acceptance and personal freedom in that, "The heightened sense of belonging requires a major yielding of autonomy" (p. 55). In these Pattern 1 families, in order to obtain the approval of their mother, the children had to relinquish their will, their autonomy, and their relationship with the father.

Typical of narcissists, however, the closeness these mothers cultivated with their children was sustained only as long as they were gratifying the mothers' needs. As soon as the mothers felt wounded or were displeased, the children were devalued and emotionally cut off. Withdrawal of love was particularly conspicuous following visitation with the father. Serita's and Ron's experiences are illustrative, "When I did see him she was horrible to me. When I came back from visits she wouldn't talk to me"; and "My mother would get really angry if, for example, my brother or I displayed any affection for my father." These mothers appeared to alternate between enveloping their children in a loving world in which they basked in the glow of maternal acceptance and exiling their children to a world of coldness and maternal rejection. This vacillation was particularly extreme for Sarah who confided, "I was afraid of her and I was afraid of losing her."

Further, these children observed first hand what happened when someone displeased or challenged their mothers, having witnessed the rage directed toward the father (and, in some cases other people as well, including grandparents, colleagues, and friends). In order to avoid a similar fate, they placed their mother first in their emotional lives. Because they were never sure where they stood and because they believed that they needed their mother's approval for their very survival, they would have done almost anything to please her, including rejecting the father. This desire to please the narcissistic parent was described by Elan Golomb as "Longing for parental love creates an invisible force" (1992, p. 49) and it was this longing for the mother's love and the fear of losing it that motivated (at least partly) the alienation of the father. Psychologist Jessica Benjamin (1988) took this line of thinking one step further when she explained that children transform the longing for their parent's approval, and the fear of losing that approval, into submission to the idealized parent. By idealizing the alienating parent, the child preserves the fantasy that this parent is actually loving and protecting them. Trauma expert Judith Herman (1992) understood this as the "formidable task" of abused children to defend the abusive parent.

Second, the mothers also appeared to their children as fragile and in need of their loyalty and emotional support. They believed that not only were they needed by their mothers but that they somehow owed it to their mothers to take care of them. Sarah's devotion to her mother is illustrative, "I didn't bring any friends home. I felt like I was supposed to be there for my mom all the time. I felt like if I associated with anyone other than her I was betraying her." This dynamic facilitated the alienation because the children believed that rejection of the father was necessary in order to heal the mother or at least stave off further damage and suffering. Thus, these mothers were able to make their feelings and needs more urgent and compelling to their children than not only the father's needs but even their own. Sarah added, "I would see her cry a lot so she appeared very fragile to me so that made me feel more responsible to be there for her." It is possible that such responsibility, although frightening, might also have been gratifying (in part) to these children because it enhanced their sense of power and importance.

PATTERN 2: NARCISSISTIC MOTHER IN INTACT FAMILY (8 families)

Pattern 2 shares much with Pattern 1. Like Pattern 1, the Pattern 2 mother was the alienating parent and the father was the target of the alienation and, also like Pattern 1, the distinguishing feature of these families was that the alienating mothers appeared to have a narcissistic personality. The primary difference was that in Pattern 2 families the alienation did not occur within the context of postdivorce custody conflict: these parents remained married.

Not surprisingly, therefore, the style of alienation was also somewhat different. The primary technique of Pattern 2 alienating mothers entailed confiding in the children about the inadequacies and failings of the father. They drew the children into their confidence in such a way as to solidify that relationship at the expense of the relationship with the targeted parent. Thus, the children had knowledge about the targeted parents that the targeted parents did not know their children had, and the parents were, therefore, unaware that it would be advisable to correct the misperceptions or tell their side of the story. As a result, the children had no alternative to the biased understanding of the marital relationship, designed to create the appearance that the targeted parent was inadequate and damaged. In addition, these confidences served to enhance the intimacy between the alienating parent and the children, further binding them to that parent. Moreover, these disclosures often induced pity for the alienating parent and anger toward the targeted parent. For example, Edward's father was a hardworking man trying to support a family of six yet his mother was relentless in her criticism of him. "She was never satisfied with what my father could provide. He worked about 12 hours a day. She was always complaining about everything he did, to him, in front of the children, and to other people."

Elaine, too, heard a constant litany of criticism of her father, which created the impression that he was fundamentally insufficient. "Almost like an us-against-him kind of thing. Treating me more like a peer or a friend rather than a child in the household. Dad doesn't do this right, Dad doesn't do that right." Larissa had become so dependent on her mother's approval, she felt grateful that her mother deigned to share her secret plans to obtain a divorce, "She made several announcements to me that she was going to be seeking a divorce and she told me how marvelous life would be once the divorce went through. I was so happy about that. I suppose I felt as though she saw me as a friend and I hoped I was worthy of her liking me." Roberta understood that her mother, "felt insecure regarding other women and I had knowledge of so many things and that was something I was really too young to know about."

One young man, Josh, recalled that when he was 5 years old his mother told him she could not cope with the demands of raising the family and she was considering taking him and running away. "She was upset and she was sharing that with me." Much of what was shared with the children about their father was designed to make them feel anger or resentment toward him and protective of the mother, furthering the alienation.

Thus, the alienating mother was able, through the force of her narcissistic personality, to cultivate an emotional alliance at the expense of the child's relationship with the father, despite the fact that the father was living in the same household. In all these cases the mother shared her discontent with the father and drew the child into her distorted perspective that the father was fundamentally lacking and was responsible for whatever ailed not only the mother but also the entire family. The following description by Larissa captured this dynamic.

She'd always made both my brother and me feel that our father was somehow to blame for everything. Every day there'd be some attempt by her, some tale she'd tell me, to turn me against my father, so many incidents it's simply impossible to list them all. Just about all aspects of the alienation worked, as far as I recall. I became my mother's puppet, her ally against my father. I grew to

*detest him, with a truly visceral hate. I couldn't stand to be in
the same room with him, or to even talk to him or have him talk
to me.*

These coalitions formed between the alienating mother and
child against the father are the types of intergenerational alliances that have long been of concern to family systems theorists. Minuchin (1993), for example, postulated that when a
child is "taller" than one of his parents (i.e., harshly and unnecessarily critical) it is because the child is "standing on the shoul-
ders of " (i.e., being encouraged by) the other parent.

What distinguishes Pattern 1 from Pattern 2 families is that
the alienation did not occur in the context of a divorce. It is
likely, therefore, that the motivation was probably different as
well from Pattern 1 mothers, for whom hurt and anger at the
spouse's rejection and abandonment seemed to be the likely
precipitating cause. In those cases, the alienation served to both
punish the father, with whom the mother was angry, and generate emotional satisfaction for the mother through the alliance
with the child. In Pattern 2, in the absence of divorce, the underlying motivation appears to have been different, although it
is possible that even in the marriage, the mother felt rejected or
frustrated by the father and retaliated through the alliance with
the child. It is also possible that the mother was not able to
maintain an adult relationship in which emotional honesty and
compromise were necessary. Perhaps these mothers turned to
their children because having the unquestioning adoration of a
child was more satisfying and less demanding than a mature
relationship with another adult. Such a dynamic was described
in D. H. Lawrence's autobiographical novel *Sons and Lovers*, in
which he wrote simply, "She turned to the child; she turned
from the father" (1913/1991, p. 13). Billie's story in Peck's (1983)
The People of the Lie is also a prototypical Pattern 2 scenario in
which the mother emotionally exploits her daughter's need for
approval at the expense of her relationship with her father (to
whom the mother is still married) as well as Billie's needs for
autonomy and independence.

Despite the differences between Pattern 1 and Pattern 2, what links them is the close emotional bond the child has with the mother which she exploits in order have her own needs met.

PATTERN 3: REJECTING/ABUSIVE
ALIENATING PARENT (16 families)

The third pattern represents a dramatic departure from the first two. The most striking difference is the tone and quality of the relationship with the alienating parent. Rather than a "fabulously close" or "excellent" relationship, as described in Pattern 1 and Pattern 2 families, the Pattern 3 alienating parents were physically, verbally, or sexually abusive. In some cases the alienating parent was alcoholic as well. The alienation occurred not through seduction, charm, and persuasion, but through a campaign of fear, pain, and denigration.

Renee's relationship with her Pattern 3 alienating mother was representative. "I just wanted to avoid her as much as possible. She was very judgmental, very hateful. Not supporting. I can count three times in my whole life that she told me she loved me." Betty too grew up in a Pattern 3 family, with a verbally and physically abusive mother.

> When I was in Junior High most of my memories come from being in Juvenile Hall. I spent time in and out of foster homes, group homes, and being locked up 30 days at a time for my mother's abuse toward me. I remember being in an overnight emergency foster home when she took my pet's cage and threw it at me for not cleaning it, stating I was just like my father, and how I'd end up just like him. My mother from that point on would hit me, call me names, and start screaming like I was beating her so neighbors thought I was hitting her, giving me 30 days lockup so she could have a break. I started working when I was 14 and she'd take my paychecks, and if I refused, she'd pull the same stunts.

Frank lived in a particularly brutal and chaotic Pattern 3 family, in which the alienating parent (his father) was physically violent toward him as well as his mother.

The last thing I remember was when I refused to climb into bed and have sex with my mother I was smashed in the head and thrown out the door and he chased me down the hallway past the bathroom. I got as far as the living room. He snatched me up again and threw me literally at my sister. As far as my father goes if he said something, and if it did not sink in to where you understood, and he could swear that he could tell whether or not you understood what he was saying just by looking at you, so if you didn't have the correct look on your face, you were going to be physically abused.

Jason, too, lived in a Pattern 3 family.

My father was a very strong patriarch. He ran the place. He was a nasty person when he drank and he drank most of the time, and he pretty much ruled the roost as the saying goes. When he spoke everyone else had to shut up and listen and he ruled with occasional unexpected violence. Mother was cowed—there was very little she could do. She had her hands full dealing with him. He would belittle her. He had a whole bag of tricks to control and one was the constant belittling of people, of me and of my sister, mocking and belittling my mother, and it was very effective because there was no escaping it. You couldn't talk back or you would be physically admonished or you would be mocked even stronger. I was never close to my mother. I didn't want to spend any time with her because I bought into some of his stuff that she was silly and mawkish or overly sentimental and unreliable or whatever the sum total of the impression that he tried to convey about her.

One way to understand why the children in these Pattern 3 families aligned themselves with their violent alienating parents against the targeted parent is within the context of identification with the aggressor, a psychological defense mechanism whereby individuals (often children) cope with the anxiety associated with feeling or being powerless by taking on the characteristics of the more powerful person—even if that person is aggressive or abusive toward them. In doing so, the child feels less overwhelmed and out of control. This defense mechanism has been used to describe why children defend abusive parents as well as why individuals who feel anxious and alone may join a cult and form an identification with its leader (A. Freud, 1936/1966; Goldberg, 1997). In the context of Pattern 3 families, the alienating parent was experienced as so powerful—through physical violence as well as sheer force of personality—that the children felt safer allying with him or her than with the rejected targeted parent. In this way, the goal of the alienation from the child's perspective was avoidance of pain and powerlessness rather than the maintenance of a close emotional, albeit enmeshed, bond with the alienating narcissistic mother (as in Patterns 1 and 2). Although the outcome was essentially the same—the child was aligned with the alienating parent against the targeted parent—the strategies the alienating parent used and the motivations for the child's choosing the alienating parent were different from those in Pattern 1 and 2 families.

Thus, it is apparent that parental alienation syndrome can take different forms, with at least three possible distinct patterns. The first scenario is the one described by Gardner (1998), but others exist as well. The underlying motivation may be different, the strategies the alienating parent uses may differ, and the motivations of the child for allying with the alienating parent may also vary. These patterns may also require different clinical and legal interventions. For example, narcissistic mothers as alienators may present different clinical opportunities and challenges than alcoholic and physically abusive fathers.

NOTABLE THEMES AND CLINICAL AND LEGAL IMPLICATIONS

The legal and clinical implications of these patterns are discussed as they relate to the following eight issues.

Co-Occurring Maltreatment

The first notable theme is that many of the adult children of PAS had been physically or sexually abused. Specifically, 17 of the interviewees reported that the alienating parent had physically abused them; and 3 reported that they had been sexually abused by that parent (an additional 5 were sexually abused by a stepparent). These numbers are considerably higher than in the general population and suggest that parents who are alienators are likely to also maltreat their children physically and sexually, although the proportion of maltreatment found in this sample may be higher than in the general population of parental alienation cases due to sampling bias in which perhaps the worst cases were most likely to want to participate in the research.

This abuse can be understood in light of the co-occurrence of various forms of maltreatment (e.g., Baker, Curtis, & Papa-Lentini, in press; Howes, Cicchetti, Toth, & Rogosch, 2000). Explanations for this co-occurrence generally focus on their shared etiology: risk factors for one type of abuse (such as parental mental illness, parental lack of impulse control, poor parenting skills, life stressors, etc.) are also risk factors for other types of abuse. Because PAS represents a form of emotional abuse (see Chapter 4), it is plausible that some of the factors that underlie parental alienation syndrome are the same as those that underlie physical or sexual abuse. The primary implication pertains to the need for assessment and intervention for co-occurring maltreatment in cases of PAS.

Co-Occurring Alcoholism

A second notable theme is the prevalence of alcoholism in the alienating parents. Alcoholism has been found to be associated with physical and sexual abuse of children (National Clearinghouse on Child Abuse and Neglect, 2003), and it now appears that it may be associated with parental alienation syndrome as well. Alcoholism is prevalent in maltreating families in part because of the negative impact of alcoholism on parental functioning. For example, alcoholism has been found to diminish impulse control such that risk for physical abuse is heightened when parents are under the influence. In addition, the basic needs of children for nurturance and supervision are less likely to be met when parents are under the influence or preoccupied with obtaining and using substances. Alcoholism is also associated with personality disorders (Trull, Waudby, & Sher, 2004) and is consistent with the fact that personality disorders were conjectured to be common among the alienating parents.

Co-Occurring Personality Disorder

Personality disorders are defined as generalized, inflexible patterns of inner experience and behavior. These patterns significantly differ from cultural expectations, and emerge in adolescence or early adulthood. Personality disorders are pervasive and persistent maladaptive patterns of perception, emotional regulation, anxiety, and impulse control. They are among the most common of the severe mental disorders, and occur frequently with other illnesses (e.g., substance use disorders, mood disorders, anxiety disorders). *The Diagnostic and Statistical Manual of Mental Disorders* (American Psychiatric Association, 2000), organized personality disorders into three groups (with three or four disorders per group). Based on the descriptions of the alienating parents, most could be considered Type B, Dramatic Personality Disorders; that is, antisocial, borderline, histrionic, or narcissistic. Individuals with these disorders have intense, unstable emotions, distorted self-perception, or behavioral impulsiveness. Many of the Pattern 1 and Pattern 2 mothers appeared to have a narcissistic personality disorder, although some may have been borderline or hysterical. What they share is an inability to see the needs of others, intense fears of abandonment, and emotional immaturity. Some of the Pattern 3 parents may have had antisocial personality disorder. Thus, assessment of personality disorders may be an important component of any PAS intervention and treatment plan. The two most likely in PAS families based on this study—narcissism and antisocial personality—are described briefly below.

Individuals with narcissistic personality disorder often have a grandiose view of themselves, a need for admiration, and a lack of empathy that begins by early adulthood and is present in various situations. In order to meet the diagnostic criteria, an individual must have at least five of the following nine characteristics: (1) an inflated sense of self-importance (e.g., exaggerates achievements and talents, expects to be recognized as superior without corresponding achievements); (2) overly concerned with fantasies of unlimited success, power, brilliance, beauty, or ideal love; (3) belief that he or she is special and unique and can only be understood by, or should associate with, other special or high-status people (or institutions); (4)

need for excessive admiration; (5) a sense of entitlement (i.e., unreasonable expectations of very positive treatment or automatic compliance with his or her expectations); (6) taking advantage of others to achieve his or her own ends; (7) lack of empathy and unwillingness to identify with the feelings and needs of others; (8) jealousy of others or believes that others are jealous of him or her; and (9) arrogant or domineering behaviors or attitudes.

Some of the Pattern 3 parents probably had antisocial personality disorder. This entails a fundamental disrespect for, and violation of, the rights of others. In order to meet the diagnostic criteria, an individual must show at least three of the following seven behaviors: (1) repeated acts that are grounds for arrest; (2) deceitfulness; (3) impulsiveness or failure to plan ahead; (4) irritability and aggressiveness, such as repeated physical fights or assaults; (5) reckless disregard for the safety of self or others; (6) consistent irresponsibility (i.e., repeated failure to sustain consistent work behavior or honor financial obligations); and (7) lack of remorse, as indicated by indifference to, or rationalizing having hurt, mistreated, or stolen from another.

Determination of personality disorders should be taken into account when devising methods for overseeing visitation schedules because such individuals are not likely to comply with court orders. People with narcissistic personality disorders tend to be arrogant, and they are therefore likely to devalue authority figures and emphasize their own ability to make judgments and decisions (e.g., Golomb, 1992; Hotchkiss, 2002). Without real teeth in a visitation or shared parenting order, it is not likely that such a person will comply. The legal system has developed measures for tracking and enforcing payment of child support; it now may be time for methods to be developed to ensure compliance with visitation.

Parental Alienation Syndrome Occurs in Intact Families

Parental alienation syndrome also occurred in intact families. The majority of the attention to parental alienation syndrome has emerged from the legal system in response to problems dealing with high conflict divorces, custody disputes, and false and real allegations of sexual abuse and parental alienation. To date, there has been minimal if any attention to the fact that parental alienation syndrome can occur outside of the legal system. The strategies that the alienating parents in Pattern 2 families used were the same as those used by parents in postdivorce cases. The experience of the alienation was quite similar as well. Despite the fact that the targeted parent lived in the same household, the children rejected, avoided, and denigrated him or her (in their hearts and minds) and essentially were denied the opportunity to have a loving and rewarding relationship with the targeted parent. Understanding that the phenomenon can occur in intact families should be useful for clinicians working with adult children of parental alienation syndrome as well as children currently receiving mental health services in a variety of settings (schools, outpatient clinics, and private therapy).

Parental Alienation Occurs in Families Not Involved in Custody Disputes

Fifth, alienation occurred in some families that were not involved in postdivorce litigation. Again, the typical parental alienation syndrome scenario is that of a family involved in intense and chronic legal battles around custody and visitation. This was not always the case. In some of the families the targeted parent did not seek remedy in the court, either because the financial resources were not available to do so or because the targeted parent did not believe he or she could win. Combined with the fact that alienation can occur in nondivorced families (see above) it appears that it is time to broaden the definition of parental alienation syndrome. Parents who feel that they are being targeted for alienation by the other parent of their child should take this seriously and not assume that because they are in an intact marriage or because they are not involved in custody litigation they are not experiencing parental alienation. These parents should become familiar with the concept and the best thinking about how to intervene and prevent the alienation from becoming entrenched. Likewise, teachers, social workers, and other mental health professionals who come into contact with parents and children should become versed in the patterns of parental alienation syndrome, and the strategies parents use, so that they can identify them when they are present. Only then can the targeted parent rethink his or her current parenting style and relationship with the child. Without knowing what they are dealing with, targeted parents may assume that there is nothing unusual about their situation or that there is nothing to be done to improve it.

Some of the Targeted Parents Played a Role

Sixth, some of the parents who were the targets of the alienation appeared to play a role in their own alienation—although the alienation itself was caused by the behaviors and attitudes of the alienating parent. In some cases the targeted parents were passive and uninvolved (even when living in the same household) and were not particularly diligent in establishing or maintaining a positive and meaningful relationship with their own children. Many of the noncustodial targeted parents did not write letters or make phone calls to their children during periods of nonvisitation. They did not attend school events and sporting competitions; they did not follow through on planned visitations; and in some respects appeared to be casual about their relationships with their children. Of course, it must be noted that these reports were made by the adult children of PAS who may not have been aware of everything that the targeted parents had done or tried to do for them. Some targeted parents might have written letters that were discarded or made phone calls that were intercepted. However, some of the targeted parents seemed to do less than everything possible. In fact, some purposefully removed themselves from the situation—apparently out of anger or a sense of defeat—inadvertently conveying to their children that they were not worth fighting for (see Chapter 8 for discussion of the role of the targeted parent in the parental alienation).

PAS Families Make a Positive Impression to the Outside World

A disparity existed between the image of the family conveyed to the world and the experience of the family members. These families, although severely troubled, did not appear to be so to others, and in fact, they cultivated an image of being particularly enviable while actually being deeply unhappy. For example, no one seemed to know that Jason's father was a raging alcoholic and physically abusive man who dominated Jason's mother.

> *He looked real good. He was sterling. . . . The difference between the inside and the outside of that house was just amazing. From the outside it looked like we were a very healthy happy family. All four of us went to college and from the outside it looked happy and all the rest of that good stuff. On the inside when he would go into his drunken rages and start picking on people, just picking them apart and just needling them, and watching his wife and children getting increasingly uncomfortable, and he would keep at them.*

Roberta, too, experienced the disparity between the inside and outside of the home. Her mother was very unhappy with her father but only shared this information with the children in the family. "She really didn't turn outside the family much for help or things like that. So we were pretty much her sounding board and her support system." The following exchange elaborated this issue:

A: I felt like I was not only expected to agree with her but to protect her identity.
Q: In what way?
A: There might have been things that wouldn't look good to outsiders' eyes.
Q: So it was your job to make her look good to the outside world?
A: Yes. We always looked good on the outside. Our clothes were always . . . there was seven of us and it was a hard thing to pull off. Nobody was supposed to talk about what went on inside the family.

In their work with "narcissistic families" Donaldson-Pressman and Pressman (1994) use the metaphor of a shiny red apple with a worm inside to describe families in which maintaining a glowing image to the outside world takes precedence over meeting the needs of family members. This metaphor appears applicable to families of parental alienation syndrome as well.

Parental Alienation is Not Always Fully Internalized

And, finally, the alienation was not always completely internalized. That is, despite the unambivalent protestation of hatred toward the targeted parent, many of the adult children of PAS held on to positive feelings about that parent somewhere deep inside of them. There was variation in the extent to which they believed what they said. This was probably unknown to the targeted parent who only saw the vehemence expressed by the child. For example, Ron was made to call his father on the phone and spout vile curses at him. "She would be telling us what to say and I remember repeating it. For the most part it was cursing. Sometimes she would make me say that he was a womanizer." Ron had no understanding of what he was saying and shared that while he was saying these things he had been secretly hoping that his father knew that he did not mean it. "I don't know whether he believed we really felt that way or not because we were saying these things to him. I am hoping in my heart he knew but it must have hurt anyway." This statement, and others like it, provides a compelling rationale for why targeted parents should not assume that what they are hearing is the complete truth about how their child feels. This should help them "hang in there" despite the intense negativity being directed toward them and should provide them with motivation for continuing to show their love and commitment to the child, who is, after all, the victim.

Chapter 2

The Cult of Parenthood

He gave us a sense of importance, and in return we handed
our will over to him.

—Deborah Layton, *Seductive Poison*

ALIENATING PARENTS BEHAVE LIKE CULT LEADERS, AND THEY CRE-
ate families that function in many respects as if they were cults.
According to West and Langone (1986) a cult (1) is a hierarchical social group in which there is a leader who requires
excessive devotion; (2) has a leader who uses emotional manipulation and persuasion techniques to heighten dependency on
him or her; and (3) furthers the aims of the leader at the expense of its members as well as others, although other defini-
tions have been offered (Langone, 1993, 2004). Utilizing this
definition provides a basis for comparing the characteristics of
cults to those of PAS families.

Most families in Western cultures are hierarchical social
groups. Power is not evenly distributed among the members of
the family. Parents have legal, physical, moral, and psychological control over their children. Even parents who respect their
children's individuality, and aim to promote competence and
autonomy, retain some authority over them. In some families,
however, as we have seen, parents exploit their inherent authority in order to alienate the child from the other parent.

A LEADER WHO REQUIRES
EXCESSIVE DEVOTION

Cults are organized around a leader, typically a charismatic individual who maintains ultimate power and authority over the group. Within the cult, the leader is considered worthy of devotion and awe because of a superior capacity to comprehend the true nature of reality. Due to this purportedly unique and valuable knowledge, it is agreed in cults that the leader understands members better than they understand themselves. It is also understood that through great personal sacrifice, cult leaders are willing to share this knowledge on behalf of the members who require the wisdom and guidance of the leader in order to function. In return, members are expected to reserve their unquestioning love and devotion exclusively for the leader who thus earns an elevated place at the center of their emotional lives. Cult leaders have been compared to both psychopaths (Tobias, & Lalich, 1994), and narcissists (Shaw, 2003). They present themselves as superior and use their extensive charm and persuasion skills in order to exploit and unduly influence others. Cult leaders tend to be charismatic, manipulative, authoritarian, and sociopathic (Tobias & Lalich, 1994). They win people over through a combination of charm and persuasion coupled with a ruthless and unprincipled willingness to instill fear as a tool to ensure continued loyalty and allegiance. Dependency on the leader is created through the promotion of the belief that this person holds a unique and irreplaceable position in the member's life; the cult leader is experienced as essential for the member's well-being. Once indoctrination into the cult has occurred, loyalty is maintained through a range of strategies such as inculcating fear of expulsion, breaking down the person's resistance and independent thinking, and creating a sense of obligation toward the leader.

The adult children of PAS described the alienating parent in much the same way. In particular, they perceived the alienating parent as needing to be the focus of attention at all times and insisting on being the center of the child's emotional life. Nancy said, "She was the center and everything revolved around her." Nicole, said, "Mainly I think she always wants to be your everything. She wants to be your center of attention. And so she liked the fact that by making me hate him all I had was her." As discussed in Chapter 1, many of the adult children of PAS described their parents as narcissistic, either using that label or precise descriptors that called the term to mind.

In cults, however, it is usually not enough to feel devotion to the leader; members are expected to demonstrate that devotion on a regular basis. Expressions of devotion include putting the needs of the leader first, never questioning the authority of the leader, confessing one's own imperfections, allowing the leader to make all important decisions, and making public declarations of faith and love. These actions reassure the leader that the member is fully indoctrinated and further solidify the member's commitment to the cult (Lifton, 1969). In many cases the expressions of devotion are made in public, with the aim of transforming a public declaration of devotion into an inner commitment of loyalty to the leader. By requiring such public assertions of faith and trust in the leader, cult leaders are exploiting what social psychologist Leon Festinger (1957) identified as the natural tendency of people to want their beliefs to be consistent with their actions. In this way saying becomes believing—although Ofshe (1992) argued that the cult beliefs adopted may be situationally based and discarded once the person is removed from the environment.

This process also occurred in the families of parental alienation syndrome. The adult children of PAS felt pressure to demonstrate their devotion to the alienating parent. Many described that relationship as one in which their parent's needs were experienced as more real and urgent to them than their own. They recalled staying home from social activities to tend to their parent, to keep them company, to take care of younger siblings, or to perform household duties. Hannah explained, "I did what I could do to make her life easier because her life was so hard because of my father. That was my mantra, Mom's life is hard. I have to try to help her." They chose friends, hobbies, and eventually careers and spouses to please their parent. Others grew up believing that it was their job to satisfy the needs of their parent, exemplified in the statement by Nicole, "I was there to help her. I learned how to be amusing at a very young age." In general, they experienced themselves as extensions of their parent, their primary function in life being to take care of, please, admire, reassure, and be devoted to them.

A particularly important expression of devotion was allegiance to and preference for the alienating parent over the targeted parent. For some, such devotion was shown by agreeing to spy on the targeted parent and keep secrets from him or her. Others exhibited devotion by denigrating the targeted parent, making negative reports to the alienating parent about the targeted parent, and saying that they did not enjoy themselves during visits, exaggerating small infractions or hurts, and making false claims of harm. Joining the alienating parent in belittling the targeted parent was another means of showing devotion. A few of the adult children of PAS recalled mocking the targeted parent, and Frank told of being encouraged to spit on, hit, and sexually humiliate his mother at the behest of his father. Devotion also took the form of making accusations against the targeted parent for real and fabricated allegations, including stealing the child's personal items and shirking financial obligations such as child support payments.

As with cults, loyalty and devotion in alienating families was extracted either through sweet seduction or through wrathful demands (and usually an alternating sequence of both). An example of the former was provided by Veronica, whose mother and stepfather were "nicer than nice," doing everything for her until she eventually believed, "that they were the only ones we could rely on, that we had to be with them." In her family, demonstrations of loyalty took the form of hiding from her father when he came to visit and being rude to people in the neighborhood whom her mother and stepfather singled out as being worthy of contempt. Kate's mother asked her, "Don't you want to stay here with me and your sister? Your sister understands that to go over there is to go with people who don't like me. I am your mother, don't you want to like me?" Through a combination of rhetorical skill and guilt inducement Kate's mother compelled Kate to reject her father.

At the other end of the spectrum of strategies for extracting loyalty was Jonah, a young man who grew up with a raging drunken father. "There was a constant ritual everyday. He would come in my room in the middle of the night and make me profess my faith to him and if I didn't and if I didn't stay away from everybody else that he was going to kill himself. He would do this and I would have nobody." Other adult children of PAS felt as if they had to constantly reassure their alienating parent that they loved them best of all, and that they did not have positive feelings for the targeted parent, as Amelia did: "She'd start crying and say we didn't love her and that's just how she is."

The ultimate sign of devotion and loyalty to a cult leader entails renouncing all other sources of influence. Just as cult leaders require an exclusive place in the hearts and minds of the members, these alienating parents seemed to want to have sole claim on their children. Allegiance to the targeted parent was not allowed in these families, and it was understood that there was to be an exclusive and all-encompassing relationship with only one parent. The children were made to feel that any contact with the targeted parent was a betrayal of the worst kind. David said of his mother, "If I talked about my dad it was like sticking a knife in her back." Oliver's mother treated him as "the enemy" when he returned from a visit with his father. Ultimately, many of the children were encouraged, if not co-erced, to renounce their relationship with the targeted parent. Loving both parents would have been unthinkable, just as be-longing to two cults at the same time is not possible. And in this way, many felt that they had to make a choice between their parents. Naturally, they chose the parent whom they be-lieved really loved them and was able to take care of them, the one who had been telling them all along that the other parent was unsafe, worthy of their contempt, and did not love them. They also allied themselves with the alienating parent to secure the relationship, which was based on the conditional love of the alienating parent, and seemed tenuous and in constant need of strengthening. Clawar and Rivlan (1991), based on their study of 700 custody cases, concluded that some children may side with the alienating parent because, "The child has observed and has been the recipient of the conditional love of the program-mer (alienating parent) and must move to cement that love through abject compliance" (p. 75). Essentially, the child becomes trapped in a futile struggle to obtain validation and love from the rejecting parent.

Whether in response to love or fear (or a combination of both), in time most of the children were completely turned against the targeted parent withdrawing their love and natural affection for them. More than one made a comment such as Mark's: "I remember thinking he should go ahead and die. I wish he'd just go get in a car accident. I wish he'd die. I didn't want him to come home." Another, Mitch, believed his father, "was a terrible, rotten person who beat my mother and thank God she divorced him." The intensity of these and other similar statements reflects the absolute lack of ambivalence (one parent is all good while the other is all bad), which is a hallmark of parental alienation syndrome.

Thus, in these families, the normal love and respect that children naturally feel for a parent appeared to be insufficient to satisfy the narcissistic demands of the alienating parent. What they seemed to want from their children was a level of adulation and exclusivity typically reserved for cult leaders.

Emotional Manipulation and Persuasion to Heighten Dependency

The second characteristic of cults is that leaders manipulate the thoughts and feelings of its members in order to promote a sense of dependency on them (Hassan, 1988; Singer, 1966). This programming or brainwashing is also a key component of parental alienation syndrome. The alienating parents functioned as "intuitive persuaders" (Zimbardo & Anderson, 1993), utilizing a range of ad hoc and informal compliance tactics to control and manipulate their children.

There were five primary manipulation techniques: (1) relentless denigration—or bad-mouthing—of the character of the targeted parent in order to reduce his or her importance and value; (2) creating the impression that the targeted parent was dangerous and planned to hurt the child in order to instill fear in and rejection of that parent; (3) misrepresenting the targeted parent's feelings for the child in order to create hurt, resentment, and psychological distance; (4) withdrawing love if the child indicated affection or positive regard for the targeted parent in order to heighten the need to please the alienating parent; and (5) erasing the targeted parent from the life and mind of the child through minimizing actual and symbolic contact. Consistent with thought reform techniques as described by psychiatrist Robert Jay Lifton (1969), these five techniques create "psychological forces within the environment that penetrate into the inner emotions of the individual" (p. 66). These mechanisms are consistent with brainwashing practices as outlined by Clawar and Rivlan (1991), who differentiate programming from brainwashing: The former consists of the content of the message, whereas the latter consists of the behaviors used to convey these messages. They found in their extensive study of families involved in custody litigation that, "Most professionals associated with the judicial process agree that virtually all cases that involve children have some element of programming/brainwashing" (p. 4).

Denigration of the Targeted Parent

The most prominent alienation strategy was denigration of the targeted parent, informally referred to as "bad-mouthing." Most of the adult children of PAS remarked on the constant litany of negative comments made about the targeted parent. Many of these comments were general statements about the lack of worth of the person such as being a "piss poor dad," a "whore and a slut," "not the man you think he is," and a "good for nothing drunk probably in jail right now." Common complaints were that the person was a cheat, an alcoholic, and someone who did not care about his or her family. No detail was too trivial to be the object of derision, exemplified by Melinda's stepmother complaining about how lazy Melinda's mother was because she served instant oatmeal in the morning. The alienating parent seemed to operate under the assumption that if a child is told something enough times, it takes on the mantel of truth in their minds, and that did seem to be the case because, "repetition is basic to all programming/brainwashing" (Clawar & Rivlin, 1991, p. 3). When asked if they believed the bad-mouthing, the following responses, made by Carl and Edward, were indicative: "Oh absolutely! At no time did I ever think my mom wasn't telling the truth"; "All of it! I believed her for a really long time, I became really angry with my father. I believed her." The barrage of negative statements was noteworthy for its apparent one-sidedness (nothing good was ever said about the targeted parent to balance out the complaints) and its lack of appropriateness. Even if true, these things should probably not be said to a child, although there might be certain circumstances in which explaining negative aspects of the other parent could be beneficial, as Warshak (2001a) pointed out. The alienating parents explained concepts or used words such as *abortion, womanizer, rape,* and *alcoholic* well before their children knew or needed to know what these concepts meant.

Bad-mouthing the other parent seemed to serve the same function as bad-mouthing the "outside world" has for cults: promotion of dependency. Bad-mouthing creates in cult members a belief that the leader is the only person who truly cares and can be trusted; everyone else is contemptible or dangerous (Kent, 2004; Lifton, 1969; Shaw, 2003). Through bad-mouthing, the alienating parents conveyed to their children that they were the only parent who loved and cared for them, and who could be trusted. Many of the adult children of PAS recalled their alienating parents explicitly inducing dependency, including Hannah whose mother told her: "I did everything for you and he did nothing," and Edward who was led to believe by his mother that, "Basically everything good that happened was because of her." After Julia's mother recited a long list of complaints about her father, her mother would then comfort her by saying that she should not be too upset because Julia had her mother to rely on. Jonah's father also used bad-mouthing in order to promote dependency, "He told me he was the only one who cared about me, the only one who wanted me, that no one else cared about me, over and over and over again." Nicole felt utterly dependent on her mother, "In my mind she was everything. She was all I had." The constant bad-mouthing created in the children the belief that the targeted parent was not worthy of their love and respect, much the way cult leaders aim to diminish all other authority figures in the eyes of members.

Creating the Impression that the Targeted
Parent was Dangerous

Sometimes the bad-mouthing took on a decidedly darker tone and these children were led to believe that the targeted parent was capable of inflicting great harm. These children were told that the targeted parent had beaten them, wanted to abort them, planned on throwing them in the river, was reckless with them when they were babies, and was intent on kidnapping them. Bonnie remembered the first time she saw her father and stepmother after a seven-year interruption in visitation, "Up to the point they drove up into the driveway my mom was sitting there telling me they would kidnap me." In all, these children were made to feel unsafe at the thought of contact with the targeted parent. Mark's mother often told him how mean and angry his father was. "If I needed help with homework she would say, 'Don't ask your daddy, he will yell at you.' I was scared of him. It was like a landmine." As a boy, Mark avoided being in the same room with his father and lived in constant fear of being beaten by him, despite the fact that this had never actually occurred. "I felt like he was hitting me all the time in my head. It was a constant barrage of how incompetent and how dangerous my father was."

Bad-mouthing in order to instill fear of the targeted parent seemed to serve at least two purposes. First, it made the child want to avoid the targeted parent and thus furthered the alienating parent's goal of severing that relationship. In addition, it heightened the child's need for a protector, a role the alienating parent seemed only too willing to play. In this way the bond between the alienating parent and the child was further strengthened and reinforced. As attachment theorists such as John Bowlby (1969) as well as Mary Ainsworth and her colleagues (Ainsworth, Blehar, Waters, & Wall, 1978) have found, when a child senses fear (real or imagined) the desire to be near and comforted by the attachment figure/caretaker is activated. This is a biologically determined protective mechanism designed to ensure the safety of the vulnerable within any species. Alienating parents exploited this innate mechanism in order to artificially induce their children's desire to be near them (see Chapter 3).

Creating fear in order to activate dependency needs is a widely used strategy in cults. False scenarios of doomsday and threats from external forces have been fabricated in order to heighten members' dependency on the leader. Jonestown, Branch Davidians, and Heaven's Gate are just a few cults that have propagated a sense of imminent danger along with a belief that the end was near (either from natural or social forces) in order to further a dependency on the leader. A survivor of Jonestown, Deborah Layton (1998), described the heightened sense of fear the membership felt as a result of Jim Jones's reference to impending nuclear holocaust. Former cult member Nori Muster (2004) reported that in the International Society for Krishna Consciousness the leaders announced that a nuclear war was imminent, resulting in a reorganization of the members into a crisis mode of dependency and fear. In this sense cult leaders behave like insensitive parents who instill fear and dependency rather than encouraging independence and competence.

Deceiving the Child about the Targeted Parent's Feelings

Many of the adult children of PAS were told that the targeted parent did not love them or want them. Amelia's mother said her father, "Didn't love nobody but himself. He didn't care about us." Growing up, Robin was regularly told that his father did not really love him. "That's another thing my mother told me was that my dad didn't want anything to do with us boys. He just walked away from us." Larissa's mother told her, "that my father wasn't my friend at all, that he had contempt for 'a lout like you.'" And Julia was told, "I was not important to him. His other kids came first. I was last on his list." In many cases the alienating parent actually engineered situations to create the impression that the targeted parent did not care and then used that very situation to convince the child that the targeted parent did not love them. For example, Bonnie's mother threw away letters her father was sending and then invited Bonnie to explain how her father could possibly love her if he could not even bother to write. Other parents refused to accept phone calls, moved away without providing contact information, and told the targeted parent that the child did not want to see them. Because the alienating parents eliminated communication with the targeted parent and controlled all information, the children had no means with which to determine the veracity of what they were being told. Eventually, they capitulated under the weight of the "evidence" and concluded that the targeted parent did not love them after all, further fueling their hurt and resentment. In addition, once they accepted this as fact, the alienating parent became even more important to them as their sole source of parental love, support, and care. In cults this use of black–white and us–them thinking promotes the belief that anyone outside the cult is necessarily wrong or does not really understand or love the members as the leader of the cult does.

Withdrawal of Love as a Punishment

A classic cult technique is to create a sense of psychological imbalance and anxiety in members so that they are preoccupied with winning back the praise and acceptance of the leader. Sometimes this is accomplished through the unpredictable use of rewards and punishments, as described by therapists Lorna and William Goldberg (1988). One particularly potent form of punishment is for the leader to withdraw love and acceptance of a member in order to create a sense of insecurity. Panic ensues as the individual scrambles to get back in the leader's good graces. Everything else becomes secondary to regaining approval and equilibrium, and considerable effort is expended in figuring out how to avoid expulsion from the leader's realm of acceptance. Steven Hassan's (1988) experience with the Unification Church exemplified this model: "Moon had a novel style of motivating leaders. He would be nice to us at first, buying us gifts and taking us out for dinner or a movie. Then he would bring us back to his estate and yell and scream about how poorly we were performing" (p. 23). Such unpredictable behavior results in an intense desire to win back the lost approval.

Many of the adult children of PAS had this same experience.

They recalled withdrawal of love by the alienating parent if they indicated positive regard for the targeted parent. They learned to pretend they had a poor visit with the targeted parent in order to avoid rejection upon their return home. This did not always work. Serita felt that her mother was not as nice to her following a visit, "She was always in a bit of a mood or temper when we came back." Many got the cold shoulder, as Nancy did, and were emotionally cut off from their parent: "She'd shut me out. It would be just silence." There was an emotional price to pay if they had contact with the targeted parent. Joanne's mother "would make life rotten for us." And Larissa said of her mother, "She couldn't stand to see me actually get on with my father. She'd make her disapproval evident if I so much as spoke to him in a civilized way. This disapproval was in the form of throwing sour looks my way, and then turning her back and ignoring me." Oliver's mother would treat him "like the enemy" when he returned from his weekly visit with his father. Some alienating parents accused their children of not loving them if they went to visit the targeted parent, some threatened to abandon their children, and one mother pointedly served her daughter an inferior portion of food upon returning from a visit. When Melinda came back from a visit with her mother (the targeted parent) her stepmother would reject her, "Oh it was very cold. She would give me the cold shoulder." For some, the alienating parent would not speak to them for several hours or the rest of the evening following the children's return from a visit. Because of the child's profound dependency on the alienating parent, these children found it very hard to tolerate disapproval and subsequent withdrawal of love. Larissa said: "I was scared to disagree with my mother. Any disagreement on my part would cause her to either turn her venom against me or threaten that 'things would never be the same again after an argument like that,' which left me heartbroken and devastated." Likewise, Roberta explained, "My mom could be very punishing in the sense that she would withdraw and not talk to you for long periods of time. I got the business; some might call it the cold shoulder. She would shut off communication. That worked pretty well for me."

When imagining what it would feel like to experience the disapproval of the alienating parents, others spoke of feeling "lost," "terrified," and "all alone." When the alienating parent withdrew love, the children became preoccupied with winning that parent back, as Hannah, did, "It was scary. It made me want to try harder." Thus, fear of withdrawal of love was a powerful threat that was used by the alienating parents to control their children and reduce their affection toward and relationship with the targeted parent.

This pattern of intermittent warmth followed by periodic withdrawal of love has also been found to be an effective strategy for keeping adult victims of emotional abuse locked in a struggle to regain the lost acceptance and equilibrium. Marti Tamm Loring wrote about this aspect of emotional abuse in adult relationships, but it is equally applicable to PAS:

> A characteristic kind of attachment binds the victim and abuser. It is not an empathic connection between two separate, equal individuals. Rather, the abuser perceives the victim in terms of his own needs and wishes, while the victim struggles to connect with him in a mutually validating and empathic manner. When her efforts are repeatedly met with scornful refusals and other forms of emotional abuse, the victim becomes traumatized and clings ever more desperately to the abuser. (1994, p. 16)

Erasing the Other Parent

Cults tend to be exclusive social environments that surround members with like-minded people. Robert Jay Lifton (1969) described this "totalistic" nature of cults as milieu control; the likelihood of contact with alternate viewpoints and perspectives is almost nonexistent. The leader controls the reality of the members by controlling the flow of information in and out of the cult. There is little opportunity for countervailing opinions and points of view to be expressed to members. There is only one shared reality, which must be accepted in order to be a member of the cult. All other ideas are excluded. Newspapers are not read, television is not viewed, contact with outsiders who might question or introduce members to other ways of thinking and believing, is strictly forbidden.

The alienating parents ran the family in much the same way, particularly as it related to the targeted parent. The children were forbidden to have contact with anyone who might speak well of the targeted parent, especially extended family members. Most importantly, contact with the targeted parent was minimized or eliminated all together. In this way, the child did not have any independent experiences of the targeted parent and the parent him- or herself had no opportunity to explain or counter the campaign of lies and denigration. Few if any of the children had pictures of the targeted parent or were allowed to talk about him or her. Mention of the targeted parent was felt to be taboo, avoided at all costs in order to keep the peace in the family. Betty experienced this, "My mother would get so mad she'd almost start shaking if the subject of my father came up" as did Renee who was pushed down the stairs when she spoke about her father. David recalled, "Every time I mentioned my dad all hell breaks loose. It was almost as if I knew if I mentioned that I wanted to go see my dad I would be brow beaten into submission." Melinda was not allowed to bring home gifts received during visits with her mother because, "It wasn't fair to the other kids. I wasn't allowed to talk about it." In all these ways, the presence of the targeted parent was minimized and their place in the hearts and minds of the children was diminished.

Through these five strategies, the alienating parents elevated themselves into an esteemed place in their children's eyes and cultivated in their children a profound dependency on their approval and acceptance.

Cults Further the Aims of the Leader

Cults operate to profit the leader at the expense of its members. While they claim to exist for the benefit of the members—who are in need of the wisdom and guidance of the leader—the reality is just the opposite: the leader gains much more than the members from the experience. The benefits of cults to their leaders are both financial and psychological. Leaders of cults have unlimited access to the accumulated wealth and assets and often spend disproportionately on themselves, justifying such expenses as the minimum compensation for their sacrifice and hard work on behalf of the members. The psychological rewards of cult membership are also plentiful. Leaders are worshipped as all-powerful, omniscient individuals who can exercise control and authority at their whim.

Similarly, the alienating parents profited from the lofty place they held in their children's lives and from the elimination of the targeted parent. First, they benefited by not having to share parenting time with someone they no longer lived with or loved. They achieved this by avoiding the complication of coordinating schedules, and by not having to secure the cooperation and make the kinds of compromises typically required when coparenting a child. As divorce researcher Janet Johnston (1994) found, concerns about the other parent's ability to care for the children is pervasive in high conflict divorces. For the most part the alienating parents had the opportunity to raise their child as they pleased without the interference or involvement of another parent. Because many remarried, they did not suffer the financial and emotional difficulties of single parenthood (Teachman & Paasch, 1994). Second, they seemed to benefit by exacting revenge on a person whom they believed had harmed or rejected them. By having the child reject the targeted parent, the alienating parent most likely had the satisfaction of the last laugh, so to speak. They had the opportunity to reject the parent in a way that was designed to maximally inflict pain and suffering. And, finally, they seemed to benefit from the narcissistic satisfaction of being the most important person in their child's life. Through the strategies described above, these parents extended the natural idealization of their children well into the later teens and for some well into adulthood. By cultivating dependency on them, these parents delayed or avoided all together the natural separation and deidealization of their children. Thus, they warded off the feelings of loss and sadness that typically accompany the process of children individuating and becoming self-sufficient adults.

Much has been written about the loss of identity, the loss of time with family, and the loss of dreams that result from extended participation in cults (Langone, 1993; McKibben, Lynn, & Malinoski, 2002; Singer, 1966; Tobias & Lalich, 1994). The costs of cult participation are profound, both psychological and financial. Many cults require hefty membership fees while others encourage if not require members to turn over all their assets and wealth to the leader. In addition to the financial costs associated with cult membership, former members describe the emotional harm done to them as by far the worst aspect of the experience, including (1) diminished self-esteem from excessive dependence; (2) guilt from having hurt friends and family; (3) depression and sadness over time lost with friends and family; and (4) difficulties trusting self and other. The adult children of PAS also experienced these negative emotional outcomes as a result of being alienated from one parent due to the actions and behaviors of the other.

Low Self-Esteem

Like former cult members, adults whose parents alienated them from the other parent also had problems with self-esteem. Some expressed the belief that they should have questioned more what they were being told about the targeted parent, while others recognized that as a child they really had no reason to doubt what their parents were telling them. "Of course I believed my mother. She was God!" explained Robin. This was not the primary source of their diminished self-esteem. For them, it came from the internalization of the hatred of the targeted parent. When the alienating parent denigrated the targeted parent, the child assumed that he or she too was bad and worthy of contempt because that person was at least in part inside him or her (genetically and psychologically). This sentiment was exemplified by the following statement by Julia: "Any parts that I did feel were like my father made me feel bad about myself because she berated him so. If I was like him how could that be good?" Thus, the alienating parent's rejection of the targeted parent was experienced as a rejection of that part of the child that was like the targeted parent. Self-esteem problems in former cult members also result from leaders fostering a belief that parents, friends, and family do not really love and care for them. Only the cult leader loves the person the way he or she deserves to be loved. This experience was also seen in the adult children of PAS, many of whom were told that the targeted parent did not really love or want them. This also resulted in diminished self-esteem because the child assumed that if the targeted parent did not love them, he or she must be unworthy of love.

Guilt

Former cult members often report feeling guilty about the harm their cult involvement caused loved ones. Once they realize that they squandered their money and assets and that they treated badly those who really love them, they feel ashamed that they were capable of behaving so callously toward people who did not deserve it. Former cult members recall the times that they were rude or belittling or rejecting of their friends and family and feel ashamed by their own behavior.

The adult children of PAS also experienced guilt at having betrayed the targeted parent. Ron, who was made to verbally abuse his father on the telephone, worried about what impact that had on his father. He described his own feeling at the time as being like "slicing his wrists." Elaine believed that she was a "horrible horrible person" for joining her mother against her father. In this way, betrayal of others becomes a betrayal of themselves. Likewise, Lifton wrote about victims of Chinese thought reform, "They were in effect being made to renounce the people, the organizations, and the standards of behavior which had formed the matrix of their previous existence. They were being forced to betray—not so much their friends and colleagues, as a vital core of themselves" (1969, p. 69).

Depression

Depression is a common experience for former cult members. They feel saddened about the time they lost with their friends and family on the outside and for the personal life dreams, aspirations, and goals they gave up. Depression was also prevalent in the adult children of parental alienation syndrome. Like former cult members, they too felt badly about the time they lost. Nancy lamented the time she could have spent with her father, "I missed many years with my father. Many wonderful years I could have had with him." Carl, who did not find his father until much later in life, said he fully expected to meet him for the first time when he stood over his grave. The adult children of PAS expressed the belief that their depression was also due to feeling rejected by the targeted parent, in addition to the time they lost with them. Carl described his experience with depression as, "I feel like I have a hole in my soul. And it is not something you can physically point to and say here it is, but you know it is there."

The impact of the loss of the targeted parent was exacerbated by the fact they were not allowed to openly mourn their loss. In general, during childhood, the adult children of PAS were discouraged from talking about or expressing interest in their relationship with the targeted parent. Their loss was not acknowledged and they received no emotional support in dealing with it. In fact, quite the opposite message was conveyed to them, that it was a positive event for the targeted parent to be out of their lives, essentially a "good riddance to bad rubbish" message. Inability to mourn a loss or significant life change is believed to be associated with subsequent depression and this was certainly borne out in the lives of the adult children of PAS (Bowlby, 1980; Kübler-Ross, 1997).

Lack of Trust

Lack of trust in themselves and others is a recurring theme in interviews with former cult members. They know that they were manipulated once and worry that it can happen again. They realize that what they believed about the cult and the leader was actually not the case, and therefore, do not trust themselves to be good judges of other's motives and character. This theme was also heard among the adult children of PAS. They did not trust their own perceptions of people because from a young age they were told by one parent that the other parent (whom most had positive memories of) was bad, dangerous, or in some way worthy of fear or contempt. Once they realized that they had been manipulated and that what they had been led to believe their whole lives about the targeted parent was not the truth (or at least not the whole truth) they became even more unsure of what to believe and whom to trust. As Serita concluded, "Everything I believed is not so true." In addition, some women who were alienated from their fathers reported not being able to trust that men would love them. They assumed that if their father (their first male love) did not love them enough to stay involved in their lives no man would find them worthy of love and commitment.

A body of knowledge has been developed about cult leaders and the strategies they use, which may help the adult children of parental alienation syndrome feel connected to a larger group, and may provide them with a way to think about their parents and themselves that facilitates recovery and growth. Parents who are currently losing a child to an alienating parent may also find this framework useful for understanding the changes they see in their child.

Chapter 3

Strategies of Alienation and Attachment Theory

Pressure put on the children to conform to their parents'
wishes can be crude or subtle, but its effectiveness depends
on the child's insistent desire to be loved and protected.
—John Bowlby, *On Knowing What You Are Not Supposed*
to Know and Feeling What You Are Not Supposed to Feel

SOME STRATEGIES WERE MENTIONED BY MANY OF THE ADULT
children of PAS, while others were mentioned by just a few, or
by only one (see Table 3.1). The lens through which these strategies are examined is attachment theory (Bowlby, 1969). That is,
the strategies are viewed as effective tools for interfering with
the developing or existing attachment relationship between the
adult child of PAS (as a child) and the targeted parent.

According to Bowlby (1969), infants develop strong emotional ties with their parents, the purpose of which is to ensure
their safety by inducing them to seek proximity to a caretaking
adult when signals of danger are present. Certain biologically
determined experiences activate the infant's need for comfort
and proximity to the attachment figure. For infants and young
children, these experiences include illness, darkness, being
alone, being in an unfamiliar environment, and the presence of
strangers. When these signals of danger are present, the attach-

TABLE 3.1
STRATEGIES USED TO ALIENATE CHILDREN
FROM THEIR TARGETED PARENT

Frequency Distribution of the Strategies Reported by the Sample

Bad-mouthing, general (n = 39, 97.5%)

Limiting contact (n = 27, 67.5%)

Withdrawing love/getting angry (n = 24, 60.0%)

Telling child targeted parent doesn't love him or her (n = 21, 52.5%)

Forcing child to choose/express loyalty (n = 21, 52.5%)

Bad-mouthing to create impression targeted parent is dangerous (n = 17, 42.5%)

Confiding in child about adult relationship (n = 16, 40.0%)

Limiting mention and photos of targeted parent (n = 15, 37.5%)

Forcing child to reject targeted parent (n = 13, 32.5%)

Limiting contact with extended family (n = 10, 25.0%)

Belittling targeted parent in front of child (n = 09, 22.5%)

Creating conflict between child and targeted parent (n = 08, 20.0%)

Cultivating dependency on alienating parent (n = 06, 15.0%)

Throwing out gifts and letters from targeted parent (n = 06, 15.0%)

Interrogating child after visits with targeted parent (n = 04, 10.0%)

Making child feel guilty about positive relationship with targeted parent (n = 03, 07.5%)

Having child spy on targeted parent (n = 03, 07.5%)

Telling targeted parent child doesn't love him or her (n = 02, 05.0%)

Monitoring letters and phone calls with targeted parent (n = 02, 05.0%)

Child calling targeted parent by first name (n = 02, 05.0%)

Having child refer to some someone else as "mom" or "dad" (n = 02, 05.0%)

TABLE 3.1
(Continued)

Not letting child be alone with targeted parent (n = 02, 05.0%)

Telling child someone else is his or her father/mother (n = 01, 02.5%)

Telling child he or she can't visit targeted parent, siblings have to stay together (n = 01, 02.5%)

Not allowing child to bring gifts from targeted parent into home (n = 01, 02.5%)

Threatening to take child away from targeted parent (n = 01, 02.5%)

Not letting extended family talk about targeted parent (n = 01, 02.5%)

Having secret signals and means of communication with child (n = 01, 02.5%)

Having child keep secrets from targeted parent (n = 01, 02.5%)

Beating targeted parent in front of child (n = 01, 02.5%)

Changing child's name (n = 01, 02.5%)

Accusing child of being too close with targeted parent (n = 01, 02.5%)

Making it appear as if the targeted parent is rejecting participant (n = 01, 02.5%).

ment system is activated and the infant seeks proximity and comfort from the attachment figure. If the attachment figure is contingently responsive to the infant's comfort-seeking behaviors, the infant learns to trust that adult and continues to seek comfort from him or her in the future.

Research conducted by Mary Ainsworth and her colleagues (Ainsworth, Blehar, Waters, & Wall, 1978) demonstrated that when the attachment figure is not consistently available in emotional and physical terms, the infant either becomes preoccupied with gaining comfort from that parent (if the parent is *un*predictably available) or learns that the parent is not available and ceases seeking comfort from him or her (if the parent is predictably *un*available). Thus, in order for infants to desire comfort from and closeness to the caretaking adult, they have to develop a belief over time that the adult is predictably emotionally and physically available. Cicchetti, Cummings, Greenberg, and Marvin (1990) postulated that as children develop and mature, the types of situations that activate the need for comfort and proximity change, but the underlying function of the relationship remains the same.

The strategies used by the alienating parents suggest that they (intuitively) understood that the way to effectuate PAS was to foster the belief that the targeted parent was emotionally and physically unavailable so that the children would cease seeking comfort from and contact with him or her. To do this, the alienating parents conveyed the message that the targeted parent was not a predictably safe, available, and comforting adult, but unworthy, unsafe, and unavailable. This process is consistent with Garber's (2004) and Thompson's (2000) observations that as children's cognitive and language skills mature, their internal working models of relationships are based not just on direct experience but can be influenced by "verbally mediated" material as well. The targeted parents had restricted opportunities to provide comfort to their children, to take care of them when they were ill, and to be with them as the primary caretaking parent. Thus, there were reduced opportunities for the targeted parents to be experienced as attachment figures. Further, the alienating parents led the children to believe that their primary attachment figure (in most cases the custodial alienating parent) would be less emotionally and physically available if they did have a positive relationship with the targeted parent. This created a sense of insecurity vis-à-vis that relationship, which could only be reduced by pleasing the alienating parent and turning against the targeted parent. Thus, a double message was conveyed: (1) the targeted parent was not safe and available and (2) pursuing that relationship would entail the loss of the primary attachment figure. These two messages powerfully combined to effectively alienate the child from the targeted parent. These messages were conveyed through a combination of strategies.

BAD-MOUTHING

Consistent with Gardner's (1998) original conceptualization, general bad-mouthing was a commonly used strategy. Derogatory statements about the targeted parent encouraged the child to feel negatively toward and unsafe with him or her and undermined the development of a secure attachment. Examples of bad-mouthing included saying that the targeted parent was a rapist, a bum, a womanizer, lazy, irresponsible, a deadbeat, a cheat, a gambler, a whore, a slut, an abuser, worthless, an alcoholic, and as Amelia explained, "Basically he was a very bad person."

It is possible that bad-mouthing was recalled so frequently because it was not particularly subtle and because it was relatively constant. Many of the adult children of PAS experienced bad-mouthing as a continuous presence in their lives. Comments by Bonnie, Mark, Iris, and Hannah are typical, "Everything she had to say about him was negative and bad"; "There was the constant bad-mouthing. What a monster he was"; "She kept telling us how bad he was. She kept telling me over and over he was a child molester"; and "It was so frequent I couldn't begin to say a specific time." Renee said, "She never said anything good about him. She said he was worthless. He was an alcoholic."

The bad-mouthing was relatively effective in creating a negative impression of the targeted parent because the children believed much of what they heard. For the most part they did not have a reason to doubt what their alienating parent was telling them. This was so for at least three reasons. First, as M. Scott Peck (1983) and others have noted, in general children believe what their parents tell them because it is too threatening to entertain the notion that the person on whom they are dependent is not trustworthy or reliable. This sentiment is illustrated by Robin's exclamation, "I believed all of it. She was God!" Second, the statements were made with considerable conviction on the part of the alienating parent, and thus were particularly believable and compelling. Tracey described her mother as "very convincing, crying, sobbing." Third, in many cases the targeted parents had limited opportunity to counter what was being said or chose not to counter because, mistakenly, they believed that it was wrong to speak ill of the other parent. For these reasons, the children were exposed to a one-sided campaign of denigration of the targeted parent. They grew up with negative images of the targeted parent that contributed to the idea that he or she was an unsafe person who was unworthy of their love and devotion. Carl's image growing up was, "of my father lying in a ditch."

LIMITING CONTACT

Preventing contact with the targeted parent reduced his or her ability to serve as a comforting attachment figure in times of illness, distress, or need. Several of the alienating mothers did not allow their children to spend time alone with the targeted father during scheduled visitation, and all contact included both parents. Nancy explained that her mother "was always around. I didn't spend quality time with him." Joanne, too "never had parental time alone with him." In other cases, the alienating parent simply did not comply with the scheduled visitation, saying the child was ill or had too much studying to do. In Kate's family, "It was supposed to be every Wednesday night for dinner but my mother kind of started going off that." Oliver's mother used grades as an excuse to limit contact: "You need to stay home more and study." Yet another scenario involved alienating parents who relocated thereby reducing the amount of contact that was possible with the targeted parent. Iris's mother moved the children from California to Oklahoma and Iris did not see her father for two years, "We were not allowed to." Others had memories of their targeted parent coming for visitation and being turned away by the alienating parent, such as in Tracey's case, "My mom and dad got into a fight because my mom wouldn't let him see us. I guess he had initiated to come see us and she wouldn't let him." Veronica's mother and stepfather, "put notes on the front door saying we were out so he would know we were not in and we would have to hide."

Limiting contact was very effective at turning the children against the targeted parent because it reduced both the intensity of the emotional tie as well as prevented that parent from countering the bad-mouthing specifically and the alienation campaign in general.

WITHDRAWAL OF LOVE
AND ANGER

Withdrawal of love and anger was particularly noticeable following visitation with the targeted parent. Kate said of her mother, "It would make her angry if I was close with him." Others shared similar experiences: Nancy, "She would shut me out. It would be just silence." Larissa, "When we returned home my mother gave a sour look. She couldn't stand to actually see me get on with my father." Melinda, "Oh it was very cold. She would give me the cold shoulder." Serita: "When I did see him she was horrible to me. When I came back from visits she wouldn't talk to me." Ron: "My mother would get really angry if, for example, my brother or I displayed any affection for my father."

Thus, there was an emotional price to pay for having a relationship with the targeted parent. It was clear that the alienating parents did not want their children to have a relationship with the targeted parents and conveyed the message that it was not possible to express love for both parents. Expressing love for the targeted parents involved a threat of losing the love and approval of the alienating parents who were also (in all but a few instances) the custodial parents. In this way, the alienating parents activated the child's attachment to them and increased their importance to the child, eclipsing the role of the targeted parents. The adult children of PAS recalled how anxious they felt when the alienating parent withdrew his or her love. It made them want to try harder to please that parent. The focus of their attention became the alienating parent not the targeted parent and this further worked to effectuate the alienation.

TELLING CHILD TARGETED PARENT
DOES NOT LOVE HIM OR HER

Some alienating parents told their children that the targeted parent did not love them. Robin said, "My mother told me that my dad didn't want anything to do with us boys, he just walked away from us." And Amelia commented, "She said he didn't love nobody but himself." While Nicole shared, "She'd say you were so misbehaved, such a bad child, look he doesn't even want to be around you." And Larissa commented, "She told me my father wasn't my friend at all." Carrie's mother told her and her brother, "that Dad left us, abandoned us. He's a bastard, he never wanted you."

This is a very specific form of bad-mouthing designed to attenuate the child's attachment to the targeted parent and to create hurt and anger toward that parent. This strategy also served to heighten the regard for and dependency on the alienating parent who was presented as the good parent who did love and take care of the child. Julia explained that after an extensive list of criticisms about her father, her mother would then reassure her by telling her, "I shouldn't be too upset because I had her."

FORCING CHILD TO CHOOSE
BETWEEN PARENTS

It was also necessary for the children to express loyalty to the alienating parent, as a preference over the targeted parent. Roberta shared, "I always felt like there was pressure to be on her side." As noted in Chapter 2, Kate's mother put it to her this way, "'Don't you want to be here with me and your sister? Your sister understands that to go over there is to be with people who don't like me. I am your mother don't you want to like me?" Peter's mother responded negatively to his relationship with his father even when Peter was an adult. "Any time I would tell her that I talked to him on the phone it was always the same response, 'Why? I am the one who took care of you. I'm the one who raised you and fed you. Why are you calling him?' That was her attitude." Likewise, even as an adult Tracey felt pressure to choose her mother over her father. "To this day I show favoritism to my mom." And Serita, too, felt guilty about having a relationship with her targeted parent, "I did seem a bit of a traitor and I felt as though I had to choose in the end."

CREATING THE IMPRESSION
THAT THE TARGETED PARENT
IS DANGEROUS

Sometimes the bad-mouthing was designed to create the impression that the targeted parent posed a danger to the child: that the targeted parent planned to kidnap them or telling stories of how the targeted parent tried to or did hurt them when they were young. Bonnie's mother frightened her by suggesting that her stepmother and father, whom she had not seen in several years, would not return her after the upcoming reinstalled visitation. "She was telling me they were going to kidnap me and never bring me back. Up to the point they drove up into the driveway my mom was sitting there telling me, 'You better watch it because they are going to take you away and they are never going to bring you back. That lady is from Ohio. Do you know anybody in Ohio? Do you know how to get back home?'" Likewise, Mark's mother told him, "how mean and angry he was." For Carl, "Sometimes there were stories about my father and when I was young he said, 'Can you wrap him up I want to take him out for a bit?' My mother said she thought he was going to throw me in the river." Two alienating parents claimed to have actually saved their child from an intended abortion (Felicity's father described the procedure in vivid detail and provided graphic illustrations of aborted fetuses).

From an attachment perspective, this strategy is one of the most damning things that can be said about a parent, that he or she is dangerous to the child. This is the antithesis of the function of the attachment relationship: promoting a sense of safety and security in the child through the presence of the caretaking adult. Many of the adult children recalled that this was an effective strategy in that they did become afraid of the targeted parent. Mark said, "I was scared of him, like a landmine."

CONFIDING IN CHILD

The alienating parent shared with their children personal details about the marital relationship, in order to solidify their relationship at the expense of the relationship with the targeted parent. These children knew things about the targeted parent that the targeted parent did not know they knew and therefore had no opportunity to correct the misrepresentation or tell his or her side of the story. The children were left with a one-sided understanding of the adult relationship, which was designed to make the targeted parent appear unworthy in their eyes. In addition, these confidences served to enhance the intimacy with the alienating parent and further bind the children to that parent. Further, these confidences often led the children to feel sorry for the alienating parent and be angry with the targeted parent for their supposed misdeeds and failings. This was particularly true for Sarah. "I believe it started when she took me into her confidence. She complained to me about how she felt he didn't care for her. I felt like I was supposed to do something, to provide her with answers and help her sort it out." Larissa, too, was the recipient of her mother's inside perspective on the marriage and family. "She made several announcements to me that she was going to be seeking a divorce and she told me how marvelous life would be once the divorce went through. I was so happy about that. I suppose I felt as though she saw me as a friend and I hoped I was worthy of her liking me."

Roberta was made aware of her mother's fears about the marriage, "She felt insecure regarding other women and I had knowledge of so many things and that was something I was really too young to know about." Similarly, Ron was exposed to more adult content and feelings than he felt able to process, "My mother would get into more of her personal life with my father, which was really not any of our business as children and in some way it had a negative effect." A particularly vivid story was recounted by Josh, who, when he was 5 years old, was told by his mother that she could not cope with the demands of her three stepdaughters and that she planned to take him and leave the rest of the family. "She was upset and she was sharing that with me. The predominant impression was incredible intensity and excitement and horror."

For Alix the confidence took the form of being told at the age of 4 by her mother that her father raped her mother and that was how she was conceived, while for Serita it entailed being taken to the lawyer's office to translate for her mother a discussion about divorce, unbeknownst to the rest of the family. Elaine explained, "It was us against him kind of thing. She was treating me as a peer or a friend rather than a child in the household." And Jonah remembered, "My father coming into my room and basically telling me that he had seen a psychologist and he wanted my opinion as to whether my father and mother should stay together." Roberta's mother, too, relied on her daughter in this way. "Our mother definitely used us as confidants. She really didn't turn outside the family much for help or things like that so we were pretty much her sounding board and her support system." As these quotes illustrate, the alienating parent drew the children into his or her perspective and created a special intimate bond, an enmeshed relationship that excluded the targeted parent, and was designed to induce anger and resentment toward the targeted parent, again diminishing the quality of the attachment relationship.

LIMITING MENTION
AND PHOTOGRAPHS OF
TARGETED PARENTS

Photographs of the targeted parents were forbidden, as was mention of their names in the presence of the alienating parents. When asked how his mother would respond if he asked about his father, Walter responded, "That obviously never happened." Although Patricia's parents remained married, she was exposed to a particularly vitriolic form of parental alienation. During a period when her parents were separated, she recounted, "He would burn her things including pictures of her." Betty's mother, too, was adamant that no mention of the father be made, "My mother would get so mad she'd almost be shaking when the subject of my father came up." Renee explained, "We weren't really allowed to talk about him. I brought up his name one time and she shoved me down the stairs." And David said, "Every time I talk[ed] about my dad all hell breaks loose." Veronica's mother became involved with another man shortly after the divorce and together the two of them banned any mention of Veronica's father. "I remember being about 5 and saying at the table that I wanted to see him and she went into her room crying." Serita, who lived with her mother, felt that she was forbidden to express positive feelings for her father, "I wasn't allowed to say I missed my father." Alix's mother was also violently opposed to any mention of the targeted parent, "I knew better than to start something like that (ask about the targeted parent). She would probably beat the crap out of me." Melinda lived with her father and visited her mother on weekends. When she returned from visitation, she said, she did not feel that she should talk about what she did or even say her mother's name, "I wasn't allowed to talk about what I did with my mom." Peter's mother conveyed to him nonverbally that discussion of his father was not permitted, "She would avoid talking about him and if you mentioned his name she would bristle."

Prohibiting talking about, thinking about, looking at pictures of the targeted parent comprised a direct attempt to disrupt the attachment with the targeted parent. From an attachment perspective, these activities (seeing pictures and talking about the person) function to keep the relationship alive in the absence of the parent. Early research on children separated from their parents demonstrated that how children make sense of a separation and how they cope with it can affect the quality of the relationship once they are reunited with their parent (Bowlby, 1969). This is because the child has inside his or her mind an "internal working model" of the attachment relationship, the sum total of the experiences with that parent organized into a belief system about whether the parent is emotionally and physically responsive (Bretherton, 1985; Bretherton, Ridgeway,

Cassidy, 1990). Separations from the parent and what they mean to the child become incorporated into the internal working model, which in turn shapes the child's interactions and responses to the parent once reunited. In general, children who are allowed to think about, talk about, and have pictures of the absent parent are better able to cope with separations and are more receptive to the parent upon reunion. In this way, prohibiting the child's ability to maintain the idea of the attachment relationship with the targeted parent during separations (through talking about and looking at pictures of him or her) interfered with the actual relationship.

FORCING CHILD TO REJECT TARGETED PARENT

Some adult children of PAS were placed in situations as children in which the alienating parent forced them to reject the targeted parent. Julia's mother was particularly creative in this respect. She wrote skits that Julia was expected to perform during visits with her father. In each there was a moment when Julia was scripted to verbally attack her father by telling him that she hated him, which was followed by a dramatic exit from the room. "She would write these little plays and he would come over and I was supposed to come into the living room and scream at him and tell him what a horrible father he was and run out of the room and cry hysterically." At the age of 9 Ron was made to telephone his father under the watchful supervision of his mother and curse at him in explicit detail about his failings. He was also forced to cancel visits. "My dad was supposed to come see us and visit and these times were supposedly prearranged with her and when the time came for these visits she would sometimes have me and my brother phone and say we didn't want him to come." Nicole was encouraged to yell at her father, repeating to him the negative statements that her mother had just rehearsed with her. Mitch recalled having the telephone put to his ear as he was told to say that he never wanted to see his father again. To this day he is not sure who was on the other end of the phone. Jonah was encouraged to call his mother from Florida where his father had taken him and tell her she did not care about him, "Basically to humiliate her." As a teenager Jonah went to the police station at the urging of his father and reported that his mother had abandoned him.

These demonstrations of rejection served at least two purposes. First, they were designed to create enormous ill will between the targeted parent and the child. Hurt, resentment, and insecurity were created in the heart and mind of the targeted parents, many of whom seemed to doubt their rightful place in the lives of their own children. Second, by requiring assertions of anger and hatred toward the targeted parent, the alienating parents were exploiting the natural tendency in people to want their beliefs to be consistent with their actions—described as cognitive dissonance by Festinger (1957). That is, the alienating parents were hoping that if they made their children behave a certain way, they would adjust their beliefs accordingly, to be in line with their behavior. In this way they aimed to make what the children said become what they believed.

LIMITING CONTACT WITH/
BELITTLING EXTENDED FAMILY

Alienating parents also limited contact with grandparents and other members of the targeted parent's family. This is consistent with what Warshak (2001a) referred to as tribal warfare and one of Gardner's eight primary manifestations of PAS. The alienating parent adopted a warlike mentality in which they and their family were on one side of the conflict and the targeted parent and his or her family were perceived to be in the enemy camp. The negative statements made by the alienating parent often extended to the family of the targeted parent, as if there was something inherently unworthy, disgusting, or unacceptable about them simply through their association with the targeted parent. As Betty noted, "My mother wouldn't let me have contact with even my father's family members." And Joanne's mother disparaged the extended family, even though she was still married to Joanne's father. "My mother was very adamant when I was a child that my (paternal) grandmother was a very bad person." Likewise, although Patricia's parents did not divorce, she recalled her father openly demeaning her mother's family. "My father never attended family holidays (with mother's family) and made us feel bad for wasting our time on 'those people.'"

From a practical point of view, limiting contact with the extended family reduced the likelihood that the children would spend time with people who might defend the targeted parent or present another side to the situation. Thus, they were prevented from being in a position in which their negative views of the targeted parent would be challenged, questioned, or tempered. According to Warshak (2001a), one way to counteract alienation is to have grandparents and other trusted adults present a more balanced view of the targeted parent. This possibility was eliminated.

BELITTLING TARGETED PARENT
IN FRONT OF CHILD

Belittling was another, subtler, form of bad-mouthing. The alienating parent belittled the targeted parent in front of their children. Patricia said: "He put her down, belittled her family, her job, her career achievements, her friends and anything that had to do with our mother." Her father made "oinking" noises whenever her mother was near the refrigerator, indicating that she resembled a pig. He also had derogatory nicknames for everyone on the mother's side of the family. A more extreme version was experienced by Frank, whose father not only verbally mocked his mother but also beat and kicked her in front of the children in order to demonstrate to them how worthless she was. Jason, too, told how his father derided his mother: "Rather than acknowledge her skills and energy and ingenuity he belittled her and put her down all the time." Likewise, Elaine's mother saw the worst in her father, constantly telling him in front of her, "Frank you were never a good father. Frank you never had any interest." Again, these putdowns were designed to induce negative feelings and ideas about the targeted parent in the minds of the child in order to attenuate the attachment relationship.

INCITING CONFLICT BETWEEN CHILD
AND TARGETED PARENT

Some alienating parents were able to create situations that induced conflict between their children and the targeted parent. Thus, when contact could not be fully eliminated the alienating parents found ways to poison the time spent with the targeted parent. This further created the impression that the targeted parent was not to be trusted. The more time spent with the targeted parent fighting and having negative experiences, the less time there was for the development of a positive relationship. This was especially true for Joanne: "We were always in conflict. She would basically do whatever she could to create conflict between us." Some, like David, were made to look for the support check in the mail and report to the mother if it was late, a strategy designed to create the impression that the targeted parent was irresponsible and rejecting. These negative moments between the children and targeted parent become part of the fabric of their relationship, and thus affected how they felt about each other. It is easy to imagine that these moments of ill will between child and targeted parent created a strain in the relationship that contributed to the alienation. For example, when the targeted parent is irritable with the child in response to these provocations inspired by the alienating parent, the child is probably only aware of the targeted parent's behavior and not of the invisible hand of the alienating parent, working behind the scenes to negatively influence the relationship. The child walks away with a negative feeling about the targeted parent. Because they were not aware that they were being manipulated, their anger felt authentic and justified to them. This is consistent with Gardner's (1998) independent thinker phenomenon in which children experience ownership of the negative feelings that they have toward the targeted parent despite the fact that they appear to others to have been manipulated into having those feelings.

SUMMARY AND DISCUSSION

Thirty-two different strategies were used to alienate the children from their targeted parent (see Table 3.1). Twelve of those strategies were described in detail above. These strategies can be understood in the context of attachment theory in that they contributed to the child believing that the targeted parent was unavailable and unsafe rather than an emotionally responsive and physically available attachment figure. The other strategies (mentioned by just a few of the adult children of PAS) included: cultivating dependency on the alienating parent; throwing out gifts and letters from the targeted parent; interrogating the child after visits with the targeted parent; encouraging the child to feel guilty about having a positive relationship with the targeted parent; asking the child to spy on the targeted parent; telling the targeted parent that the child does not love him or her; monitoring letters or phone calls from the targeted parent; calling the targeted parent by his or her first name; encouraging the child to refer to someone else as "mom" or "dad"; not letting the child spend time alone with the targeted parent; telling the child that someone else is his or her father or mother; curtailing visits because a sibling does not want to visit; not allowing the child to bring gifts from the targeted parent into the home; threatening to take the child away from the targeted parent; not letting the alienating parent's extended family talk about the targeted parent; having secret signals and means of communication with the child while with the targeted parent; having the child keep secrets from the targeted parent; beating the targeted parent in front of the child; changing the child's name; accusing the child of being too close with the targeted parent; and making it appear as if the targeted parent is rejecting the child.

These alienating strategies worked together to give the child the following three-part message: (1) The alienating parent is the only parent who cares; (2) the alienating parent is needed in order for the child to feel safe and good about him- or herself; (3) the targeted parent—who is dangerous and does not love the child anyway—must be disavowed in order to maintain the love and approval of the alienating parent. Boldly stated this way, the message resembles the message cult leaders convey to cult members (as discussed in Chapter 2).

There appears to be a wide range of actions and behaviors that constitute parental alienation. No one behavior characterized the full sample and no alienating parent utilized just one strategy. Thus, parental alienation syndrome can be effectuated through many possible combinations of strategies and there is no one formula for doing so. This means that counteracting it will be difficult because the targeted parent may not even know all the strategies that the alienating parent is using. Most alienating parents probably participate in bad-mouthing, but bad-mouthing alone may not be sufficient to effectuate alienation and countering the bad-mouthing may not be enough to counter the alienation. Thus, parents who believe that they are the targets of parental alienation should assume that the alienating parent is utilizing an array of strategies. In the absence of tested interventions for parental alienation syndrome, it may be advisable for targeted parents (or parents who suspect they are being targeted) to address the underlying goal of the alienating parent rather than the specific behaviors (which may be unknown and/or may change over time). Thus, rather than saying to a child, "I think your mother/father may be saying bad things about me to you." To which the child may accurately respond, "That is not true." It may make sense to say, "I think that your mother/father wants to come between us or make you feel unsafe/uncomfortable with me or have you believe that you can only love one of us at a time." If there is any chance that alienation is occurring, such a statement is more likely to reflect reality than any statement about a specific strategy. In order to avoid the appearance of bad-mouthing the alienating parent, which might backfire, a targeted parent might also want to consider saying to the child "I really want to be close with you and help you feel safe and good about yourself." In this way, the targeted parent is aiming to fortify the attachment relationship without bringing the alienating parent into the picture at all. (Additional ideas for targeted parents are presented in Chapter 11.)

It is also important to bear in mind that the list of strategies generated by the adult children is limited by what can be remembered by the adult children of PAS and by what they understand to be the actions that led to the alienation. It is quite possible that some of the strategies used by the alienating parents were so subtle that they remain outside the awareness of the adult children. This line of thinking is supported by a study conducted by Baker and Darnall (2006) in which targeted parents were surveyed regarding the strategies that they believed the other parent was using in the service of parental alienation. While there was considerable overlap, there were also some strategies only known to the targeted parents, including letting the child choose when to visit, not letting the child see the targeted parent at targeted parent's extended family's home, calling or visiting during parenting time, early pick ups and drop offs, intercepting calls, not providing targeted parent with information, not providing others with information about the targeted parent, refusing to communicate, using child as messenger, rewarding children for rejecting targeted parent, bad-mouthing targeted parent to others, bad-mouthing targeted parent to authorities, having stepparents call themselves mom or dad to others, not allowing child to bring to targeted parent's home items from alienating parent's home, preventing targeted parent from attending parenting functions, and undermining targeted parent's values and hobbies. These too seemed design to attenuate the attachment relationship between children and targeted parents and to enhance the child's dependency on the alienating parent, although some strategies may be more salient for the adult children than for targeted parents. The ways in which these strategies and parental alienation syndrome in general constitute emotional abuse are explored in the next chapter.

Chapter 4

Parental Alienation Is Emotional Abuse of Children

> When parents mind batter, it is frequently in an unmalicious but concentrated attempt to forge the ties that bind.
> —Ruth Ingliss, *Sins of the Father*

THE IDEA THAT PAS IS A FORM OF EMOTIONAL ABUSE WAS PRO-posed by both Gardner (1998) and Rand (1997a, 1997b), and resonated with the experiences of the adult children of PAS. Some focused on an unnecessary level of drama and fear being injected into their lives, others spoke of the loss of the targeted parent, and others used the phrase *emotional abuse* to describe their relationship with the alienating parent. Hannah expressed this belief, "I think it is abusive to a child to tell them they shouldn't enjoy being with their father." Robin, too, felt he had been emotionally abused, "I was physically abused, mentally abused, emotionally abused by my mother and stepfather when I was growing up." Carrie said, "The majority of our suffering was psychological/emotional," like Joanne who felt, "Our real issues, and I think all my brothers agree with me, is the emotional abuse of having the kind of self-absorbed mother that we had. My mother using and abusing my father and, conversely, having her use us to get to him was more painful than being spanked." For Patricia, "He stopped abusing her [the mother] physically, but it turned all to inward scars of mental abuse, for all of us." Roberta, too, believed that she had been emotionally abused. "I think this was emotional abuse, having to deal with adult situations as a child and not being fully developed." Ira experienced, "Emotional violence to the extreme."

In the field of child maltreatment, different types of abuse have been delineated including physical, sexual, and emotional abuse. Although researchers have made great strides in operationalizing physical and sexual abuse and documenting its precursors and sequelae (Cicchetti, 2004; Sedlack & Broadhurst, 1996), emotional abuse has been relatively less studied, partly because it is harder to define, document, and observe. There is no physical evidence of emotional abuse; the scars, as they say, are on the inside. In addition, emotional abuse is more difficult to assess because parents may intermittently use some of the actions associated with emotional abuse, without being emotionally abusive. It is the repetition of these actions that makes the experience abusive, unlike physical or sexual abuse in which a single incident can be designated as abuse. For these reasons, the study of emotional abuse has lagged behind other forms of abuse and maltreatment of children. In fact, the American Psychiatric Association's (2000) *Diagnostic and Statistical Manual* contains no diagnostic criteria for emotional abuse although it does so for other forms of maltreatment. On the other hand, the Federal Child Abuse Prevention and Treatment Act (P.L. 93-247) does include a definition of emotional abuse as "a repeated pattern of caregiver behavior or extreme incidents that convey to children that they are worthless, flawed, unloved, unwanted, endangered or only of value in meeting another's needs." Hamarman and Bernet (2000) offered a specific set of actions that characterize emotional abuse, drawing on the earlier work of Garbarino, Guttmann, and Seeley (1986), including: (1) rejecting, (2) ignoring, (3) isolating, (4) corrupting/exploiting, (5) terrorizing, (6) verbally assaulting, and (7) overpressuring.

This definition provides a useful framework for understanding the experiences of the adult children of parental alienation syndrome. Each of these components of emotional abuse is described below, accompanied by examples that demonstrate the specific ways in which emotional abuse was experienced by alienated children. Following this discussion a list of seven additional behaviors are presented that could also be included in a definition of emotional abuse as it pertains to PAS: (1) sharing personal details about adult relationships with children, (2) making children feel responsible for adult problems and well-being, (3) exposing children to use of alchol and drugs, (4) threatening abandonment, (5) exposing children to domestic violence, (6) making children feel that the other parent does not love him/her, and (7) making children feel that the other parent is unworthy of their love. But, first an analysis of the 7 components of emotional abuse as defined by the field.

PAS AS EMOTIONAL ABUSE: SEVEN CORE COMPONENTS

The seven core components of emotional abuse are examined as they pertain to the experiences of the adult children of PAS.

The Child is Rejected

Parents who reject their child refuse to acknowledge the child's worth and the legitimacy of the child's needs, telling the child in a variety of ways that he or she is unwanted, unloved, unworthy. According to emotional abuse expert Ronald Rohner (2004), rejection is organized around four themes: coldness, hostility, indifference, and lack of love and care. Rejecting parents convey to the child his or her general lack of worth. The parent may also tell the child to leave, call him or her names, and tell the child that he or she is worthless. The child may become the family scapegoat, being blamed for all the family's problems.

Rejection was prevalent in the childhoods of the adult children of PAS. Not only were they misled into believing that their targeted parent rejected them but in many cases the alienating parent as well was rejecting of them when they were young children. Iris, for example, felt rejected on a regular basis by her mother, "According to her my brother and I could do nothing right and I remember her at times telling us she wished we were never born." Jason's father, "was impossible to please and I never knew what he wanted and I never stopped trying." Larissa said of her mother:

She once burst into my bedroom (she never used to knock), sobbing and boo-hooing loudly, and said that my father had told her that all she'd ever done for him was land him with two creeps (my brother and me). The moment she saw that I'd been hurt by that comment, her boo-hooing stopped, and she started to smirk. . . . I had no idea how easily some mothers and daughters interact, and I suppose looking back I simply wanted some sign that she genuinely cared about me. In fact I most likely wanted her affection and good opinion more than anything.

Serita felt no warmth or connection with her mother.

We had no emotional tie. We didn't sit down and talk about things. She would tell me to do my chores if I forgot. There was no place for me to voice my concerns or my hurt. There was nowhere for me to speak about my pain, I think she was afraid that my letting all these things out would hurt her. She tried to counteract that by trying to say things . . . which really stick in my mind like "I am on my own; why are you relying on me? Is it my fault he's not coming to see you? It's him. I didn't have any money I am on my own, you know, it is very difficult for me."

Alix's mother rejected her by comparing her with her father:

Q: So to tell you that you are just like your father was an insult?
A: Yeah I did hear that actually. She always wanted me to stop smiling like him because I looked just like him.
Q: How did you feel when she said that? What did that mean to you?
A: I felt like I was ugly.
Q: Undesirable in some way?
A: Yeah!

Iris explained that through the constant disparagements by her mother, she grew up with low self-esteem and a sense of worthlessness. "She always told us we were failures and would never amount to anything, that we were just like him. We would always be losers," and when Ira expressed interest in living with his father his mother responded, "You want to live with him? Don't let the door hit you in the ass," reminding him that he was not a valued member of the family.

The Child is Isolated

In this form of emotional abuse, the parent limits participation in normal social experiences, preventing the child from forming friendships, contributing to the feeling that he or she is alone in the world. Isolating behaviors include not allowing the child regular contacts with peers, restricting the child's participation in routine family activities, and locking the child in a room, basement, or attic.

None of the adult children of PAS remembered being locked in a room, but several shared that the alienating parent instilled in them a belief that they were alone in the world and should not or could not have a life of their own. As Jonah explained, "I had no life. I had no existence. I didn't even care to be doing the things he wanted me to be doing. I was threatened and told if I don't go with him to do the painting we are not going to have any money and that I don't love him." Others spoke of declining invitations to social activities in order to stay home and be with the alienating parent, of not being allowed to play with friends because the alienating parent wanted them to remain nearby. Iris was under the constant observation of her mother and siblings to make sure she never made contact with her father. If she ever tried to sneak out to the local store to make a phone call or send her father a postcard, her brothers and sisters "always intercepted it. Any time I went anywhere I had to have one of my siblings along with me." As a young boy Edward was not allowed to play in the neighborhood. His mother wanted him to stay home:

Q: What would she say if you said you want to go play with that boy?

A: She would say, no. Can't do that.
Q: Did she say why?
A: She's got to keep her eyes on you.
Q: Is that what she would say?
A: She probably wouldn't say it. But that is what was moti-
    vating her.
Q: She liked to have you around at all times?
A: Yes.
Q: Was she more focused on you because you were the
    youngest?
A: Probably, yes.
Q: What do you remember feeling when she would say you
    can't go down the street?
A: Lonely. Especially when my brothers were in school. I
    was by myself.

Oliver's mother isolated him by not allowing him to leave
the house, "Basically she wanted me to not see him, keep me
away from him [his father], I guess out of her desire to control
me. She wanted to have that much control over me and from
8 to 15 I was pretty much in her control. She drank and she
told me to stay home."

The Child is Ignored

Parents who ignore their children may not show an attachment to the child or provide him or her with nurturance. They
show no interest in the child, and express no affection or even
acknowledgment of the child's presence. The parent may be
physically present, but remains emotionally unavailable.
When a child is ignored it is a passive form of rejection; too
little rather than too much is said; and can be likened to Rohner's (2004) indifference component of parental rejection.

The adult children of PAS felt that their alienating parents
had ignored them, particularly when they associated (in word
or action) with the targeted parent. In Jason's family there was
a pervasive lack of demonstrativeness, "My family did not
show affection that way. There was no hugging and very little
touching at all." Others got the cold shoulder, were treated

like "the enemy" or "a traitor" when they came back from visits. Most found this form of punishment to be extremely painful and frightening because it felt like the loss of their own identity. If the alienating parent did not see them, perhaps they did not truly exist. For Maria, the best way she could describe it was to say, "I was invisible. I was invisible to my mother. To this day I am still invisible to my mother."

The Child is Terrorized

Terrorizing entails singling out one child for criticism and punishment. Parents who use this form of emotional abuse ridicule the child for displaying normal emotions and have expectations far beyond the child's capabilities. The child may be threatened with death, mutilation, or abandonment. Terrorizing may be one of the more overt and aggressive forms of emotional abuse and most likely represents a complex trauma "that occurs repeatedly, cumulatively, over time and in the context of a specific relationship" (Courtois, 2004, p. 412).

This degree of hostility and violence was less common in the alienating families but not all together absent. Several of the adult children of PAS had been physically abused by the alienating parent, including Jason:

I don't remember for what, probably back talk. I was like 3 or 4 years . . . and his favorite little saying was, "I'll give you a dose of strap oil." And he took his belt out and folded it over and whacked us a couple of good ones with it. That was life in the . . . family house for many many years. My younger sisters escaped that because as he got older and got more into his alcoholism he kind of mellowed a little bit but he had me completely terrified for most of my boyhood.

Jonah said:

I believe there is some history to that. I don't have any memory. I think things were very chaotic when I was very young probably until around age 5 according to my brother. I guess I was pretty much . . . there was a lot of abuse going on by my father, physical, verbal, and even sexual against my mother and I guess I actually did sleep in the same bed with them for many years, probably until I was close to age 5.

He added:

My father would basically when he would home drunk at night would make me confess . . . espouse my faith and allegiance to him and that if I didn't do that he would kill himself, and during the rages when he came home drunk—this continued for about three or four years—he would get his gun out and say he would kill himself if I didn't do that.

Renee was "terrified" of her mother and Frank's experience was particularly frightening:

Well the few times I remember talking to him, having a human conversation she was always downgraded, called the worst things, slut, whore, no good, and so on. The times that he wasn't talking to us was pretty much either myself or my brother getting slapped around. I can remember one time in particular when we were told, "You are going to stand right here and watch" and he lined all four of us kids up in the living room and proceeded to literally beat the hell out of my mother and turned around and told us that is what a "no good bitch" is worth.

The Child is Corrupted

Corrupting parents permit their children to use drugs or alcohol; to watch or participate in animal cruelty; to watch pornographic materials or adult sex acts; or to witness or participate in criminal activities such as stealing, assault, prostitution, or gambling. Another form of corruption involves forcing children to verbally abuse or demean their other parent.

This form of corruption was identified by both Warshak (2001a) as well as Waldrin and Joanis (1996) as particularly relevant to PAS. Teaching children to disrespect and demean their other parent corrupts the children's values and personality by encouraging them to be rude, selfish, and ungrateful.

This was the case in the alienating families. For example, Ron's mother required him to use foul adult language with his father. Jason shared that in his alcoholic family, he was allowed to drink from an early age, "And everybody was drinking at the time. I was drinking then too." Another form of corruption was experienced by Jonah who was asked to spy on and keep secrets from his mother. "What he would do is have me spy on my mother when I was younger and report to him at night what she did during the day and who she talked to when I was home from school and stuff like that."

Sarah spoke of being taken with her mother to meet other men (while her mother was still married to her father), and Oliver was asked by his mother to obtain alcohol for her. "She wanted me to go to the liquor store and get her some beer but . . . at the grocery store they wouldn't let me have anything. She said she would beat me if I didn't get her some beer. She was that type of person." Thus, these children were exposed to alcohol use, adultery, cursing, and were asked to spy on and keep secrets from the targeted parent, behaviors that are unsavory, unwholesome, and not appropriate for children.

The Child is Verbally Assaulted

Verbal abuse consists of name-calling, harsh threats, and sarcastic comments that continually "beat down" the child's self-esteem, and create feelings of shame and humiliation. Verbally assaulting behaviors also entail openly telling the child that she or he is worthless and calling the child derogatory and demeaning names.

Verbal assaults were common experiences for the adult children of PAS when they were young. They were yelled at, called names, and were the recipient of a litany of negative statements about their worth and character. Ron and his brother, "would be chastised and yelled and screamed at." Betty's mother was physically and verbally abusive to her, "My mother from that point on since I had a juvenile record would hit me, call me names, and start screaming." And Oliver said that his mother "would start crying and cussing and cussing me out."

The Child is Over-Pressured

Parents who overpressure their children emotionally abuse them by making them feel that their age-appropriate accomplishments are insignificant and meaningless. The parent imposes constant pressure for the child to grow up fast and to achieve too early in the areas of academics, physical/motor skills, and social interaction, which leaves the child feeling that she or he is never quite good enough. Overpressuring behaviors include excessive expectations of the child, and criticism and punishment of age-appropriate behaviors as inadequate.

Patricia's childhood was marked by overpressure by her (alienating parent) father, who compelled her to excel in several sports.

> I was really controlled by my father. When I was about 9 he started to coach my softball team. I had some natural ability, so he took the team, and pushed me to succeed for the next 15 years. Everything revolved around sports. I was a pitcher, so I pitched and hit every day! If I did not get my pitching in, I was yelled at, and sometimes hit. I also took karate, and played soccer and basketball. I always practiced pitching, even during the other sports seasons. I did not have any friends outside of sports.

Nancy too felt pressured to produce successes and accomplishments for her mother. She spoke of showing her mother that she loved her by doing things for her. "Folding the clothes, straightening the room, getting great grades in school, it was more her achievement than mine. Everything I did in my childhood she bragged about." These adult children of PAS only felt loved as long as they achieved and performed for their parents, even if what was asked of them was beyond what they should have been required to or were able to deliver.

The Child Witnesses Parental Abuse
of Drugs and Alcohol

Allowing children to watch parents hurt themselves or be out of control is a form of emotional abuse. This was experienced by several of the adult children of PAS. Their parents got drunk or began drinking in front of them. This was very stressful and frightening for many, including Alix. "So I got home and she decided to smoke cigarettes and make me watch her and she knew I didn't like her doing that and she decided to get drunk that night and it was all to spite me because she knew I didn't like all that. She made me watch her." Robin's mother and stepfather were both still in active addiction, something that caused Robin great pain and sadness. "They are both still drunks as is my older brother. He is in active addiction I am sorry to say." Oliver said of his parents' marriage, "They fought all the time. I have a lot of memories. Both of them were alcoholics. I have pretty good memories of their battles and they would hit each other and in turn hit me." Ron, too, had memories of parental substance use. "My mother had a problem with alcoholism and prescription drugs and I remember her and my father fighting constantly and I also recall my mother not coming home often." Both of Tracey's parents drank. "When they fought we heard them. They were both big drinkers at that point. My mom would just get so drunk and get stupid I guess and my dad more or less tried to stop her from hurting herself and other people but she would get violent when she would drink." These children experienced extreme discomfort, embarrassment, and sorrow at having to witness their parents' self-destructive and selfish behavior.

The Child is Threatened
with Abandonment

Threatening to leave a child is a form of emotional child abuse because it instills in the child a deep-seated fear of being uncared for, unworthy, and unsafe. This was not uncommon in the childhoods of the adult children of PAS, especially when they expressed a desire to have contact with the targeted parent. Such threats, for example, were frequently made by Ron's mother. "She would say things like, 'You can go live on the street with your father' and stuff like that." David's mother made similar threats: "I remember one time I mentioned about talking to Dad and she said, 'I'll kick you out.' That sticks in my mind because at the time I was thinking about calling him."

For Veronica, the threats of abandonment came in response to her mentioning her father. "I remember being about 5 and I remember saying at the table that I wanted to see him and she went into her room crying to my stepdad and he came out and shouted and said 'You are not going to see him and if you mention his name you're out.'" Ira's mother's response to his interest in his father was to imply that he would be expelled from the family. When Robin was 13 his mother tried to contact his father because she wanted to send him away, "Oh yes. Oh yes. It was like a threat: 'You kids are pieces of crap. You are just like him and it is time for you to go. I am going to try to find him and you are gone.'"

The Child is Exposed to Domestic Violence

Exposure to violence, even when it is not directed toward a child, is frightening and traumatic. Domestic violence is particularly disturbing because children do not know whether they will be the next victim and because they are watching someone they love (one parent) hurt someone else they love (the other parent). Making matters worse is the fact that the person most likely to comfort the child (a parent) is preoccupied with either being the perpetrator or the victim of the violence. Thus, the child is frightened but unable to receive comfort.

The parents of the adult children of PAS had highly conflicted marriages, which often rose to the level of violence in the home. Both of Frank's parents were alcoholics, "and there was a lot of fighting. "Oh lord . . . they were fighting about just about anything and everything. Once it was because a glass was not in the right place. My father seemed to get physical as often as he opened his mouth." Kate also witnessed a lot of fighting. She did not know what they were fighting about, but she remembered feeling "a little freaked out and scared and I remember the yelling and I remember hands flailing. I remember mostly the loudness of it. I don't remember the words." In Oliver's home the domestic violence would often turn to child abuse, "They fought all the time. I have a lot of memories. I have pretty good memories of their battles and they would hit each other and in turn hit me." For Carl, exposure to domestic abuse occurred after his mother remarried. The marital conflict was so great Carl voluntarily moved into a foster home. "She remarried when I was 12 and I ended up leaving home when I was 15 because of their fighting." In contrast, Maria stayed at home despite the violence and chaos, "I don't recall them being that loving towards one another. There was a lot of emotional I would say instability and a lot of anger, a little violence. Really the screaming was mutual." Before Ron's parents' divorced, he was exposed to their escalating conflict. "I would hear them yelling and screaming and I would see them yelling and screaming. It was in front of us, that's what happened." Carrie, as well, saw violence between her parents, "Both of them equally were very violent in terms of pushing, shoving. I remember there was a kitchen knife block on the counter and they actually pulled knives on each other. I can visualize that. I was about 3 at the time." Tracey shared a poignant account of what it felt like to be a young child witnessing conflict between her parents,

A lot of times it was my mom who would just drop bombs on him, just cursing him out, she didn't care what she said, every curse you could imagine and that was all you heard and the next thing you hear my mom calls us down to help her cause my dad is hurting her. There was one day when we lived in our two-story house and I was literally running up and down the steps cause my mom would call and I would make it about halfway down and then my dad would tell me to get back up the steps and I had to run back up the steps, and then I hear my mom calling me again telling me to run back down the steps, and all I can remember is seeing my dad sitting on top of my mom and my mom naked because they were fighting, and she was trying to get away from my dad, and my dad just sitting on top of her and keeping her down so she won't go ballistic and her just screaming.

Clearly, this level of conflict and strife is unhealthy for children to witness. They cannot make sense of what is happening and are placed in an untenable position of feeling they have to protect or rescue one parent from the other parent.

The Child is Told That the Targeted Parent
Does not Love Him or Her

Children need to feel loved and accepted by both of their parents. Thus, for one parent to tell a child that the other parent does not love him or her constitutes a form of emotional abuse by creating unnecessary pain and suffering for the child that can damage his or her self-esteem and sense of worth. Telling the child that the targeted parent did not love him or her was a consistent feature of the parental alienation strategies employed by the parents of the adult children of PAS. It is part and parcel of parental alienation syndrome and was pervasive in the experiences of the adult children of PAS. This aspect of PAS has been described elsewhere in the book (see Chapters 1 and 2) and only a few additional examples are provided here, the first by Veronica, "They always told us that he was bad, had always beaten us, and was having an affair with his best friend, was beating my sister. I was told that before I was born his mother wanted to get rid of me when I was in the belly and that when my brother was born with a hair lip they said that my dad hated him and wanted nothing to do with him and things like that." Hannah shared, "The first thing we were told was our father didn't love us. We were led to believe that our financial hardships were due to our father. He didn't love us and he abandoned us." Carrie's mother, "Would tell my brother and I that Dad left us, Dad abandoned us. He didn't love us. He loved Joan and he wanted to build a new family without us. That we were the problem." Her mother was particularly cruel when she told her children, as she put them on an airplane to visit their father, "If this plane goes down you are going to die and your dad doesn't care."

The Child Is Told that the Targeted Parent
Is Unworthy of Love

A corollary of telling children that one of their parents does not love them is to tell them that a parent is unworthy of their love and respect. Children identify naturally with both parents, and will, therefore, internalize negative beliefs about the denigrated parent and feel bad about themselves. As described in Chapters 1 and 2, the alienating parents were quick to suggest that the targeted parent was a dangerous, unwholesome, and unworthy person. According to Kate, "Growing up I got the idea that my dad was everything she ever hated and he was a horrible monster and I was just like him." Likewise, Robin shared, "I was told he was very abusive and that he was an alcoholic, that he used to beat me and my brother and my mother and he would come home drunk and take money and would go out drinking with it, that he was a womanizer." Carl's mother spoke so often of his father's alcoholism, he said, "The impression was always that he was an alcoholic and he was probably living on skid row. I grew up with images of my father lying in a ditch." Ira said of his mother, "She wanted to make it clear that he (Ira's father) was a loser."

Personal Details Are Shared That Exceed the Child's Cognitive and Emotional Capabilities

Telling children personal details about adult situations is a form of emotional abuse because it exploits their inability to walk away from a parent. They are a captive audience and are, therefore, unable to protect themselves from information that they are not able to handle cognitively or emotionally. As an example, Alix's mother explained to her when she was a little girl that she was conceived from a rape. "I didn't ask. My mom was very vocal about everything. She was like, 'Oh he beat me around and he was drunk and he drank a fifth of vodka and he held me down and I was crying and he wouldn't let me up' and all this I consider lying now." Even if this story were true, it would still be considered emotional abuse because Alix did not possess the cognitive skills or emotional capacity to process such information. Hearing such stories most likely overwhelmed and frightened her. The fact that it was not true simply added insult to injury. Kate said, "She talked a lot about how he did her wrong and she made up a lot of stories and it was difficult because I couldn't really figure it out. It was a little too adult of a situation for me to understand." For Hannah,

"My mother did nothing but complain about him. I knew inappropriate things about their relationship. I knew he was beneath her. He was an inadequate lover. I knew that his size was a problem before I knew what that really meant." Roberta explicitly understood that her mother's confiding in her met her definition of emotional abuse, "I think this was emotional abuse, having to deal with adult situations as a child and not being fully developed."

The Child is Made to Feel Responsible for an Adult's Well-Being

One outgrowth of sharing personal details is that it conveys to children an expectation that they are responsible for solving their parents' problems. This places a heavy burden on them, with an expectation that they cannot possibly achieve, resulting in shame and guilt for disappointing their parents. Sharing personal details and making children conscious of their parents' problems also clues them in to the fact that their parents are unhappy, something else children should not have to know. When the parents seek emotional support and guidance from their children, they are "parentifying" them, asking the child to be the parent of the parent. Family therapists Boszormenyi-Nagy and Spark warn that when this happens, "In extreme cases, the child becomes so overburdened with demands for responsibility that he is never given the chance to be a child. Such children become specialists in dealing with infantile adults while they become depleted as children in their own right" (1983, p. 22).

This experience was common among the adult children of PAS, many of whom felt that it was their job to make their parents feel better and to help fix their parents' problems. This is, of course, consistent with the likelihood that many of the alienating parents were narcissistic (see Chapter 1). For Sarah, when her mother confided in her, "At first it felt ok. It felt nice because at least that way she was acknowledging some of my feelings. Later I started to feel burdened and frightened with the information she was giving me." Josh recounted the story of when he was 5 years of age his mother would share with him that she was overwhelmed with having to care for three stepdaughters and that she was thinking of taking him and leaving the rest of the family.

Mark felt, "Responsible. I felt sorry and very responsible. I had to take care of everything. I remember Grandma always telling me my mother was very sick." Edward exploded in anger at his father because he felt that his father was the cause of all his mother's unhappiness and he felt he had to do something, while Maria felt burdened by her mother's, "constant playing the martyr. Oh poor me for her whole life. It was all about what I do do and don't do for her and how horrible life is for her and what she needs and what she feels." If Amelia mentioned her father, her mother would, "Fall to pieces so basically [I didn't] don't bring him up. She'd start crying and say we didn't love her and that's just how she is. I could never tell her the truth about anything because if I did she would emotionally break down so it put a lot of stress on me." These children were encouraged to assume responsibility for their parents' well-being, something in reality they had no control over. Donaldson-Pressman and Pressman (1994) describe this assumption of responsibility for parental happiness as the key to long-term negative outcomes for children raised in narcissistic families.

Not surprisingly, the adult children of parental alienation syndrome, as well, suffered negative outcomes. As Garbarino and colleagues (1986) noted, "The psychologically maltreated child is often identified by personal characteristics, perceptions, and behaviors that convey low self-esteem, a negative view of the world, and internalized and externalized anxieties and aggressions. Whether the child clings to adults or avoids them, his or her social behavior and responses are inappropriate and exceptional" (p. 63).

PART II

BREAKING THE TIES THAT BIND

Chapter 5

Rethinking the Past: The Process of Realization, I

A journey of transformation has no real beginning.
—Salvatore Minuchin, *Family Healing*

TO DATE LITTLE INFORMATION IS AVAILABLE ABOUT WHETHER AND how individuals leave the "cult of parenthood" and come to terms with their childhood. According to work with former cult members, people either walk out, are thrown out, or leave as a result of counseling. Walkouts are people who become disenchanted with the cult and come to the understanding on their own that what they are experiencing no longer makes sense for them. As one former cult member explained, "It is as if there is a shelf where all your doubts and misgivings are placed while you are in the group. Over the months or years you observe so many conflicts with your original beliefs and values, or you see things done by the group or leader that are just not right. Because of the indoctrination and not being allowed to ask questions, you just put it on the shelf. Eventually, the shelf gets heavier and heaver and finally breaks and you are ready to leave" (Tobias & Lalich, 1994, p. 53). Layton, too, a survivor of the People's Temple in Jonestown, spoke of having a space inside her mind that was reserved for doubts and misgivings. "As always, I stashed my own fears into the secret compartment that rational thought couldn't penetrate" (1998, p. 131).

Cult members who are cast out have violated a fundamental principle of the cult, and have become a threat to the leader and the stability of the cult. They are forced to leave the cult in order to preserve the cult. Casting people out of a cult serves a secondary purpose of instilling fear in the remaining members that they need to obey the rules in order to avoid being cast out as well.

A third group of cult members leave after having been convinced to do so by family and friends. Originally this was accomplished through intensive "deprogramming." The individual was removed from the cult, sometimes forcibly, and subjected to a reverse brainwashing campaign that undoes the influence of the cult and compels the person to realize what has happened. More recently, exit counseling, a less coercive intervention, has been found to be effective in helping cult members rethink their cult involvement (Clark, Giambalvo, Giambalvo, Garvey, & Langone, 1993; Hassan, 1988).

What remains unknown is the process by which adults who were child victims of parental alienation syndrome leave the "cult of parenthood." Whether one walks out, is cast out, or counseled out, confronting the reality of PAS is probably more difficult than leaving a cult because a cult leader is a parent substitute while the alienator is an actual parent. Realizing that a parent is abusive or harmful is in all likelihood considerably more difficult than realizing that about a cult leader. M. Scott Peck noted that, "To come to terms with the evil in one's parentage is perhaps the most difficult and painful psychological task a human being can be called on to face" (1983, p. 130). Recognizing parental limitations when one is still a child is nearly impossible, and something children will avoid at almost any cost. Trauma expert Judith Herman wrote that for an abused child, "To preserve her faith in her parents, she must reject the first and most obvious conclusion that something is terribly wrong with them. She will go to any lengths to construct an explanation for her fate that absolves her parents of all blame and responsibility" (1992, p. 101). Similarly, Fairbairn (1952) believed that children will readily assume the "burden of badness" upon themselves as a way to defend against recognizing parental limitations.

Nonetheless, at the time of the interview, all of the adult children of PAS had come to realize that they had been alienated from one parent by the other. Eleven reported becoming aware of the alienation when they became teenagers, while three-fourths of the sample reported that they did not become aware of the PAS until they were well into adulthood. Length of time alienated ranged from 7 to 47 years, with an average of about 20 years, although of course these are approximations.

How did PAS individuals come to realize that their parent had turned them against the targeted parent and that the alienating parent had put his or her own needs (for revenge, for control, for emotional satisfaction) above the needs of the child? The term *realization* is used because it indicates that some truths had not been available at a conscious level to the adult children of PAS. The realization entails becoming aware of these truths, and then of undoing the brainwashing and programming. This conceptualization draws on the literature on denial and defense mechanisms, and assumes that it is possible to *not* know something that has been true all along. Reality does not change, but a person's ability to recognize it does change. This can be thought of as an awakening, a disillusionment, an opening of the eyes, and a listening to the small voice inside that says something is not right.

Regardless of what the process is called, it must be asked what exactly is *not* known in cases of parental alienation syndrome. What are the truths that are being denied? According to the adult children of PAS, some of the truths denied included that: (1) the alienating parent was actively interfering in their relationship with the targeted parent; (2) the alienating parent was doing so for selfish or irrational reasons; (3) the alienating parent had harmed (emotionally abused) them through the diminishment of the relationship with the targeted parent and through the strategies used to effectuate the alienation; and (4) the targeted parent may not be as dangerous or unworthy as the adult children had been led to believe.

As children, they denied the reality of PAS because the alienating parent demanded that these truths be denied. Submission to the alienating parent's reality was the price of admission into that relationship; and they paid that price, as most children do, without questioning. In order to avoid withdrawal of love, they had to subscribe to the alienating parent's version of reality in which the targeted parent was the villain and the alienating parent was the hero-victim. The children also denied the truth because the truth was too painful to know. Most children cannot bear the thought that their parents are hurting them, and they will do almost anything to avoid that reality, including taking on the blame themselves. It was easier to think that they were unworthy or in some way at fault or that the targeted parent (who had less importance in their life) was unworthy, than to think that the parent on whom they were dependent was hurting them. Submission to the parents' version of reality preserved the children's fantasy that the parent loved them and would take care of them. To subscribe to the alienating parent's reality allowed the children to avoid the painful truth that the alienating parent was abusive.

Until the realization, the children were blind to the real intentions of the alienating parent. As object relations theorist Fairbairn (1952) explained, "It is better to be a sinner in a world ruled by god than a saint in a world ruled by the devil" (p. 65), by which he meant that children would rather preserve the notion of an ideal parent even if that entails absorbing the blame and hatred wrongly directed at themselves. Research and theory regarding information processing has supported this line of reasoning by demonstrating that information that produces anxiety may be filtered out of consciousness (Goleman, 1985) and research on the psychobiology of trauma suggests that experiences too painful to acknowledge or integrate become stored as sensory fragments that cannot be summoned at will (van der Kolk & Fisler, 1995).

Reaction formation (Freud, 1930/1961), another defense mechanism, also appears to be applicable in parental alienation syndrome. In this way, negative or ambivalent feelings about the alienating parent were transformed into a wholly positive (exaggerated) assessment and attitude toward that parent. This was accomplished through complete repression of all negative thoughts associated with this parent. Because it was unsafe to acknowledge any negative feelings about the alienating parent (because of threat of loss of that parent's love), these negative thoughts and feelings were banished. The vehemence with which PAS children are willing to defend their alienating parents can be seen in this light. As Gardner (1998) observed, they will often make the case for the alienating parent better than that parent does for him- or herself.

In addition to denial and reaction formation, a third defense mechanism, identification with the aggressor, was also at play. This occurred when the children took the fear of the alienating parent and turned it into an allegiance with that parent against the targeted parent. In this way the child transformed him or herself from a victim to a victimizer. In Anna Freud's (1936/ 1966) view, "A child introjects some characteristic of an anxiety object and so assimilates an anxiety experience. By impersonating the aggressor, assuming his attributes or imitating his aggression, the child transforms himself from the person threatened to the person who makes the threats"(p. 113). It was better to join the alienating parent's side in rage against the targeted parent than to stand alone (psychologically speaking) as the recipient of the alienating parent's anger, scorn, and rejection.

The defense mechanism of denial played a pivotal role and the alienation would probably not have taken hold without it. In order for the alienation to be successful, victims of PAS must deny the truth of their experience, and this is exactly what they did. At some point, however, for the adult children of PAS, denial no longer was possible. The truth emerged. They longed for an authentic self, as opposed to what Winnicott (1960) referred to as the false self, the person who out of fear of loss chooses to be controlled by others. Hassan, in his experience with cult members, also believed that there is a real self that is buried inside the cult identity and that, "As much as cult indoctrination attempts to destroy and suppress the old identify and empower the new identity, it never totally succeeds. Good experiences and positive memories rarely disappear entirely" (1988, pp. 73–74).

The realization process, then, can be understood as a way of becoming reunited with one's authentic self.

CATALYSTS TO REALIZATION: 1–5

Eleven different catalysts for the realization process have been identified by the adult children of PAS. With a few exceptions, this reunion with the authentic self preceded reunion with the targeted parent. This chapter explores that "reunion with the self."

Catalyst 1: Maturation (n = 8, 20%)

Maturation as a catalyst is consistent with Gardner's (1998) assessment that although some older teens are still susceptible to PAS, many have sufficient cognitive and emotional maturity to defend against manipulation. This is also consistent with the normal deidealization of parents that occurs as a function of development (Erikson, 1964). Teens and adults are more able to question their parent's beliefs and attitudes than younger children.

> There are few children who haven't strained to accommodate themselves to their parents' image of who and what they are. However, in adolescence, as the child develops a growing sense of his own personality, the effort is often abandoned, leading many parents to believe that their children have undergone a drastic character change. What is really happening, in many cases, is that the child is feeling and being himself for the first time." (Inglis, 1978, p. 145)

Thus, one part of normal development is to question the values and beliefs of one's family of origin, and questioning the statements made about the targeted parent would probably be one aspect of a larger process of separating from the alienating parent. In addition, the physical—and eventually financial separation—concomitant with reaching adulthood probably enhanced the individual's capacity to tolerate psychological distance. Further facilitating the maturation process was increased time spent observing other families and other ways that parents interact with their spouses and ex-spouses.

According to Smullens, "The one primary challenge of leaving home and becoming an adult is to take back the power that we have given our parents and family" (2002, p. 37). Recognizing PAS for what it is, is one way to take back that power. Below is a case vignette that illustrates Joanne's experience with outgrowing the alienation.

At the time of the interview Joanne was 47 years old. She had been born in Iowa. Her parents were in their early 20s when they met. Neither had been married before. Joanne was the second born and the first girl of five siblings. Joanne explained that in many respects her parents were not well suited to each other.

My father is a very, very classic introvert, and he is a scholarly, studious man. My mother is of Sicilian background and her family is voluble and expressive. My father was the only child of his mother who married very late in life, and she only had one child so he was probably pretty spoiled and pampered. When he married my mom it was probably one of those opposites attract things. He was thrown into this tumultuous emotional subculture, which he really did not understand. I remember they (mother's family) would be very rude to my father and they would speak in Sicilian or Italian around him so that he couldn't understand them, and this caused a lot of conflict for my parents because we lived in the same town that my mother's family lived in. They (mother's family) all lived together in the same neighborhood and they did just about everything together, and my father did not have that kind of family background or even that wide a range of relations; he had very few relations and so there was a lot of conflict due to just the integration of the two families. Between the two of them (her parents) there was constant fighting. Some of my earliest memories are of them fighting about so much of what went on in our daily life.

Despite the conflict, Joanne's parents remained married. There were periodic threats of divorce and even a trial separation when Joanne was in her 20s. However, at the time of the interview her parents were still married to each other.

Joanne's mother was the alienating parent who used constant bad–mouthing of the father to the children as the primary strategy. "To anyone who would listen she would say bad things about how she would get over things but my dad was the one who stayed mad. It was a way of explaining her own behavior and trying to put herself in a better light. That was really the main strategy although she had permutations of it." Her mother also complained frequently that she did not have enough help in taking care of the family and that her father was to blame for much of what went wrong in their lives. "That was a repeated mantra. . . . My mother since the time I can remember talked my father down, whereas I can only remember my father saying one negative thing about my mother."

Sometimes the bad-mouthing seemed designed to draw the children into the mother's confidence, to make them feel sorry for her and angry and disappointed in the father. To that end, Joanne's mother would share personal and intimate details about her marriage and complaints about her relationship with the father. "It was not appropriate for a mother to talk about her sexual relationship with the other parent in front of the children. That was one thing she would do."

Joanne also recalled that her mother tried to create tension and disagreements between her [Joanne] and her father.

She would basically do whatever she could to create conflict between us. We, as children had several pets (as all children want to keep animals and the five of us were no different), and she always resented all our pets. My father, as a child, always had many pets. He would regale us with stories of all the many different animals he had had. He loved showing us animals. But I think Mom hated all animals. She would say, "I hate dogs." We never had cats because she hated cats. "Get that damn dog out of here" was a constant refrain in our home. She always complained about them and made us feel bad for wanting them, and she got rid of every dog we had until we were in our teens and picked one up on the side of the highway once, coming home from a trip. The way she got rid of the dogs was to blame my father for their bad behavior (fouling inside the house being an easy kill since she refused to train them), and then complaining about how we treated

the animals. Yeah. . . . unsupervised kids, doing the odd thing
with a pet. Again, an easy kill for her. . . . She refused to train us
or the pets and it is somehow my father's fault.

Another strategy Joanne's mother used was to incite the father
to become so angry with the children that he would hurt or
frighten them. "He would discipline us on her behalf and she
could act like she wasn't the injuring party. . . . She would get
over it and leave him fuming. I can't tell you how many days
he would come into the front door, smiling, hopeful, us de-
lighted to see him, and she would just rip in." Looking back
Joanne could see that there was a difference between when her
father was mad for his own reasons and when he was mad on
behalf of his wife. "It had a different texture. It was more about
his own disappointments and frustrations, it had more of a de-
featist tone, 'What did I do that I didn't get you to understand
what I wanted from you.' or whatever. It wasn't that fury. The
fury was hers."

Another strategy was to limit the amount of time that Joanne
spent with her father. "My father was a distracted person, but
seemed to enjoy the kids. He didn't discipline much except
when pushed to it and we children enjoyed spending time with
him." But if Joanne wanted to spend time with her father, her
mother made it clear that this was not to happen. "I knew intuitively that someone would be punished, either me or him, if I
showed *any* preference for time with him."

The sum total effect of these strategies on Joanne's relationship
with her father was to, as she explained, "Shut us off from him.
We knew that we could not risk being close to him because there
would be a price to pay. She (her mother) would make life rotten
for us. She would escalate. She would get angry about little
things. She would go off on us. And she would get our dad mad
if we risked any closeness with him, then she would punish
someone." Because of the parental alienation, throughout her
childhood Joanne felt isolated from her father.

Two events occurred that resulted in Joanne realizing that
her mother was trying to turn her and her siblings against their
father. The first event was the death of her father's mother, a
woman whom Joanne adored and her mother despised.

I think it was a slow steady thing with an epiphany at some point but I can't tell you when that epiphany occurred. A lot of this gradual understanding of the profound level of her problems occurred when my grandmother died. My mom hated her but would let me be with her a lot, and then it was like she transferred that hate to me.

Joanne recalled that her mother, who had always made her disdain for her mother-in-law clear, put on quite a show of her grief at the funeral. "She hated my grandmother and now she was faking that she cared about her. It was so twisted." Her mother's blatant fraudulence opened Joanne's eyes to the other ways in which her mother had been dishonest and hypocritical.

The second experience that allowed her to gain perspective revolved around the planning of a 50th anniversary party for her parents.

We have recently been through the ringer with my mother because their 50th anniversary came up and she expected this big elaborate party and I thought they hated each other for 50 years and you expect us to throw some $5,000 party to celebrate what? Forget it! It turned into this enormous family conflict and we saw these things happening and we thought, "My god this is just what she did when we were kids. Oh yeah! This is so familiar and so it was quite an epiphany for the four of us this past year to 18 months."

Joanne summarized her maturational experience this way:

I am in my mid-40s. It took me this long to understand what my mother was like, and why. I don't think I could have seen it clearly in my 30s and certainly not in my 20s. I now see past all the excuses and rationalizations that she, my father, and my siblings (and even myself) all engaged in. She is just a lousy person. I am not sure you have the distance and life experience to really wrap your mind around the sort of things that a lousy parent does to you when you are only in your 20s or 30s. At this point in my life, I know enough about myself as a woman and a mother, and enough about other women as mothers, and enough about their mothers, and also, add into that, enough about my mother to see that it wasn't that she was busy or that we were poor or anything else. It was that she was a narcissist and that she sucks as a person. I'm done with her. I didn't have that figured out until recently.

What was particularly helpful for Joanne was when her siblings came to the same understanding that she had. "I think it was *their* ability to see through the drama that helped me move on." As she concluded, she needed life experience, decreased dependence on her mother, increased sense of her own worth gained through positive experiences with friends, colleagues, and her own family, and more opportunities to compare her mother to other mothers, before she could gain the kind of perspective necessary to rethink her entire childhood and become aware that her mother had been trying to alienate her from her father.

Unfortunately for Joanne this awareness did not lead to an improved relationship with her father who defended her mother against Joanne's confrontations and accusations. At the time of the interview she was not on speaking terms with either of her parents.

Catalyst 2: Alienating Parent Turned on Child (n = 7, 17.5%)

For these adult children of PAS, the precipitating impetus for the realization was that the alienating parent turned on them and became hostile or intensely controlling. Thus, these alienating parents revealed their true relational style over time as they began to treat the child in the same rejecting and manipulative fashion that they had treated the targeted parent. Without the targeted parent as a focus for their rage and desire to control, the alienating parents turned their animosity and need for control onto their children. Once the children had a taste of being on the receiving end of this behavior, they realized that the targeted parent was probably victimized in the same manner.

This process is best understood in the context of the alienating parent's character disorder. As noted earlier, a significant segment of the alienating parents appeared (based on descriptions of the adult children) to have had a personality disorder, notably narcissism. This narcissism fueled the alienation but was not satisfied once the alienation was achieved. The personality structure of the alienating parent remained the same except now the alienating parent did not have the targeted parent as a focal point. Thus, the need to remove the targeted parent from the child's life was part of a larger, more enduring desire to control the child, which was not attenuated with the removal of the targeted parent. The adult children described it as something of a rude awakening to realize that the anger and hostility once directed toward the targeted parent was subsequently turned on them.

Felicity exemplified this experience. What makes her story somewhat unique is that the noncustodial parent (her father) was the alienator. Although less common, noncustodial PAS is possible according to Gardner and borne out in this story. Felicity was 18 at the time of the interview. Her mother was 19 and her father was 23 when they met. Neither had been married before. They dated for less than a year before marrying, and 10 months later her mother gave birth to Felicity. She was the only child of a marriage that lasted less than two years. Felicity lived with her mother and had regular visitation with her father throughout her childhood. During much of that period, her parents were involved in an acrimonious court battle over custody and visitation.

During the interview Felicity recalled that for much of the time she spent with her father he was preoccupied with anger and hostility directed toward his ex-wife. He tried to and, in fact, succeeded in creating considerable bad feelings between Felicity and her mother. Bad-mouthing was his main strategy. "The most common type with my dad was telling me stories about my mom that I now think are untrue. It was pretty much every time I saw him. I can think of two really bad stories off the top of my head although there are a few others as well." The first story Felicity's father told her was that her mother was dangerous and violent.

He has a scar on his forehead and he told me that the scar was caused by a rocking chair that my mom threw at him during an argument. And I believed that for a long, long time, actually until recently I found out from a family member that he actually got the scar when he was a teenager. So there was that and he also told me she wrote "I hate you" in blood on the wall after she broke a dish. She was doing the dishes one time when they were arguing and I . . . well I probably did believe it as a little kid and I definitely don't believe it now.

Felicity's father also took bad-mouthing to a new level by telling her that her mother did not want her to be born and that he saved her life by preventing her mother from terminating the pregnancy. "The worse thing is that he told me that my mom wanted to have an abortion; she didn't want me." This bad-mouthing was an integral part of her relationship with her father. "Yeah, the same stories. I remember those stories because he told them to me more than once. He told them to me several times. Maybe I asked him about them, but I don't remember that. I was told those stories when I was between 5 and 10."

Felicity's father also utilized guilt as an alienation strategy to garner her sympathy, at her mother's expense.

He used to passive aggressively mention to me how little he was able to see me and how that was my mom's fault, and mention to me custody issues when I was pretty young. He kept a logbook of all the hours that I saw him and he would show it to me and say, "I have seen you xx hours this year so far, compared to this is how much time your mom sees you." I think he actually still has those logbooks, although he might have thrown them out by now. He used to write it down every week, every phone call we made. That was all logged in and I guess he was expecting me to blame my mom for the fact that he didn't get to see me all the time.

Eventually the alienation strategies took their toll. Felicity felt sorry for her father and angry with her mother.

When I came home I would be angry at my mom. I felt like she was the bad guy and that came up in our arguments a lot. Yeah, I did think my mom was bad. I did join him and I did feel bad for him. I would think, Wow Dad has it really hard and my mom is such a horrible person to do all these things. He was also a member of a support group for divorced fathers and he would take me to that group and I would feel guilty that I was living with my mom, thinking, you know, dads have a right to see their kids too.

Felicity especially resented her mother for wanting to abort her. "It wasn't just that he told me that she wanted an abortion. He actually explained to me what an abortion was and took me to an anti–abortion rally at one point." Her father showed her graphic pictures of aborted fetuses and explained how he had rescued her from that fate. These vivid descriptions made a strong impression on her young mind. She came to resent her mother and, over time, came to believe that her mother did not really love her and had not wanted her to be born.

She explained that the weight of all this negativity contaminated her relationship with her mother.

When I was young I think it was pretty tough. For a long time I guess I felt like I was opposed to her instead of living with her. Every time I came home from my dad's we would argue, with me feeling like she is this terrible person. She told me later that it would take a week or week and a half to deprogram me to be how I would be before I'd see him. I mean we got along sometimes, but a lot of times there was a lot of fighting and there was a lot of me resenting her and believing those things that he said and thinking in the back of my head that she really is a terrible person.

When Felicity would return from visits with her father she would be rude and hostile toward her mother. Her mother tried to explain that Felicity's father was creating these problems between them, but that was not Felicity's understanding of the situation. "My mother said that he was lying, but I didn't believe her for a really long time. And I think there were a couple of times when I was a little older when I did run away to his house when I had arguments with my mom." For Felicity, these feelings of hatred toward her mother were real. "Well I thought she was full of crap. I wanted to believe my dad. My dad was my hero and my mom was like this evil person who yelled a lot and didn't want me to see my dad." Not only was Felicity unrealistically harsh and negative with her mother, she was un- realistically positive and forgiving of her father. "I idealized him, I looked up to him. He was my hero for a really long time." This idealization of the alienating parent is consistent with Freud's (1930/1961) account of reaction formation and with Gardner's (1998) third manifestation of PAS, lack of am- bivalence toward the alienating parent.

The turning point in Felicity's life came when she was a teen- ager and her father was sent to prison for physically abusing her younger brother (from another marriage). At first, Felicity ardently supported her father and refused to believe that he was guilty of the abuse. When he was released from jail, he became a born-again Christian. "He was pretty intent on con- verting me so it was around then that I started to resent him a little more and a year after that he pretty much confessed to me that he did actually break my brother's leg." Felicity elaborated further about the ways in which her relationship with her father deteriorated over time.

> I decided I was a wiccan and Dad wasn't too happy with that. He told me I was a demon, and that I was going to hell and terrible things that you really shouldn't tell your daughter. After a cer- tain point visitation was up to me. It became a terrible experience. I would always come home crying after I saw him and I finally told him, "I am not going to see you anymore if you keep this up." After that he sort of calmed down a little, but he asked peo- ple to tell me their stories of salvation and how I should convert and all this stuff, and it was becoming so difficult for me to be with him. It was easier for me to see how he manipulated me when I was younger. It is kind of hard to think about idolizing somebody who's not being nice to you.

Ultimately Felicity concluded that her father did not want to see her mother happy, and that the denigration and guilt- provoking episodes were not motivated by her father's desire to have a better relationship with her. "He was trying to get revenge on her. It was not really directed toward me in terms of seeing me more or some ultimate end other than causing havoc in our family." Thus, she realized that his behaviors were not motivated by a true love and commitment to her. As she came to accept this idea, her relationship with her mother improved dramatically. "I think we did get more close after that. I mean we still have problems but I resolved to work with her. That's what Mom said, 'We are a team.' After that it was a lot easier for me to get along with her." At the time of the interview, she and her mother were close while she had only limited contact with her father.

Catalyst 3: Experiencing PAS as a Parent
(n = 4, 10%)

Becoming a targeted parent themselves served as a catalyst for some of the adult children of PAS by helping them realize that what they were experiencing was comparable to what their own targeted parent had gone through. Making this connection allowed them to rethink much of what they had been told about the targeted parent and set in motion the process of recognizing that they had been lied to and manipulated by their parent.

David's story is representative of this scenario. David, 48 at the time of the interview, was born in Ohio. His father was 27 and his mother was 23 when they met. His father had been married before for a short period of time, but there were no children from that marriage. His parents dated about one year before marrying and David was born one year later. He had one younger brother and one younger sister. He was 5 when his parents separated and 6 when they divorced. He had limited memories of the marriage. "At the end there was a lot of fighting. That makes a pretty strong impression. I overheard it." His father worked the third shift at a machine shop and was not around that much, but David did have warm memories of time spent with his father before the separation.

After the separation, his father moved out and there was an initial visitation schedule. A few years later his father remarried.

Mom got custody of the three of us and Dad would come by on Sunday and we would be gone most of the day. A lot of times we would have dinner at Grandma's house and then within a couple of years Dad remarried and we had dinner at their house. I looked forward to it. It was fun. I looked forward to seeing him and doing things. At Grandma's house she had a cord carpet and we used some speed cars and you could just sit there and make like a highway there on the carpet and I remember her house was a little bigger, had higher ceilings and bigger rooms. And that was for the first couple of years and then Dad remarried.

After his father remarried, David's mother started to have a negative response toward visitation. "That was when things were a problem. The first couple of years wasn't so bad but once Dad remarried that's when things became a problem." The primary alienation strategy used by his mother was overreacting to minor incidents that occurred at David's father's house, building a case for the fact that his father was careless or dangerous.

Something would happen at Dad's house, like even the littlest thing. I remember one time we were at Grandma's house and my sister had some jacks, and we were playing jacks, and we went off to do something else. When we came back into the room and we were kind of running around, she fell on one of the jacks and one of them kind of hit her thigh and went in a little bit. I remember it wasn't that big a deal, but when we got home you would have thought someone had beat her. I was 7 or 8 at the time and my sister was 5. I remember thinking at some point after this happened several times that . . . on my way home and it was about a 30 to 40 minute drive, I remember just dreading it and thinking what will it be . . . what is going to be the thing that upsets her this time.

David's mother had a way of finding out about what happened during visitation and then zeroing in on the most negative aspect of the visit to the exclusion of everything else. She would inquire about the visit until she heard something negative.

She would ask me and I would tell her but downplay it, but then my brother and sister would tell her more and she would take that information and kind of use it to get more. Dad had remarried and his wife had a couple of kids and the daughter was older than me, and the boy was a pretty good sized kid, and kind of a bully, and he would push my little brother around a little bit, and one time in particular my brother was being pushed around a little bit but you would have thought that my brother was beaten to a pulp by this kid.

Another way that David's mother tried to create the impression that his father was dangerous was to tell him stories about his father that he no longer believed to be true. For example, she would tell him that his father was physically abusive toward him when they lived together before the divorce. She also told him that he was mean to children who lived on his street.

When Dad and my stepmom moved to their house I was 9. My mom knew in a very casual way the people who lived two or three doors down the street even though they lived on the other side of town. Mom would say things like, "Oh the boy who lives next door to your dad accidentally threw a ball into your dad's yard and your dad kept it." That story was told to me a couple of times.

Although seemingly minor, the story of his father hoarding the neighborhood youngster's toys stayed with him as a kind of emblem of his father being an untrustworthy man who was not good to children.

A second strategy utilized by his mother was to invoke a rule that if any of the three children did not want to visit, then none could go. Eventually, David's younger sister became resistant toward visitation, something that was exploited by his mother to cancel visitation for all three children.

I didn't mind going. In fact it was kind of fun, but my sister started to not want to go and Mom would say that if the girl didn't want to go, and the kids stick together, no one is going. I never quite understood why my little sister didn't want to go other than the fact that she said the food my stepmom cooked was kind of spicy and so that was always a problem that the food was too spicy.

David did not think that this information was shared with his stepmother so that she would have an opportunity to prepare more appealing food, nor did he recall the food being too spicy for his tastes. Such a frivolous complaint about the targeted parent is consistent with Gardner's (1998) description of the second manifestation of PAS: weak, frivolous, or absurd rationalizations for the alienation.

Another alienation strategy was to involve the children in discussions of financial matters designed to put David's father in the worst possible light.

> *There were things with the support checks. The checks came once every two weeks through the court. It was always a big deal when the check arrived. We had to check the mailbox and call Mom as soon as we got home from school and let her know that the check was there and if it wasn't there it was a big deal. I remember it always showed up the next day if it was late, so it was not like it was [really] late. We needed the money and it was very important that the money be there, and I guess I know now as an adult to get the kids involved is just counterproductive.*

It appears that she took advantage of a one-day delay in the arrival of the check to create the impression that his father was negligent. She was able to create the impression that he was a deadbeat father unwilling to provide the financial support necessary for the care of his children. His mother also used financial issues to create a wedge between David and his father by arranging for David to make a surprise request to his father about camp payments.

> *There was one incident . . . one year we went to camp. . . . I can't remember if it was the next summer or two summers after that and we called Dad up and asked him to pay for camp, and I remember I got on the phone and my brother got on the phone, and my mom got on the other phone, and it was real quick and dirty: "Dad can you pay for camp?" and either he said no or I'll think about it or something, and then Mom blurted in—there was no negotiation at all. "If you can't pay for camp then forget it" and we hung up and it was like wow that was fast and it was a big*

deal, one of those things where there was zero negotiation and no
details. I was even crying after the conversation was over and my
brother and sister were just bawling.

At some point David's mother moved away with the three children. She tried to prevent the father from finding where they had moved.

When we moved from the house where I lived with my parents be-
fore, it was eight or nine months after the divorce, we had a single
car garage and we had windows on the garage door, and then
Mom had them taken out and replaced them with solid panels.
The telephone number was changed to an unlisted number, and it
just seemed like . . . like it was a secret where we lived and the
phone number. We weren't allowed to give out the phone number.
She told us not to give him the number. Then we moved a second
time and I hadn't seen my dad in several years and it was a big
secret and I wasn't supposed to tell anyone where we lived. She
just didn't want him to know, something bad might happen. She
always said that she was afraid. She wouldn't even say that she
was afraid of him, just that she was afraid and not to let your dad
know where you live. I wasn't supposed to talk to him.

After the move, visitation stopped altogether. "When they first got separated there were day visits. When he got married then there were overnight visits, and then there was a break, and then we started seeing him again, and then there was a big break and then we saw him a handful of times, and then there was a permanent break. Shortly after they moved into the house we stopped going over altogether. I don't remember why."

David also shared that there was an emotional price to pay if he showed any interest in his father. It was not enough for his mother to have eliminated all visits, she also had to eliminate any discussion or mention of the father as well. She made it clear that to talk about him was a betrayal of her.

Even when I was in high school and college if I talked about my
dad that was like sticking a knife in her. It was just something

you did not want to do. It was almost as if I knew if I mentioned that I wanted to go see my dad I would be browbeaten into submission. I was thinking this is crazy, that it seems like every time I talk about my dad all hell breaks loose and it was almost easier . . . it was easier to not broach the subject. It became about survival . . . at that point in my life to survive you just don't talk about him at all.

At some point David's feelings for his father changed. Although David did not recall having negative feelings toward his father initially, he eventually did turn against him. He admitted that much of what his mother said about his father took hold inside of him and he came to believe most of the negative things said about his father.

David only began to reconsider his negative attitude toward his father when he became a father himself and witnessed his ex-wife behaving in ways that were reminiscent of his mother. When David was 23 he married and became a father. When his daughter was 2 years old, David and his wife divorced.

Initially there were some problems with the parenting time but then I was always able to get things worked out. I started keeping pretty good notes so that if I had to go back to court I would be prepared. When we did go back to court they would slap my wife's hand and I would see my daughter for a while until the next time. I noticed this from an adult perspective and I started to remember things that had happened to me and there started to become a number of similarities. For example, little instances would happen (between him and his daughter) and they would be blown up way out of proportion and out of context, and then I wouldn't be able to see my daughter. I started to see too many similarities. And actually my current wife started to say that I should get back in touch with my dad, and then I called him up and made arrangements to get together.

David came to understand that his negative feelings toward his father were, to a considerable extent, manufactured by his mother.

Spurred on by his second wife, David made plans to meet his father for the first time in several decades. "It went pretty well actually. I called him up and introduced myself and he said, 'Fine. Great.' We talked for a while and made arrangements to meet for lunch, and we went there and we sat and talked, and ate lunch and really things couldn't have gone smoother. We talked a little bit about that (the alienation) but never really in detail like maybe we could have because I never really felt like we had to."

David pointed out that his mother had passed away three years before he contacted his father. "Only then was I beginning to feel comfortable talking to my dad. It still felt like I was betraying her. It took three years for her to be dead."

Although he reestablished a relationship with his father, things did not go as well in David's relationship with his own daughter. At the time of the interview she was 25 years old and David had not seen her in over 10 years. David described the various strategies he used to try to repair and maintain his relationship with her:

While she was in high school I would go to ball games where she would be a participant and I would send her letters. I would go to parent–teacher conferences and I would go to the school once every couple of weeks and pick up classroom assignments and get copies of grade cards if they didn't send them to me. When she got into college she went out of state several states away and about once a quarter I would send a big package. I would include some of her things that she left at the house and then I would include a check, a very respectable amount of money, and the check would be cashed within a day or so without any thank you or anything. After about a dozen of those checks I guess when she was into her junior year at college I stopped doing that. I made some effort. I thought I tried to balance not being overbearing but yet still trying to let her know I loved her. I took a lot of photographs when she was little and I made duplicates of the photographs and I made a binder. At one time there must have been 20 or 30 pages of pictures and I sent that to her.

In my case even though I was an adult it was still taboo to have any contact with my father and now I am seeing something similar with my daughter. I have taken a different approach than my dad took but it is not working either. My dad laid back and waited for the kids to come to him, and in my case I am trying to reach out, but not to the point of being intrusive; my intention is to reach out a bit but that is not working either. Nothing would please me more than for her to call or show up at the door or e-mail. That would tickle me to death.

Catalyst 4: The Targeted Parent Returned
(n = 5, 12.5%)

The return of the targeted parent into the lives of the alienated children sparked the realization process. At that point the child was able to directly experience the targeted parent and was able to take in the reality that she or he was not the toxic person that the alienating parent had portrayed.

Bonnie was 28 years old, born in Texas. Her parents were 19 when they met. They dated less than a year before marrying. Bonnie was born about two years later and her younger brother was born about seven years after that (by a different father). She did not recall much about the marriage except that both of her parents drank. "When they would drink it would get nasty." When Bonnie was 3 years old her father discovered that her mother was having an affair, ending the marriage. Her mother took Bonnie and moved out of the house.

There was a standard visitation schedule that was followed for about two years.

Then there was an incident when I was about 5. I was with my dad and we were having fun. We were out on the lake and I was on the marina where they park the boats, and he had asked a friend of his to watch me for a couple of seconds. I remember sitting there fishing and all of a sudden my mother was driving down the road causing all kinds of dust and ruckus, and she slammed on the brakes and she is yelling at my dad and yelling at his friend, and she grabbed me and threw me in the car and that was it for a good seven years. She was trying to say that my dad wasn't watching me. I was small but I specifically remember him telling his friend, "Please watch her." I had a life jacket on and I was set to go. I was very confused. I didn't know what was going on. I was crying because I wanted to stay there and fish with my dad but it didn't happen that way.

So for the next seven years Bonnie had no contact with her father.

My dad tried several different tactics to talk to me but my mom foiled his plans I guess you could say. At the time I sort of knew what he was doing. In a way in my head being a child to me it felt like he was trying to contact me but she would stop it. For example when I was in middle school in 6th grade I think my dad went up to the school to have lunch with me and she had told the school that if he would ever go up there they were to immediately call the police and I remember it was a big production. They came and got me out of class and they put me in the principal's office and they locked the door. I found out later he was escorted off the grounds by the police.

Another alienation strategy employed by her mother was bad-mouthing.

Everything she would have to say about him was negative and bad. She was saying, "He's bad he's bad he's bad and he's an alcoholic and he doesn't care about you and don't you think he would come to see you?" and things like that. She would tell me he was a drunk and that he was no good. What kind of father was he if he couldn't even keep a job to send a measly $100 every month to take care of his kid? When I was younger she would tell me that he was an alcoholic and that he beat her.

When Bonnie's father remarried, the bad-mouthing focused on the stepmother. Her mother tried to instill fear in her about the dangers that her father and stepmother posed to her.

My mother told me that my father had remarried and this other woman was trying to take me away from her and they were trying to go to court and make me live with them. She was trying to tell me bad things about them, that they are alcoholics. She would

*say that I don't know who this woman is, and I don't know what
she is going to do to me and I don't know how she is going to
treat me and maybe I should think about those things. She was
telling me they were going to kidnap me and never bring me back
and she would tell me things like, "You think you have fun with
him but just wait when it comes down to it he's going to choose
her over you." Insinuating that . . . he would choose his new wife
over his daughter.*

When Bonnie was asked how much she believed of what her
mother said about her father, she responded:

*I was a kid and my mom was telling me these things. As a child I
was afraid. Deep down I did think maybe they really are going to
take me and not bring me back and what am I going to do? And
sometimes I would think maybe he really is like that. Maybe he is
a mean, evil person the way she makes him sound. Maybe he
really doesn't want to see me. That was another thing she would
tell me: "Do you think he really wants to see you? He can't even
send the money. If he wants to see you he would send the money
like he's supposed to." Sometimes I would think maybe he doesn't
want to see me. I would hear her saying that she didn't get any
money and then I would start to think well maybe he doesn't
want to. Maybe he doesn't care. Maybe he did forget about me.
She would say "Does he ever call you? Does he ever write you?
Where are your gifts on your birthday and Christmas?" How do
you answer that as a child? You can't, you know. I would sit
there and I would seriously wonder. When she was talking she
would say, "Don't you think if he wanted to see you he would
send the money? Don't you think if he really wanted to talk to
you he would write to you?" She would tell me bad things like
that and I said, "Yes I guess he would if he really did care."*

Sometimes during these bad-mouthing sessions, Bonnie's mother
wanted Bonnie to actively side with her against her father.

*She wanted me to agree. I know that for certain. I do remember
one vague memory. I don't remember what she was talking to me
about but I do remember I was sitting on my bed and she was*

standing in front of me and she was saying something about him and she was dogging him and saying things over and over and over again and she was like, "Why are you sitting there agreeing with him?" I remember her saying that and I remember sitting there and crying. I didn't want to tell her yes because it would feel like I was betraying him, and he hadn't really ever done anything to me that was bad and she was telling me over and over again "How can you sit there and not see that?" And she wanted me to say yes yes yes and I didn't want to say it, and I didn't say it, but it made me feel terrible and I was sitting there crying and crying. It was almost like a loyalty bind. I remember at that point I hadn't started seeing him yet but I remember through my whole childhood he's there and I don't ever remember him doing anything bad to me. She put the doubts in my head, of course, and I thought maybe it is true and maybe he really doesn't want to see me. But I never knew, I never knew ever, and that was the worst part.

Shortly before her father returned to her life she found out that he had been writing to her. "He did send a couple of letters. I never got them but my grandmother told me about them. They were letters addressed to me not my mom, but of course she opened them, and my mom said she read them and she burned them so I never knew what they said."

As a teenager Bonnie began asking questions about her father. She wanted to know why she couldn't see or talk to him. Bonnie recalled that her mother did everything she could to discourage her interest in her father. Around that same time her father and stepmother went back to court. She later found out that they paid up their debt (although they claimed that there should have been no debt because they had paid monthly support directly to Bonnie's mother. However, without proof of payment, they had to repay $4,000).

So I know that it came out that my stepmother, the lady that my father married, went ahead and said, "I don't care. Tell us how much we owe and we will pay it." So they ended up paying my mom like $4,000 that she didn't even deserve, but because he hadn't been sending it through the DA's office and he was sending it directly to her, and he had lost his receipts, they said ok you *don't have proof of this so you have to pay it. I remember that she got that money and that next weekend was when I was supposed to be able to see my dad for the first time in forever.*

This did not sit well with Bonnie's mother.

Up to the point when they drove up into the driveway my mom was sitting there telling me, "You better watch it because they are going to take you and they are never going to bring you back. They are going to kidnap you. That lady is from Ohio. Do you know anybody in Ohio? Do you know how to get back home?" I mean I was like 11 or 12 years old and I hadn't seen my dad in like forever and I really didn't care about this other lady but as a kid it was hey, whatever, somebody helped me get to see my dad so . . . it worried me and it stressed me out and I was real anxious and almost afraid, but the whole thing of being able to see him again overtook it.

And as soon as they got there my dad got out of the car and I hugged him and I hadn't hugged him in forever and ever and ever, and my mom was just standing there glaring at them from the back porch. We had a really long driveway and they had to drive all the way down the driveway to where the back porch is, and that's where I got into the car, and it is like 30 feet but it was ice all the way across. My dad didn't really say anything to her. She said, "Ok, she should be back on Sunday." We left and drove up to his house and I met his new wife and I had a blast. After that there was no ifs ands or buts about it.

There was regular visitation from that point on.

Bonnie's mother did not take well to the renewed visitation schedule. "At that time my mom started drinking again. I would come home and she'd be plastered, and there were snide comments such as, 'I hope you had fun. You think they are fun but just wait until they get tired of you. Just wait until you act up and then we'll see how much they want you.' She would get pretty dirty when she was drunk." Bonnie's relationship with her mother deteriorated after that and she spent the entire summer with her father.

Bonnie explained that she was able to experience her father for who he was rather than how her mother wanted her to see him. Facilitating this was his and her stepmother's ability to respect that she was just a child and that they did not impose their beliefs onto her. "I was only 12 years old. They didn't drag out all the terrible things about her [mother] and try to make . . . they didn't set up to prove anything against her. They were just there. They wouldn't bring her up if I didn't bring her up and it was almost like a reprieve to be out there." Bonnie had the opportunity to experience her father and stepmother for who they were rather than how her mother wanted her to think about them. She did not perceive her father and stepmother as having an agenda to interfere with her relationship with her mother, and this allowed Bonnie to hear what her father was saying. Through this experience she learned to trust and value him.

At the same time, Bonnie's relationship with her mother became increasingly conflicted. This was likely due to her mother resenting Bonnie's interest in having an ongoing relationship with her father (see Pattern 1 families in Chapter 1). In response, Bonnie pulled away from her mother. At the time of the interview, there had been a significant breach between them.

> I haven't spoken to her in 10 years. She did a lot of bad things to me. My dad is just a part of it. I don't have resolution. When we sat down, I asked her, "Why did you do this? What is wrong with you? What was your whole purpose behind it?" Ten years ago when she did what she did that caused me to stop talking to her is when I went ahead and closed that chapter myself. Well, my dad ended up passing away in 1998. He passed away of cancer. He smoked himself to death. But up until that point it was really good. I was talking to him and he even told me a couple of times toward the end, I could have whatever I wanted of his, it had always been like that, that he loved me. It was almost like he was my parent the whole time rather than my mother had been. All the way up until the time he passed away, we were fine.

Catalyst 5: Attaining a Milestone
(n = 5, 12.5%)

For some adult children of PAS reaching a significant milestone in life allowed them to realize that they had been manipulated

by one parent to turn against the other. Mark's experience typi-
fied this pattern. Mark was a 39-year-old man who recalled his
parents' marriage as "very combative, very cold. My mom was
antisocial and he was very social and she pretty much ran all
his friends off. There was a lot of arguing and some violence.
No love. I don't ever remember seeing them kiss. I remember
he worked as a salesman and she didn't like his traveling, she
was jealous of his traveling. I remember her saying, 'I hope
you're having a good time.' He worked his butt off I came to
find out."

His parents remained married throughout his childhood but,
because of the alienation strategies of his mother, Mark had
only a minimal relationship with his father. As he explained,
"With Dad, I barely knew him." The chief alienation tactic was
bad-mouthing designed to create the impression that his father
was a wrathful and dangerous man.

*I only remember him whipping me one time but I felt like he was
hitting me all the time in my head. I can't explain that. I was
very clingy to her and very close to my grandparents, because she
was very close to her parents, but my dad, I was scared of getting
a whipping. I was always told he was getting mad. We didn't
play ball. We didn't have very much to do with each other. I remember her always telling me how mean and angry he was.
Homework was a big thing. I needed help and she said, "Don't
ask your daddy he will yell at you" so I remember never going to
him with that. There was constant bad-mouthing. This was constant and my grandparents did it too. What a monster he was.
My grandfather said he threw me up in the air and I was made to
feel like he was dangerous. I do remember fishing with him one
time and I slipped in the mud and went under the water and his
friend was sitting there and he pulled me out, and they had been
drinking, he grabbed me by my hair and pulled me out and the
way I remember it was he didn't care enough to save me. I must
have told my mom about it, I was pretty young, and I remember
being really mad at him because he almost let me drown. Everything was blown up. I remember him being this terrible oppres-
sive man. I was very scared of him. I just hated him. He was
probably on the other side of the lake fishing and I was with his*

friend, but all I could remember was you weren't there and Jack had to pull me up.

Another strategy Mark's mother used was to ask her son to spy on his father. In the evenings when his father was at a local bar having a drink with friends, Mark's mother would pay Mark to ride around town on his bicycle and see if he could locate his father. Then he was to return home in order to make a report to his mother about what he found. In this way Mark developed the idea that his father was shirking his familial responsibilities and hurting his mother. This pattern created an alliance between mother and son against the father. "She would send me out on search and hunt missions where I would have to go and look for him and find him and then when I found him I had to come back and report and she would tell me what she thought he was doing. I was her spy." This activity also served to create secrets between Mark and his mother to the exclusion of his father, further creating psychological distance and mistrust between father and son.

Mark's mother drew her son into her confidence by complaining about his father to him. "Her main complaint was his cheating. I remember her saying 'We are going to get a divorce, who are you going to go with?' It was always, 'You, of course.'" In this way Mark was privy to information about the marriage and about his mother's intentions well before his father. This too served to create a special bond between Mark and his mother. It is also notable that his mother created loyalty tests for him by asking him to affirm his allegiance to her in the event of a divorce. She extracted from Mark a promise of loyalty well before he could really know what it was he was promising. The impression given was that his mother was not really asking him what he wanted. Rather she was asking him to reassure her that he would choose her in the event that the marriage dissolved.

Another way she garnered her son's support and sympathy was to imply that his father was having too much fun on his sales trips rather than working hard as a responsible family man.

He was a salesman and he would go to home shows and demonstrate machinery. I was always hearing about this big party he was on and she'd always tell me he was out there having a great time. He'd go for one or two weeks at a time and she would say he was having a big party and he is out there with women and drinking and doing all this stuff and he's eating great food and having a great time.

In this way, Mark's mother conveyed her resentment of these business trips and her belief that his father wanted to escape the family.

Mark's mother also limited actual contact between Mark and his father. He explained that as a traveling salesman, his father would take business trips, and he would sometimes invite Mark to go along once the boy was old enough. His mother would not allow this. "When he was on the road and I wanted to go on the road with him she wouldn't let me do it and I wanted to get to know him and she would flatly refuse." Between telling Mark not to ask for homework assistance and refusing to permit him to go on work trips, Mark's mother made sure that Mark and his father had little time together in which they could establish an independent and positive relationship.

And, finally, Mark's mother engaged her extended family in the campaign against her husband. For example, she created loyalty conflicts by telling Mark that his grandparents would not approve if he went on trips with his father. "She would tell me if I went with my father, her parents wouldn't like it and wouldn't speak to me again." Mark also recalled that his grandparents denigrated his father. "My grandfather would tell stories and he was a big talker, and the only story I ever heard about my father from him was when I was a baby and my dad used to pick me up and throw me in the air and catch me and how worried they were that I would fall down. A constant barrage of how incompetent and how dangerous my father was." Getting her parents to join in the bad-mouthing helped to solidify in Mark's mind that all the important people in his life believed that his father was a dangerous man and a bad father.

Eventually this barrage of negativity took hold inside of Mark. "Hatred. I remember thinking he should go ahead and die. I wish he'd just go get in a car accident. I wish he'd die. I didn't want him to come home. I just wanted to be with my mom." When asked whether he believed what his mother and grandparents told him about his father, Mark responded, "Oh yeah, totally, until I was an adult." Even living in the same house did not allow for father and son to have a relationship. Based on what he was told about his father, he avoided him at all costs. "He'd be in one room and I would be in another. I tried to stay away from him. I just remember him watching Westerns all the time. It was uncomfortable to be around him. It was tense. I was afraid of him that he was going to explode. I was scared of him. He had a deep voice and a presence about him." Thus, the alienation strategies worked. Mark had little if any relationship with his father during his childhood.

It was not until his son was born that Mark became aware that he had been misled about his father. At that point, he decided to reach out to him.

> I lived in California at the time after I got out of the service, and he and I started talking on the phone. We started to get to know each other. I came out on vacation and I was very miserable in my marriage. In fact I had divorced and then remarried my ex-wife in order to be with my son and to be a full-time father. I came to find out that he did the same thing back when my parents first got married. Then he found out she was pregnant and he stayed with her in order to be with me, and then they kept having babies after that. I remember that there were periods of calm and then there would be a lot of turmoil and fighting and she would come up pregnant. About every six years. So in talking to him I come to find out he is a great guy and he did love me. We have gotten to be friends. We could never have done it face to face with her there because I felt like I was betraying her, because if I did want to go do something with him I felt like Mom was going to be upset, Mom was going to be mad, and I am not supposed to do this. I am supposed to hate this guy. So on the phone we talked—my phone bill was $60 or $70 a month! We'd spend an hour at a time just talking and getting to know each other.

Facilitating Mark's relationship with his father was Mark's admission that his mother had tried to come between them.

> Yes. That was a breaking point, the first vacation back in 1993. We were out on the front porch. I was on vacation and I

brought my son there and it was the first time I had been home in eight years. My father liked to sit on the porch so I snuck out there to talk to him. My wife was very clingy too, and Mom was always there, so everybody was always around so we couldn't talk unless I snuck outside to talk to him. I asked him whether it was right for me to stay with my ex-wife and the kid because I knew that was what he'd done, and he answered my question and he said he did the best he could, and I said I knew that he had.

At that point Mark confided in his father some of the ways his mother tried to interfere in their relationship. Mark told his father about the spying and the secrets. "I said you know this happened. Mom always sent me out on these missions." He explained to his father that it was not his father's fault that they had not been close growing up. "I kind of broke it open at that point." It was then that his father shared with Mark that he had stayed in the marriage to be near him. "He stayed strictly for me and he did the best he could." Mark had not known that. "I didn't know why he stayed. I thought it was money. Mom would always say he wouldn't have paid child support."

From that point forward, Mark maintained a close relationship with his father. "And then when he was dying I came out and spent time with him and talked with him more and really broke down. I had seen her jealousy at the hospital when he appointed me the executor of his living will. He really confided in me and told me things that made sense; we got to be very close. I am glad that I found out who he was."

After his father's death Mark spoke to people who had known his father and learned even more about him from that experience. "A lot of the way I found out who he was happened after the fact from his friends. I went around and started talking to them. I didn't know anything about him, his time in the military, or when he was younger. There were some pictures of him when he was a teenager." In this way Mark further undid the alienation and opened himself up to learning about his father from an unbiased perspective.

After his father died Mark tried to confront his mother.

What happened was, my mother all of a sudden was saying that my father was this white knight on the horse and they had this dreamlike romance that never happened and it angered me. I asked her, "Why are you all of a sudden saying you had this dream marriage when you never said it then?" And I got mad and I hurt her feelings pretty bad. That was just recently. I told her, "You're saying we had this wonderful family relationship that never existed." She still won't admit to it. So right now my mother and I don't talk. We don't get along at all.

In sum, having a son and being in a difficult marriage allowed Mark to rethink his own childhood and opened him up to the idea that perhaps his father stayed in the marriage just to be with him. If so, he realized, then his father must have loved him much more than he had been led to believe as a child.

Chapter 6

Rethinking the Past:
The Process of Realization, II

The truth is cruel, but it can be loved and it makes free
those who have loved it.
—George Santayana, *Little Essays*

THE PRECEDING CHAPTER PRESENTED FIVE POSSIBLE CATALYSTS TO
realizing that one was a child victim of parental alienation syndrome: maturation, becoming the object of the alienating parent's
hostility and abuse, becoming alienated from one's own children,
the return of the targeted parent, and attaining a major life milestone. This next chapter describes the final set of six catalysts.

CATALYSTS TO REALIZATION 6–11

Entering therapy, the intervention of an extended family member, the intervention of a significant other, seeing the alienating
parent mistreat others, discovering that the alienating parent
was dishonest, and becoming a parent were all pathways to
realization.

Catalyst 6: Therapy (n = 5, 12.5%)

Entering individual psychotherapy provided a platform that allowed some of the adult children of PAS to rethink their child-

hood experience, including their feelings and beliefs about the targeted parent. Therapy was not pursued in order to examine that relationship, but that is where therapy took them, and these adult children of PAS eventually understood that such an endeavor was critical to their mental health.

Maria was 50 years old at the time of the interview. She was born in Florida. Her father was 25 and her mother was 35 when they met. Maria's mother had been married before. Her parents knew each other for about a year before marrying, and Maria was born two years into their marriage, the only child of this union. She was 11 when they divorced, they were living in Florida. Her mother was the alienating parent.

She remembered the marriage of her parents as stormy and fraught with conflict. "I don't recall them being that loving toward one another. There was a lot of emotional I would say instability and a lot of anger, a little violence, that is something I don't know the truth of. . . . I don't know if I am still brainwashed, I just don't know."

She had some positive memories of being with her father before her parents separated.

> Well, he was very involved with me as far as reading. We would read together and he would . . . I was way beyond where I should have been at that age because he had me reading and he was teaching me to read, spending time together. We were very close. I was Italian and there was a lot of demonstrative type of stuff, things like going in the car and watching the planes take off at the airport. We were close.

When Maria was 11 years old, she and her mother moved away. "We got on the train and went to Chicago and stayed with my mother's sister for three months. Then we left Chicago and went to Ohio near her family." There was an initial visitation schedule hammered out so she could spend time with her father.

> There was summer and holidays. But it didn't happen. He came up to see me several times which I remember, two or three times. I have been told by him and others that he came up more than

that but I didn't know about it. There was a visitation where he came up shortly after settling at my aunt's and there was a visit the following year when we were out of my aunt's, and that was it as far as him coming up.

Maria understands now that her mother exacted an emotional price from her for having any kind of relationship with her father.

Basically I was a chess piece between the two of them and it was very hard, and upon returning to Ohio (after visitation with her father) and the aftermath with my mother. I knew I would never ever go down and see him until I was much older. At that point I started picking up on signals from my mother that showing any kind of affection or love for my father could be a problem for me. If I showed any positiveness toward him it was, "How could you do this to me? How could you do this to me after all I did for him? You are betraying me." When I go to visit him and I come back, to this day, my mother still says, "How can you do this to me? You are betraying me. You are slapping me in the face any time you have anything to do with this man. How could you do this to me?"

In this way, Maria's mother created a loyalty conflict in which any contact Maria had with her father was interpreted as a betrayal. She was led to believe that thinking about, talking about, and being with her father was causing her mother harm.

Bad-mouthing was also a frequently used strategy.

It was all bad-mouthing my father about the violence. How could he treat her that way? How could he treat us this way? Look how he does this. He never really loved her after all she had done for him. She would be talking to my aunt, not speaking directly to me. My first present that he sent me, and he did send me presents, was a little portable stereo. And my mother said he deliberately put a receipt in the box for a $300 suit he had bought because she was trying to get child support and how horrible he was, how could he treat her that way after all she did. She put him through medical school. She had nothing. That was spoken directly to and around me. Not just to me but in my presence. All *of this was directed toward me. She harbored a great amount of feelings toward him, saying things like, "Have you heard from your father? Look he hasn't sent support."*

Maria's mother also recruited her sister to reinforce the campaign of denigration.

She even went so far in that situation to enlist the help of my aunt who was like, "How can you do this to your mother. Your mother really doesn't want you to have anything to do with that man the way he treated her. And your father doesn't want anything to do with you." And my father didn't have anything to do with me after that letter I wrote him about the child support other than a few phone calls and some promises that he would call and then he didn't. So of course that was just ammunition for my mother who constantly kept that in my face.

Interrogating her after visits was also a part of the routine. "Then when he came up there was a big argument as to whether I would be allowed to spend time alone with him and I did for a few hours then afterwards it was just . . . drilling session, drilling. 'Oh did he say anything about me? What did he say about you? Did he say he loved you? He can't really love you when he treats you like this. Did he hit you?' Was he physical with me [Maria] the way he had been with her."

At some point Maria's mother brought her to a psychologist. The apparent purpose of the meeting was to extract from Maria a statement that she did not want to have a relationship with her father. "I do remember the specific questions the psychologist asked me and I do remember overhearing my mother and the psychologist talking afterwards. The psychologist was a friend of a friend and she asked me whom I loved the most. I remember them talking and I hid between a curtain. I remember that very vividly."

And, finally, Maria's mother involved Maria in the intricate details of financial arrangements between her parents.

A couple of times there were problems with support and she got very upset and I ended up getting very angry on her behalf and

*writing him a very nasty letter about the support and he wrote
me a letter back saying, "Your mother has basically reduced me to
a biological father." I still have that somewhere. "I am not really
your father any more. All I am is a donor." So obviously he took
it that way when I was just trying to stand up for my mother because that is what I heard from her.*

Evidenced by the letter she wrote, Maria relented under the
weight of the alienation strategies. She went from having loving
feelings toward her father to just the opposite.

*My dad and I were very close and then after a time and all of this
stuff from my mother and then I think I took on a lot of her anger
toward him, feeling responsible for her because she was so, "Oh
poor me. I am so broken and so wounded." Like writing him that
letter and I think there was a whole lot of anger toward him I felt
after hearing all of this stuff that my mother had said. I thought
he must have horribly mistreated us. From my mother's constantly ingraining [this in] me I took on a lot of what she thought
and felt about him, and I threw that back at him the times that I
did communicate with him, whether consciously or subconsciously
he picked up on that. I think I almost borderline hated him for a
while. And even if I would have desired anything to do with him,
I would not have acted on it because of how my mother would
have reacted. She just instilled so much in me that I just felt so
alienated and so far away from him I couldn't have reached out if
I had wanted to.*

Further contributing to the alienation was that her father, perhaps because of his cultural background and own system of
beliefs, did not reach out to his daughter. Maria has come to
understand that what felt like rejection when she was younger
was her father acting on his belief that a daughter should reach
out to a father—that he, as her father, deserved her respect.
Unfortunately, his passive behavior was interpreted to Maria
by her mother as lack of caring, and Maria did not have a sophisticated enough understanding of his motivations to offer an
alternative explanation, even to herself.

For Maria the realization that she was being manipulated emerged over the course of her therapy.

The therapist started out by asking me about my parents and she asked how the divorce affected me. Without thinking and very flippantly I said I was one of those people who got through a divorce without being touched. Apparently from her point of view that told her a lot. She brought to my attention the abandonment issues. She said, "It looks to me like you grew up without any nurturing care. You had parents who had their own problems and didn't know how to be adults let alone a parent." And then as we began to explore this she would ask me why I had so little contact with my father and I would say that I had no idea. But I did have a lot of anger that came out about why he didn't call me, why all these years went by and he wasn't a part of my life. I decided to go to Florida, so I made a special trip. It was awkward. We sat around the table and I asked him, "Where have you been the last 20 years?" And he said, "You don't understand. Your mother took you away and I was hurt. You're my daughter " and I just looked at him and I said, "You were the adult and I was the child. I'll ask the question again, where were you for the last 20 years?" And that opened the discussion.

From that point on Maria slowly rebuilt her relationship with her father.

Slowly, slowly we have a friendship. I told him that is all we can have. It is too late for him to play the father–daughter relationship. We can't start out with that and I don't want any more idle talk about you are going to call me. Either you will call me or you won't but don't tell me you will and then don't. I set the boundaries to keep myself from getting hurt and for his part he has been pretty good. The problem was when he fathered a child in his last marriage and I freaked out. I don't know why. I just came out in a rage.

Maria realized that it was hard for her to see her father be a devoted and involved parent with this new child when he had not been that way with her. Eventually they moved past their difficulties and have established a satisfying relationship.

Maria described another factor in the realization process.

Yeah. I was talking to my father's first cousin who came up to visit me. She is about 10 years older than me and we have always had a closeness, and I was talking to her. She was my way of keeping in contact with that side of the family. She said it was not the way I remember it. And I asked her what she meant and it was through her that I got a picture. That was about eight years ago. It has only been in the last 10 years that I have come to realize that probably things were not as I remember them.

This cousin described her father as being devoted to her and her mother as being controlling and abusive. This was a new perspective for her, but one that made sense in light of her on-going relationship with each of her parents, and in light of the work she was doing in therapy to put the pieces together.

Since then she had developed a more trusting relationship with her father.

I have had conversations with my father in the last year when I opened up to him. When I was ending a 23-year relationship I reached out to him and I talked to him about it, and in talking to him about it we also talked about our relationship and I said, "It looked like I took Mom's side against you but it was just easier that way to keep the peace." And I tried to explain to him the kind of relationship I had with my mother and she can be certain ways and he just said he understood. And he asked my forgiveness for not being there, for abandoning me. We had a very good conversation but it has taken all this time.

With the aide of her therapist Maria came to realize that her mother was probably a narcissist who had placed unreasonable demands on her daughter. She finally understood that she could never be good enough or give enough to her mother. Her mother cannot be pleased and so Maria stopped trying to live her life for her mother.

My therapist said even if I were everything my mother wanted me to be it would never be enough. My mother has to have something to worry about. I have such intense resentment toward her. I have gotten enough courage to confront her about some things but she just falls apart. "How can you do this to me!" All emotional, whatever. She cannot see anything but herself. She must be a horrible person for me to do this after everything she has sacrificed. I can't stand her. I can't have a conversation with her. I am just full of resentment toward her. But to tell her that, she would fall apart. She would literally fall apart.

In this way, Maria has not been able to gain a satisfactory resolution with her mother and she lives with the knowledge that they will probably never resolve their differences.

Catalyst 7: Intervention of Extended Family (*n = 4, 10%*)

The intervention of an extended family member was the key to developing a new understanding of the past for this group. Robin, 39 at the time of the interview, exemplifies this pathway. Robin was born in Rhode Island, the second son of his parents, who were teens when they met, and just 20 when they married. When Robin was 4 years old his parents separated and then divorced. His mother was the alienating parent.

Like most of the other participants, Robin recalled a campaign of denigration as the principal alienation strategy. "What I was told was that he was very abusive and that he was an alcoholic, that he used to beat me and my brother and my mother and he would come home drunk and take money and would go out drinking with it, that he was a womanizer. He was in the Navy and [I was told] that he had been AWOL a few times, and that was what eventually got him locked up in jail." His mother described a man who was not a good father and was not worthy of his son's love and respect. She also created the impression that his father was a dangerous man who was likely to hurt him.

Soon after his parents divorced, Robin's mother remarried and moved the family to Michigan.

*I just remember the next guy showing up and my mom saying to
me: "This is your new daddy. I can remember when we had gotten to Michigan, and I had gotten this new daddy, I asked my
mother what ever happened to my old daddy. I can remember her
telling me he was a bad man and she said, "You can't have a bad
man for your daddy. You are going to have a good man for a
daddy and that is why I got you a new daddy." I don't know if at
that time she told me he [father] was in jail or if that was later
on, but that was kind of how it was explained to me, that I deserved to have a good daddy. My old daddy wasn't a good daddy
and that he used to spank me all the time and he would hurt her
and that he was just a bad daddy and he had to go.*

After the move to Michigan there was no visitation or contact
of any kind between Robin and the man who used to be his
father. Nonetheless, the disparagement of him continued.

*The thing is that she attempted to erase him out of our lives like
he never existed. Almost like he was dead. If we questioned her
about him then it was put to us, "Well he was a bad man. He
beat me. He beat you boys and you deserve a better dad." And
then once she got to drinking a lot and me and my brother got
older, then it really started coming out. She told us all sorts of
stuff about him. He used to be a womanizer and he had girl
friends on the side, and the only reason she ever married the piece
of s**t was because she was pregnant with my brother and her
brothers wanted to kill him and she begged them not to. He was
having an affair with one of her cousins and one time he black-
ened my brother's eye. She told me one time that my grandparents had given me these silver dollars which were very special
that they saved for me, and that my dad came home one time and
broke open my piggy bank and stole my silver dollars so that he
could go out and get drunk, and how he used to beat us and on
and on and on.*

There were no pictures of his father in the house and no casual
discussion of his father. It was either relentless bad-mouthing
or utter silence. "I had never seen a picture of him. It wasn't
just her either. It was my maternal grandmother and my uncles

on my mom's side, everybody." Robin explained that growing up it was taboo to mention his father's name. "Oh. Absolutely. That would have been an insult to Pete, my new father. For me to bring him up in any way, shape, or form was a betrayal of this man who now took me into his home, the piece of crap that I turned out to be, took me into his home out of the goodness of his heart and is raising me." If Robin did mention his father, his mother's response was quick and decisive.

> She said, "How dare you. How dare you. You are talking about somebody who always treated you like garbage. Who always treated me like garbage. And now you've got a good man. Now you've a good father. He puts food on the table and a roof over our heads. How dare you even mention his name in this house." You know, that kind of thing and it got to the point where I didn't even mention it.

Robin eventually gave in to the conditioning and began to hate his father, exemplified by the following exchange.

Q: How much of what your mother said took hold inside of you?

A: All of it! She was my mother. She was God!

Q: What would happen if someone asked you about your dad?

A: I'd tell them about Pete.

Q: What did you think of your father? He was no good?

A: He must have been. My mother told me so. He had to have been. My mother wouldn't have lied to me.

Q: Is that part of why you didn't ask to have contact with him? Was there a time when you lost interest in him because you believed he was no good?

A: Yes. There was that and why would I want to have contact with somebody who was a dirty rotten piece of crap who beat me and beat my mother!

Q: Did you ever have a memory of being beaten?

A: I never had a memory of it. The only memories I had of him were good memories, but if my mother said it, it must have been true.

The tide turned unexpectedly when Robin's mother placed a call to his paternal grandfather. At that point, the family was in turmoil and Robin's mother was struggling to control her two sons who were acting out and getting into trouble. She decided to try to locate Robin's father and ask for assistance. The first step in this process was to speak to the grandfather. This conversation was the turning point in Robin's awareness of the alienation, although it must be noted that Robin shared many features with Catalyst 2 families in that his mother became emotionally abusive toward him. The negative relationship between Robin and his mother probably facilitated his ability to separate from her and question what she had been telling him about his father. But Robin recalled the conversation with his grandfather as pivotal in the realization process.

> My mother made contact with my grandfather and I was actually allowed to talk to him. I remember her saying, "Your father's dad is a good man. He was always nice to you boys. So I can't see you not being able to talk to him and he would probably like to hear from you boys." So I remember talking to him on the phone and he was crying and he was like, "I can't believe I am talking to you after all these years. I miss you so much." He told me stories about taking me hunting for periwinkles (little snails). He used to take me to Horseneck Beach and go for clams and stuff like that, stuff that grandpas do with grandkids. He said he used to do that stuff with me and my brother. He said, "I didn't know where your mama went. Your mother just disappeared and she took you boys with her. I had no idea where you were. I didn't know where you were. I would have called you. I am sorry. I didn't know where you were."

Hearing that sparked a thought in Robin's mind. "I got to thinking. I thought hmm, you know if my grandpa had been trying to find me, what if my dad was looking for me all this time. What if my dad was looking for me and he couldn't find me either? Because we moved to Michigan then to Washington all the way across the country." This suggested to Robin the possibility that perhaps his father had not abandoned him. Perhaps his father really did love him after all.

It was like a revelation. I remember thinking at the time what if my dad was looking for me? That's another thing my mother told me was that my dad didn't want anything to do with us boys, he just walked away from us. My mother told me and my brother that my dad didn't want anything to do with us.

Unfortunately for Robin it took many years after that revelation to reunite with his father, whose whereabouts at that time were unknown even to Robin's grandfather, and life with his mother and stepfather continued to deteriorate.

By the time I was 17, my parents' drinking had gotten pretty bad and they had gotten pretty abusive and it was real apparent they didn't want me and my brother there anymore. My drug abuse had gotten pretty bad and I had to get out of there or I was going to die and I knew it. I joined the military and I spent seven years in the military. While I was in the military I continued to drink and was slowly destroying myself and I had a lot of problems with identity, who am I, where do I come from? I only had contact with my mother and Pete one time while I was in the military. I basically wrote them off. It was pretty obvious they didn't want me. I met my first wife in the military. I've had a real hard time accepting love, one of the impacts this has had on me. I had major abandonment issues, major fears of intimacy. I didn't think that my mother loved me and if my mother can't love me who can? I thought my real father didn't want me. He was someone who hated me, despised me.

I got out of the military at 24 years of age and I had met a woman who was a good Christian woman from the Midwest, a good Catholic girl, college educated, and she wanted to marry me and take care of me, and god knows I needed someone to take care of me. I finally broke down and told her, "I have got a major problem. I am addicted to drugs and alcohol." I sought help; finally at 26 years of age I went to a drug treatment center and that's where the majority of my recovery and life started. This is where my real father comes into my life. I was in a drug treatment center and I got a card in the mail that was sent to my home and my wife brought it to me at the treatment center. It was a letter from my real father. It said on the card "No matter how much knowl-

*edge we gain we still can't make the sky turn bright or the rain
go away. Sometimes you just have to walk through the storm."
And then I opened the card and it said, "I have been looking for
you for years. I finally hired a private investigator who found
you. I know where you are right now and I just want you to
know that I have traveled the road you are traveling now and if I
can ever be of help give me a call. Your dad Jack." And it had his
phone number and an AA medallion in the card, and I picked up
the phone and called him and that was the first time I talked to
my dad in 22 years.*

That was the beginning of repairing the relationship.

*It was kind of scary. I was scared. But it was good. We both cried
and I told him basically that I thought he had abandoned me and
that he didn't love me and didn't want me. I told him the things
my mother told me and he said, "I am not going to tell you that
all the things your mother said aren't true. What I can tell you is
that who I was and who I am aren't the same people anymore. I
can't ever remember beating you boys. I always loved you boys. I
have been looking for you for years. We'll have to get together and
talk." He said, "Right now the most important thing is that you
are going to die if you keep doing what you're doing. I am here to
help you with whatever I can through that." I said ok and I said
"I'll accept your help."*

Not surprisingly, his reunion with his father resulted in increased conflict with his mother.

*It is not that she really comes right out and says it, but she basi-
cally says, "Are you still talking to Jack?" and I will say, "Yeah,
I am still talking to Jack." And she says, "Oh well how's he doing?" "He's doing fine. He's not drinking anymore. He's got
about 16 years sober now. I've got 13 years clean and sober." We
are not the best of friends, but we get along and we talk and that
is better than I can say for me and my mother. She has pretty
much let me know that as long as I am talking to him there is no
room in her heart for me.*

To this day Robin has not been able to resolve this conflict with his mother.

> *I have confronted my mother about a lot of things. I have con-*
> *fronted her about the abuse of me when I was a child and I have*
> *confronted her about her alcoholism and her emotional abuse of*
> *me and my siblings and everything. My mother lives in a cloud of*
> *ambivalence and a cloud of denial and that is just where she is. It*
> *is kind of useless when you are dealing with someone who is in ac-*
> *tive alcoholism. There isn't going to be any closure for me on that*
> *end. I have to find my own closure.*

Robin was currently feeling very positive about his life. He was about to marry again and he described having a close relationship with his 8-year-old daughter from his first marriage. He was an active and involved father. He summed up his life in the following way. "It might have been better, it might have been worse. Things happened the ways things are supposed to happen. I think I am a pretty good man today and I wouldn't be who I am today if I hadn't gone through everything I have been through. And that is what counts. I wish things had happened a little differently I suppose, but there is not a whole lot I can do about it now."

Catalyst 8: Intervention of Significant Other (n = 4, 12.5%)

For these adult children of PAS, the major catalyst was a significant person in their lives encouraging them to reconsider their feelings about the alienating and targeted parent. Nicole was 19 at the time of the interview. She was born in California and her parents were in their early 20s when they met. Neither had been married before. She was the first-born child, followed by three younger siblings. Her memory was that the marriage was stormy, with frequent fighting and screaming. "I think mainly it was money. I remember my father worked two or three jobs and was gone a lot and that upset my mother. Later on he quit and then they fought about the lack of money. It was kind of back and forth like that. He would get another job and then they would fight about him being gone." Nicole had memories of being close with her father when she was a little girl. "When I was really young I remember being closer to him than my mother. He would take me all over and do all kinds of things with me. He would go to the store and I would be up in a minute putting on my shoes and I guess that's when I was really young like 4 or 5." After one particularly heated fight between Nicole's parents, they divorced and her father subsequently moved away. There was a brief reconciliation during which her father committed fraud in order to buy her mother a new car. This resulted in his arrest and conviction and he served some time in jail. Her parents remained separated from that point forward.

According to Nicole her mother was the alienating parent. The alienation strategies began prior to the divorce but escalated after that. "Her style changed dramatically after he went to prison. Before he went to prison, when they were fighting she would make all of us come in and sit down and she would say, 'Can you believe he is doing this? Look, he never wants to be around. He is always trying to leave us. He doesn't love any of us.'" Nicole described how her mother would draw the children into the conflict in order to have them feel sorry for her and angry toward their father. It seemed important to Nicole's mother that the children share her disparaging view of him.

Another strategy Nicole's mother employed was to encourage her to reject her father by actively aligning with her mother during parental conflicts. Understandably, this resulted in her father becoming hurt and angry with Nicole, further driving a wedge between them. "She would say something bad about him and want me to agree. And we would say these things in front of him and he would get angry with us and scream, 'I can't believe you just said that to me.' And he would turn and walk away." Exhibitions of allegiance to her mother were frequent occurrences in Nicole's life. "That happened all the time."

Nicole's mother also accused her of having an inappropriate relationship with her father.

She constantly used to harp on that thing like I was trying to . . . I don't know if seduce is the right word. . . . She would say I guess seduction. She'd say I positioned myself so he would have to look at me and I positioned myself so he had to brush past me. Just crazy. If you're told that enough times you start wondering about yourself, especially as a young child . . . Before he left she would make these crazy accusations. . . . I was 8 years when he left so you can understand why it was a little insane. So she would get angry about that and say I was trying to seduce him and then a whole scene would erupt about that so we . . . my dad and I, pulled away from each other probably a year or two before he left.

Following the divorce, Nicole's relationship with her father was further diminished. "After he left he would write us and every once in a while he would address it to me but usually he would address it to one of my younger brothers and sisters. Then we just lost contact." At that point the alienation strategies used by her mother evolved.

After he left, her campaign was different. A lot of the time she would complain about him leaving and deserting us. She would say, "Look. Your father deserted you." and different stuff like that. Mainly she would say, "Look, look he never writes you, why can't he send you any money to help take care of you. Look he doesn't care. He has a nice life. He doesn't even send any money. He doesn't help out with child support." and stuff like that. She'd bring up the money thing a lot. She'd bring up the lack of him writing me. She'd say every once in a while, "You were so misbe-haved, such a bad child, look he doesn't even want to be around you." Different stuff like that. Her main campaign was probably just . . . as I got older . . . you were such a bad child didn't do as much damage as saying, "Look he doesn't write you." Because that had some type of proof to it.

As far as Nicole knew her father was not writing to her.

Nicole speculated about her mother's motivations and con-cluded that her mother alienated her from her father in order to satisfy her own needs. "Mainly I think she always wants to be . . . she is very self-centered and vain. She wants to be your everything. She wants to be your center of attention. And so she liked the fact that by making me hate him all I had was her. So that worked good for her." And the alienation did work. Nicole came to hate her father. "I hated him. I remember times when I really hated him." Nicole did not have the opportunity to actively reject her father because he was already out of her life, but her heart had closed to him.

Nonetheless, Nicole's relationship with her mother became increasingly abusive and conflict-ridden. "There was hitting and screaming and a lot of crazy stuff." These incidents of hostility and rejection, however, alternated with episodes in which Nicole's mother tried to win her over.

She kind of went through periods of ups and downs. There were times whether she was drinking or sober she would tell me how much she loved me. How great I was, how smart I was. Whatever, you know, whatever compliments. I was there to help her. It would make me want to try harder to please her. I learned how to be amusing at a very young age. During good periods I felt like if I could just be funny enough or cute enough, sweet enough, good enough whatever then she'll stay happy, but for whatever reasons she would go back down into anger and sadness and then it was over.

The remarriage of Nicole's mother added further conflict and hardship to Nicole's life.

My mother's and stepfather's relationship was worse than my father's and mother's, a lot worse. My father never drank and never did drugs, but her second husband was a drug addict and so it turned into a really bad situation. I saw a lot as a child and most people should never see that kind of stuff, and I was real young.

At the age of 17 Nicole married her high school sweetheart, partly as a way out of the home situation. "I had married my husband at 17 to escape from my mother. I love my husband and I wanted to marry him, but I probably would have waited until I was a little older if things had been different." Despite wanting to create some emotional and physical distance between her and her mother, Nicole was still not quite ready to acknowledge that her mother had engineered the alienation from her father.

What precipitated this awareness was the input and perspective of her fiancé.

It wasn't too long ago really. As far as that . . . probably actually just recently. I talked to my husband about my childhood and different things and I talked to him about my father and I was still in denial about my mother and he would say stuff like, "It sounds like he was the better of the two." At first I thought he was pretty stupid. No way. And at first I was like, "No. You don't understand." I guess I would get really angry because he would push at it when we were dating and he would push things like that saying, "Your mom is the horrible one. Your dad doesn't sound that bad." And we'd get into a fight about it. And I'd go home and just kind of think about what he said. I guess the first time it really hit me was when we were discussing something and it was kind of related. We were actually discussing my mother, and my father didn't really have anything to do with it. When I was 17, she was arrested for drinking and driving, and so she was put in jail, and I called up my husband (fiancée at the time) and said, "What do I do? Can you give me a ride down to the jail so I can bail her out?" We went down there and he said, "Why do you pretend she loves you when she's doing stuff like this?" And I said that she does love me she just doesn't know how. He goes, "I don't know why you equate love with just being there. If I hang around you but kick you in the teeth every time I see you that's not love." And we just went on talking like that and it just kind of hit me and I went home and kind of reevaluated everything and just thinking about that definitely made me see that she didn't love me or didn't have any idea what love was. I guess that is when I started thinking about my dad and just wondering different things and seeing her manipulation for what it was, different ways that she tried to . . . and just seeing different ways that she manipulated me, analyzing the different ways she manipulated me with my dad and with my aunts and uncles and everything. It wasn't so much that I was in denial of her it was just everything. I don't know why it was so hard to see that, why it was so hard to see the manipulation. I guess because I felt there was a basis of

*it. I have a fear of being unlovable. And so it was so easy to be-
lieve when she would say obviously he doesn't love you. He's not
writing. When she would say stuff like that, "Look it isn't easy
for me either but I stick around here and do it and I sacrifice everything." And so I concluded she loves me and he doesn't. I
guess I heard that so many times. . . . I equated sticking around
with love. So it was kind of hard to digest what my husband was
saying.*

Nicole struggled with this new way of thinking about her
parents.

*It was actually really hard. It was hard realizing I had been ma-
nipulated into letting go of those relationships with my father,
grandparents, and aunts and uncles. That was hard, but I had
really pretty much already let those go, so that wasn't as hard as
admitting that there really wasn't any love from my mother. That
was a little more hard because I guess she had done her job well. I
relied on her. She was . . . in my mind she was everything. She
was all I had. It was really hard coming to grips with that.*

In the end, Nicole developed a more realistic understanding of
her mother, whom she described in the following statement,
"She wants all different things, someone to bail her out when
she is in trouble. She wants someone to tell her she is right no
matter what. She wants someone to fall back on. She wants a
12-year-old kid to take on a grown man when he is hitting her.
She wants someone she can control. All of those things. She
wants someone she can hurt when she is hurting. I think mainly
it is about control; she wants me to be all hers."

As noted above, Nicole's mother was probably narcissistic
and felt threatened by Nicole's positive relationship with her
father. She conducted a campaign of alienation designed to
drive a wedge in their relationship, even prior to but especially
following the divorce. Once the father was pushed out of their
lives, Nicole's mother turned her wrath on Nicole (as with Catalyst 2 participants). However, for Nicole, the catalyst was a
loving and supportive boyfriend who offered her a new way of
thinking about both of her parents. At that point she was able

to understand that her mother was in large measure responsible for the loss of her father. A loving boyfriend who became her husband provided her with the emotional support and perspective she needed to accept the reality of her mother's narcissism and manipulation.

Catalyst 9: Seeing the Alienating Parent Mistreat Others (n = 2, 5%)

For these adult children of PAS, the major catalyst was witnessing the alienating parent treat other people much the same way as the targeted parent had been treated. In this way, they began to understand that the problem was with the way the alienating parent interacted with others, not with the targeted parent.

Sarah was 41 at the time of the interview. She was born in Arkansas. Her mother was 17 and her father was 25 when they met. Neither had been married before. They dated less than a year before marrying. Sarah was born during the first year of the marriage, followed by two younger brothers. Her parents separated when she was 12 years old and the family resided in Arkansas at the time.

Sarah recalled a troubled marriage. "They had a very rocky relationship. They fought a lot. They were not affectionate with each other." She did not know what the fighting was about but her impression was one of constant conflict between her parents, some of which she observed first hand. "I heard them fighting and I saw them fighting. They fought a lot over other people. They fought over people that my mother knew and people that my dad knew. They fought a lot over other men and women."

Despite the marital discord, Sarah recalled being close with her mother. "I was very close with my mother and very distant from my father." She also reported that the alienation began prior to the separation.

My mother confided in me a lot about their problems and how she was feeling, and I didn't talk to my father very much at all. Oh yes, it started way before the actual separation. I was drawn in to my mother's confidence and she talked to me about a lot of prob-

lems and how she felt and what she wanted to do, and I didn't talk to my father very much at all—even before they started having problems. My father was very unaffectionate and he is a very reserved, very quiet person so I didn't speak to him very much or talk to him a lot even before their problems started. I have always been closer to my mother even before their problems started.

The primary strategy utilized by Sarah's mother involved drawing Sarah into her confidence.

I believe it started by the way she took me into her confidence. She criticized my father to me. She criticized his family. She would tell me that he doesn't care about her. She didn't like the things he believed in. She said he was not faithful to her and that he didn't care about her. She would get pretty specific at times. Not all the time but she did tell me that she saw him with someone else. She would accuse him in front of me of not caring for her and not caring for the family.

Being her mother's confidante was a complicated experience for Sarah. "At first it felt ok. It felt nice because at least that way she was acknowledging some of my feelings so at first it felt ok. At first I liked it. It made me feel safe. I felt safe with her. I felt safe in that position and at least that way she was listening to me." However, there was a downside to this experience as well, because these conversations created anxiety in Sarah. Knowledge of intimate details of her parents' marriage confused her and made her feel responsible. Sarah felt that her mother was asking for advice, something she was ill-equipped to offer.

Later I started to feel burdened and frightened with the information she was giving me. I felt like I was supposed to do something and that I was supposed to provide her with the answers and help her sort it out and help her find solutions to what was going on. I felt like I was supposed to give her advice. I really felt like I was supposed to do something for her but I didn't know what. She took me into her confidence. She wanted me to give her permission, I felt like, to divorce my dad. She would ask me a lot

whether she should divorce him. I told her I don't know and then
I would feel guilty because I wouldn't know what she should do.
And so I felt really awful.

Another strategy her mother used was to limit the amount of
time Sarah and her father spent together. "She didn't allow
very much time with him alone. She took me everywhere with
her. She completely controlled my life." In this way Sarah and
her father had few occasions to develop an independent relationship that would have provided Sarah with her own understanding and experience of her father. Because there was little
time together, there were few opportunities for her father to
counter the bad-mouthing either by directly correcting Sarah's
ideas about him or by just showing himself to be different from
how her mother was portraying him.

Sarah's mother also limited the amount of time Sarah spent
with friends. Sarah felt obliged to put her mother's needs first
at all times. This resulted in Sarah being more emotionally dependent on her mother than she might otherwise have been,
because she did not have a strong relationship with her father
or with friends. This heightened her mother's importance for
her well-being. "I didn't have any friends. I didn't bring any
friends home. I felt like I was supposed to be there for my mom
all the time. I felt like if I associated with anyone other than
her, I felt like I was betraying her. I was real afraid then. I was
afraid that I would lose my mom if I said anything to anybody
that I felt like she wouldn't approve of it. If she found out that
I told anyone about her problems."

Because her mother was all she had, Sarah became vigilant
about not displeasing her. If she lost her mother's approval, she
felt she would be completely alone in the world. "I was afraid
of her and I was afraid of losing her." Typical of individuals
with personality disorders (as was probably the case for Sarah's
mother), her mother's behavior and moods were unpredictable.
Sarah never knew whether she would be on her mother's good
side or her bad side, whether her mother would be loving toward her or disapproving and rejecting. In this way, Sarah became preoccupied with winning her mother's approval. "She
easily lost her temper at times, and I remember that she drank

a lot, and I would see her cry a lot, so she appeared very fragile to me so that made me feel more responsible to be there for her."

Another behavior that functioned as an alienation strategy was bringing Sarah along with her on her adulterous liaisons. This resulted in Sarah having secrets with her mother at her father's expense, further binding Sarah to her mother.

She took me with her to see other men. I spent several nights with her when she met other men and would contact other men. Oh gosh, she had a female friend that she went to stay with a lot, and she would take me with her and at her friend's house she would call other men on the telephone and I remember a couple of the times where she met other men there at her friend's house. She never told me to not tell him (her father) but I knew I shouldn't.

When Sarah was 12 years of age her mother moved away, leaving Sarah and her brothers in the care of their father. Shortly after she moved, she contacted Sarah and asked her to secretly pack her belongings, plan a bus trip, and move to another state to live with her.

When she left the state after she and my father separated she contacted me at school and she arranged with me to come live with her and she didn't contact my father about it. She went behind his back. She went behind the school authorities' back, and she didn't talk to any other adult to make arrangements for me to come stay with her. She contacted me, just me, a 12-year-old child alone, to come and get on a bus and relocate to go live with her.

It took a little planning but eventually Sarah left her father's house. "I didn't leave immediately. I didn't take anything with me. I remember I took very little. Mostly I left everything behind. I told one friend of mine but I didn't tell my father or any family. She told me I shouldn't say anything to anybody about it." In light of the relationship established between Sarah and her mother, in which her mother's approval was paramount, it is not surprising that Sarah complied with her mother's wishes. In case there was any doubt in Sarah's mind, "She told me that she couldn't live without me, that since I was her first child my rightful place was with her, which was where I was supposed to be. I understood that."

Sarah left her father's home and moved in with her mother partly to please her mother but also in part because she did not have a close relationship with her father. There was not much holding her there. The alienation had worked. She explained, "I really did see him as she did. My father is very quiet, reserved, and she flipped that over and made it seem he didn't care for her or us, and I adopted that view about him too. He wasn't quiet and reserved because that was who he was, in my mind he was quiet and reserved because he didn't care. So I did take that attitude toward him that she did."

The alienation strategies continued even after Sarah cast her lot to live with her mother.

Well when I went to live with her sometimes she would discuss him with other people and she would criticize him in front of me to her friends, so I don't know if she did that intentionally to cause further alienation but it had that result that . . . it was more reason for me to stay away from him and not care about pursuing a relationship with him. [Unfortunately, her father was not able to actively engage Sarah in a relationship.] My dad had remarried during that time, so when I would go back to visit him I primarily spent time with his wife. I didn't spend quality time with him. I spent most of my time during those visits with the wife he had at that time. So there was very little time spent with him actually.

Eventually Sarah came to the realization that her mother was at least in part responsible for her negative feelings toward her father. This occurred when she came to understand that her mother created conflict and negativity in all of her relationships. It took some time for Sarah to gain this insight because she had to experience firsthand how her mother treated her and how she treated other people in her life. At some point it became clear to Sarah that her mother was the root of the problem. This occurred for Sarah after seeing her mother have several other failed relationships in the time between Sarah moving out to be with her and turning 18 years of age.

*That didn't happen until much later, around 18 years old, when I
started planning on moving out of her home I started realizing
that. So it wasn't until I was an adult. . . . During the time I was
living with her until the time I was 18 she married twice and divorced twice and so . . . before she married her third husband I
was pretty sick and tired of having to adjust to a new family situation, so I started thinking differently about her because she was
having so much trouble staying in a marriage, and then I was
thinking at that point . . . I started asking questions because I was
becoming . . . I was experiencing depression myself because I was
having to adjust and readjust to another stepfather so I started
having symptoms of depression. At that point there was so much
changing homes and whatever. I had started asking questions because I was depressed a lot.*

Seeing other people have trouble with her mother helped her
realize it was not all her father's fault; that perhaps there was
something wrong with her mother in her ability to sustain relationships.

Sarah has never confronted her mother about the alienation,
she felt that there would be a heavy emotional price to pay if
she did:

*I could imagine her cutting me off. If I were to say, "Mom, what
happened wasn't right. It wasn't right for you to take me into
your confidence and turn me against my father." I can imagine
her retaliating and saying, "Well, if that is how you feel then you
don't need to have anything to do with me." I could imagine her
justifying her actions and distancing herself from me. I don't
know if she would say, "Well you are not my daughter anymore."
But I could imagine her becoming very distant. She would distance herself and run away from what I was saying.*

Sarah was able to repair her relationship with her father.

*Just recently I admitted to my father that I believed everything
Mother said about him. I did that just a couple of months ago.
That went pretty well. I told him that. Actually what happened is
that I asked him to forgive me for completely taking my mother's*

side when I was small and I admitted to him that I believed every-
thing she said about him, and I asked him to forgive me for taking
her side in everything. And it went well.

She explained that she waited 20 years before asking for his forgiveness, "because we didn't have a close relationship and it didn't feel safe to approach him about this subject." Just recently Sarah moved in with her father and she felt ready to clear the air. Living with him led her to become aware of her feelings of guilt for having betrayed her father. She was experiencing depression and guilt. "When I started having a relationship with my father. I just discovered that in my interaction with him. I discovered the guilt. It was through frequent contact over the last several months that I realized I felt that way. I felt like I had to reach out to him and apologize because it was wrong for my mother to do that. And I felt like I owed that to him. I owed him an apology."

Catalyst 10: Discovering that
the Alienating Parent Was Dishonest
(n = 2, 5.0%)

Catching the alienating parent in a significant lie sparked the realization that the alienating parent had lied about the targeted parent as well. For Julia the lie was not about the targeted parent but it nonetheless alerted her to the possibility that other things the alienating parent had said might also not be truthful.

Julia's story begins with the fact that she was the product of an affair, which began when her father, a 31-year-old police officer with a wife and family, met her mother, a 38-year-old single mother of four children. Julia was born 2 years into the affair, which lasted 15 years.

According to Julia, the alienation occurred as far back as she could remember. "My earliest recollections were when he would not show up for visits. My mother would let me know when he was coming on a Saturday and if he did not show up she would tell me I was not important to him, and his other kids came first, and I was last on the list, but I shouldn't be too upset because I had her." In this way, Julia's mother tried to diminish her father's importance in her life.

As with the other alienating families, bad-mouthing was central in the alienation campaign. Julia's mother would tell her that her father was a liar, "that he wasn't going to leave his other family for us, and he kept saying he was going to do that and he didn't, and basically that he was a liar and he couldn't be trusted and he never showed up when he said he was going to."

Julia only saw her father when he came to the house to visit her mother (as part of their ongoing affair). Julia and her father were not allowed to have any parenting time alone together.

I only saw him when he came to the house. He never took just me anywhere. We never had any one-on-one time. My mother wouldn't allow that. She always had to be there. They had a 15-year affair so I saw him when he came really to see my mother. I don't know how often he was there, once a week maybe. When I was in school he was there more I think during the day. If I was there I saw him, and if I wasn't he didn't go out of his way to see me.

Julia's mother limited and controlled all contact between Julia and her father. She had no independent relationship with him.

None. None. One time he took me to the dentist and then he took me to his house and I met his wife. I was 4 and my mother had a fit and that was the last time we ever did anything by ourselves. My mother threw the fit in front of me. When we got back and I said . . . my mother used to call her the witch so, of course, I said "I met the witch" and my mother was really furious. From that point on she always had to be there if we did anything.

Another alienation strategy was to limit contact with her father's family and to create ill will between Julia and them. "She didn't allow me to see any of my siblings, my stepbrothers and sisters that were from my father's side. She basically told me that they all hated me and so I was never allowed to meet them." Julia believed that they hated her because she had no independent experience with them. All she knew was what her mother told her and she had no reason to doubt what her mother said.

Because of the limits her mother placed on visitation, Julia's relationship with her father was severely constrained. "It was very awkward." Her mother saw to it that her father did not play a significant role in her upbringing. "So it wasn't like I ever felt like I knew him." Her mother also created enmity between Julia and her father by claiming that her father did not support her participation in talent shows and beauty contests.

> *At some point she started putting me in beauty pageants and talent contests, that was something that she used to do and something she really wanted, and she used that to drive a bigger wedge between myself and my father. Well my father really basically thought that the dancing and all the pageant stuff was a waste of time and money. . . . I know that he said that once. I remember, you know, him saying that once but she would reiterate that, "Oh every time I talk to your father he says you are just wasting your time and you have to be really talented to get anywhere and he doesn't feel that you are." And she said she would buy him a ticket to every event that I was in, and he never showed, and she would say, "See he doesn't support you. He doesn't understand that you have natural talent and he can't be bothered to come and even see you." Basically that, and in my teen years that made it even more obvious to me that he wanted nothing to do with me, not only nothing to do with me but that he completely did not support what I was doing.*

In this way, her mother created the impression that Julia's father did not love and care or her. It was only much later that Julia learned that her father never received tickets to these shows.

An additional alienation tactic was to induce in Julia feelings of anger and resentment toward her father, which she then was encouraged to demonstrate to him.

> *If she was angry with him then I was supposed to be angry. She would write these little plays and he would come over and I was*

*supposed to come into the living room and scream at him and tell
him what a horrible father he was, and then I was supposed to
run out of the room and cry hysterically. She would write these
skits that she would want me to perform. I guess I never really
felt that it was appropriate to love him because she was almost always mad at him anyway.*

In this way Julia and (probably) her father as well came to believe that each was unloved by the other.

Thus, Julia's mother was the center of her emotional life and
her father's role was vastly diminished. She described the relationship with her mother as, "Very enmeshed. I was her favorite child and so I was the child who was supposed to be
everything she wanted to be. So she had very high expectations of me and she didn't ever let me out of her sight. There
wasn't any independence that was allowed. She was extremely
controlling."

Eventually, the weight of the alienation overwhelmed whatever relationship Julia had with her father. She felt for her father exactly what her mother wanted her to feel.

*I hated him. I hated him. I never called him dad. I always called
him by his first name. I hated him. I thought that he was just an
evil person. I mean my mother told me that they both decided to
have me, that it was a mutual decision to have a child, so for me I
could never really understand how they could mutually decide to
have a child and then he just had no interest in me, and I thought
that was really horrible to purposefully have a child and then ignore that child. So I really just hated him.*

Julia lived with her mother until she married her first husband
at the age of 20. During this period of her life, even though she
was an adult, she barely had contact with her father. As she
explained:

*I went to visit my father when I was around 22 and that was the
first time [since age 4] I met my siblings and my stepmother. I
had never heard from any of them again, my father, my siblings,
nobody and I concluded that they did not like me. But what had*

*happened was my mother had called my father when she found
out that I had met everybody, and she told him that I did not feel
comfortable at his house with his wife and my stepsiblings and
that I didn't have a good time and I would prefer not to do that
again. My father stupidly believed her and I did not have contact
with him for another five years.*

Julia began to think about her father differently only after she
found out that her mother had purposefully misled Julia to
believe that she (Julia) had leukemia. At some point Julia began to wonder whether this was true. "When I was in my mid-
20s and I started to question whether I had leukemia since my
mother brought me up to believe that I had leukemia. I was
working in a hospital right next to the children's leukemia ward
and it didn't really seem to make sense to me, and so I started
to think about it. I was also getting divorced, and so when my
father found out I was getting divorced he actually called."
The conversations between Julia and her father at that time
confirmed that she had not been born with a fatal illness.

*I asked him when I was getting my medical records because I
started getting concerned, and I wanted to know what kind of leukemia I had, so I asked him what did he remember the doctors saying when I was born about the leukemia and he was like, "I don't
know what you're talking about. You were healthy when you
were born." And I said, "No Mom said I was premature and I
had leukemia." and he said, "You weren't premature. You were
born the week they said you would be born." And so he was very
shocked and he said, "You know, your mother has always been
very sick and it got her a lot of attention to say you had leukemia."*

Julia concluded that her mother fabricated the illness in order
to gain attention and sympathy. Her father explained that her
mother had always needed a lot of attention. "So he figured
right away her whole reason for going around and saying I had
leukemia was to get herself more attention over the fact that
she was with this man who tricked her and wouldn't leave his
wife and now she had this child who was ill."

Julia also concluded that the fictitious illness was designed to engage her father in ongoing contact with her mother. When she was born Julia did have some minor medical complications that her mother used to try to engage her father. "I was called a blue baby. I think the two blood types of my mother and father weren't compatible and it does something to the baby. I needed a blood transfusion. So there was a little something wrong, but it wasn't life threatening, but my mother would call my father."

This pattern continued throughout Julia's childhood, with her mother trying to draw her father into invented medical dramas. "When I was in fourth grade she called him and said there was something wrong with me and they couldn't find out what was wrong with me. I was having stomach problems and I went through a large number of invasive tests and she would call my dad and want him to come to the hospital. And there was nothing wrong with me."

Around the time that Julia was concluding that she did not have leukemia, her father contacted her, and they began a more open and loving relationship.

He contacted me when he found out I was actually getting divorced and was moving back into my mother's house. Then he started taking me to breakfast, he took me to lunch, and then I ended up being invited to dinner at one of my siblings' house. That was what actually started the relationship that I have with him now. We had a very long and open conversation about that and he knew that was happening, he had known all along that was happening.

These conversations put some of the pieces together for Julia in a new way.

I think that in my heart I always sort of knew that everything didn't make sense. It didn't make sense to me that they purposefully had me, so when he admitted that he did not purposefully have me it was actually a relief to me because that felt more responsible than having a child and treating her the way I was treated. It was a very odd conversation. He admitted he shouldn't have been having an affair, but the pieces more or less made sense because he had tried to visit me, and he had wanted me to be with my other siblings, and I also learned that my siblings never hated me, that they all felt growing up that they weren't allowed to meet me.

Julia also learned that her father and stepmother had taken her mother to court for increased visitation and custody. This also helped Julia understand that her mother's statements that her father did not love and care for her were not true.

Eventually Julia confronted her mother about not having leukemia.

Yeah well, I confronted her about the leukemia specifically and I told her I had looked into it and I talked to my father and I brought my sister with me when I did it so I wouldn't be alone with her. I said I don't believe I ever had leukemia and she looked at me and said, "Well maybe the doctors said you had anemia. So now you don't have anything to worry about." Since that time . . . actually she proceeded to say, "Your father is a liar and the truth is you are not his only illegitimate child," and she got up and walked out of the room. She was angry that my father had told me the truth or that it made her look bad, and my mother never wants to look bad. So for me to have figured this out and for my father to have supported it, she was very angry because basically I should be so grateful to her that she raised me by herself, and so because of that I shouldn't question her. So she felt hurt that I was saying this and she was angry that I had anything to do with my father, and so she wanted to be hurtful back. Except for the conversation very briefly about the leukemia where she said probably it was anemia, to this day she still stands by the fact that I had leukemia. She went right back to saying that. She is absolutely convinced I had leukemia and works hard to try to get me see that.

Over time Julia developed an understanding of why her mother behaved the way she did and why she tried to alienate her from her father. "Fear of abandonment. I think she was scared that I would want to be part of that family and that ultimately maybe

I would want to live there." Even though there were four other children in the family, Julia played a special role in her mother's emotional life.

I was the favorite. All growing up I was told that I was the favorite child. She loved me more than she loved the others. She always said I was the only child she conceived out of love. The others she had because she was a good Catholic girl and you're supposed to have children, so she had her two boys and then she had my two sisters with a father figure, but my father was the only man she ever was in love with so that made me different. Also, as a child I was much more the girl personality that she had wanted. My sisters were more tomboys both of them and I was more the real girl. I liked hats and dresses and stuff and that was more her thing also.

Currently, Julia and her mother were still in touch.

It's tense. It is very superficial. It is very strained. It is like walking on eggshells. I have to be extremely careful with what I say. I work really hard not to say how much involvement I have with my father's side of the family. So it is a difficult relationship. It goes in spurts. She was actually not talking to me for about 10 months. Now we are speaking again and so on average I would say we talk about once every three weeks.

Julia reported having a closer relationship with her father. "We do family function things so we see each other at least every three months if not every other month. A lot."

Catalyst 11: Becoming a Parent
(n = 1, 02.5%)

Having a child of one's own initiated the realization process for Veronica, by highlighting the importance of both parents in the life and development of a young child. When she went through her divorce, Veronica worked hard to keep her husband engaged and involved with the children, and through that effort she came to the awareness that her mother could have and should have done more to promote her father's relationship with her.

Veronica, 40 years old, was born in Wales. Her parents were quite young when they met; neither had been married before. They dated a short while, married, and had three children within a few years. Veronica recalled a stormy relationship between her parents, with considerable conflict and fighting, although she did not know what they were fighting about. When Veronica was 3 years old, her parents separated and her father left the house.

The alienation strategies of her mother began soon thereafter. From the beginning, there was constant denigration of her father. Her mother said that her father physically abused the three children and that he ran off with another woman. She painted a picture of herself as the victim and her father as a terrible villain who hurt everyone in the family. "They always told us that he was bad, always beating us, and having an affair with her best friend, beating my sister." In addition, the badmouthing focused on how her father had not done anything good for her or her brother and sister. "They (her mother and stepfather) would say, 'If it weren't for your stepdad you wouldn't have this or you wouldn't do that, or go there,' continually saying, 'Your father did nothing, never gave us no money.'"

Veronica and her siblings were also told that her father and his family did not want them to be born and were disgusted by the fact that Veronica's brother had a minor cosmetic complication at birth.

Another alienation strategy used by Veronica's mother was to interfere with visitation by making it uncomfortable for him to come to the house. "She didn't want us seeing him, she made things awkward for him." At some point Veronica's mother moved the family away, making visitation even more difficult. When her father came to pick up the children for visitation, Veronica's mother and stepfather instructed the children to pretend that they were not home. "And I always remember my mother and stepdad putting notes on the front door saying that we were out, if it was the catalog man then put the catalog in the door. So he would know we were not in and we would hide. We'd have to hide." She maintained vivid memories of what it felt like to hide in the house, partly wishing that her father would leave and partly wishing that he would never stop trying to be with her. Eventually he did stop knocking on the door.

Veronica was also led to believe that in order to preserve her mother and stepfather's love and approval, she would have to reject her father altogether. "We had to do it for my mom and stepdad. We weren't supposed to like him. I never could hate him even though I had to say I did. The only reason I'd say it was to please my mum." She explained what would happen if she expressed interest in or positive feelings toward her father. "I remember being about 5 and I remember saying at the table that I wanted to see him and she went into her room crying to my stepdad and he came out and shouted and said, 'You are not going to see him and if you mention his name you're out.'" To further ensure her place in her mother's heart, Veronica made up stories about her father's girlfriend. "I did tell my mother that his girlfriend at the time (eventually his wife) slapped one of our legs. My mother would say, 'You're not going there then if they going to be like that to you.' It seemed to make her like more yeah . . . more loving." When asked what would have happened if she came back from a visit and said she had a lovely time, she responded emphatically, "I would never say that."

Veronica's mother solidified the alienation by threatening to withhold contact between the children and their grandparents if the grandparents mentioned the father's name or encouraged contact with him. The paternal grandmother agreed to these terms, in order to maintain contact with her grandchildren. "My mother would threaten his mother that if she involved us with him she wouldn't see us, you know."

As was true of many of the other alienating parents, Veronica's mother was probably narcissistic. She was able to instill in her daughter a keen desire to please her and a sense that her approval was critical to her well-being and sense of self. Veronica described her early relationship with her mother in glowing terms.

We were really good friends. It was brilliant. There was a lot of past abuse and she told me everything. She was abused by her

*brother when she was about 11. I used to follow her. I was called
her shadow by Stepdad because wherever she went I stayed with
her. When I was little, when I was a teenager we'd do everything
together.*

Despite the fact that her mother made it impossible for Veronica to sustain a relationship with her father, Veronica still felt close to her mother and believed that they had a good relationship.

Eventually, her father gave up trying to maintain a relationship with his children. The fighting over visits when he would come, and the children hiding from him and pretending they were not home when he would knock on the door, perhaps led him to believe that any efforts on his part would be futile. Once the attempts at visitation stopped, Veronica came to truly believe that her father did not love her or want a relationship with her. For many years, there was no contact between them and the alienation hardened inside of her.

It was not until several years later that Veronica came to believe that her mother had interfered with her relationship with her father. She attributed this understanding to having children of her own. She came to see that both parents are important for children, that her children needed their father in addition to needing her. Soon after her own divorce, Veronica's ex-husband started pulling away from her and the children and she saw that she could either accept his lack of interest or fight it and encourage him to stay involved with the children. "I would really try to push him to see the kids. I just knew it wasn't right. I knew it wasn't right. You should be with them. They both done nothing wrong. I always used to try to explain to my kids, "Me and your father doesn't love each other and that is it. It has nothing to do with the kids.' I think it was then that I started. . . ." This led her to conclude that her mother also had a choice. Her mother could have facilitated or interfered with her relationship with her father and Veronica understood that her mother chose to interfere. She recalled feeling inside herself a desire to support her ex-husband's relationship with her children, and that set the wheels in motion for what turned out to be a slow process of Veronica coming to understand that her mother did not want the same for her when she was a little girl. Her mother did not want her to feel loved by her father.

Further facilitating the awareness was that her mother and stepfather eventually won custody of Veronica's two children. In this respect her mother turned against her (Catalyst 2) and Veronica observed firsthand the alienation strategies her mother used against her father now being used against her (Catalyst 3). She noticed how her mother and stepfather made themselves important emotionally to her children and convinced the children to come live with them. "I just didn't see that she was doing the same thing she did with me and my dad. I thought she had changed but. . . ."

When asked to describe in more detail how her mother turned her children against her she offered: "I have been looking at that and trying to figure that out, these last few years my mind has just been nonstop. They'd been doing it since they were babies. I think the last straw came when I could really see my mom and stepdad controlling my children was when my daughter fell and I was kneeling on the floor at the time, he just pushed past me, I went flying just so he could grab my daughter and give her a cuddle. I felt like I wasn't a mother." Veronica recognized the same dynamic at work that she experienced as a child. She came to understand that mother and stepfather were emotionally needy and it made them feel powerful and special to have children align with them against someone else. "They wanted them for themselves. They needed my children to be their kids." As she did with Veronica's father, Veronica's mother waged a campaign of denigration against her. "They told my children that I didn't let them see their father but I wouldn't do that."

Experiencing the alienation as a parent allowed her to come to this understanding that she had been alienated from her father. With this new outlook, Veronica sought to reestablish contact with him.

I tried phoning, I did find him on the net about a year ago. I spoke to him twice. But he didn't want to know . . . so I wrote a letter saying I was sorry for what I put him through because I do understand he was in pain because I am feeling it. I said it wasn't his fault, I know it wasn't his fault, and I do feel bad about that. I think my mother told him we hated him, that we didn't want nothing to do with him. I think that hurt, that hurt him. I understand that my kids are not saying that (that they don't love her) because they feel that. I know why they're saying it, because of my mother and my stepdad. But he (her father) didn't know what was going on, what was happening. He just thought we did hate him. He wanted to explain himself and I said, "You don't have to explain, I know exactly what they did, I know what they are like."

Veronica has had no contact with either of her children for quite some time. "No not at all. They don't want to." She has drawn on her experience as a child of alienation in her decision to never stop trying to reach out to her own children. She knew that even though she had behaved as if she did not want a relationship with her father, in her heart she had never wanted him to stop coming to the house and knocking on the door. Thus, Veronica decided that she would continue to write to and seek contact with her children. She did not want them to ever think that she gave up on them. "I have not stopped writing letters. I was about to give up and then I think, I can't. I have letters to write." The letters come back with her mother's writing on them but she writes anyway, in the hopes that her children will somehow know that their mother is still thinking about them and loving them.

SUMMARY

There were 11 identifiable pathways or catalysts for the adult children of PAS to realize that one parent had alienated them from the targeted parent. In many cases this led to a reunion with the targeted parent and a distancing from the alienating parent. Most of the adult children of PAS mentioned only one catalyst. But it is likely that a confluence of factors were present. Their memory may not provide a complete understanding of what actually allowed them to become aware that they had been manipulated. The good news is that there are many ways to get from manipulated alienation to awareness and autonomy. Targeted parents currently alienated from a child can gather hope from these stories that it is possible for alienation to be reversed and that there are many ways that this can happen. The bad news is that it is not clear what the specific steps are to make this process more likely to occur. Some of these stories are so idiosyncratic that it is not possible to draw definitive conclusions about how the process of becoming aware of the alienation occurred.

It is also notable that most of the adult children of PAS experienced this process as slow and painful, although in the end they were grateful to know the truth and to have a more balanced understanding of their parents. They were happy to have found their way back to the targeted parent and to learn that for the most part this parent was not the dangerous, unloving person they had been led to believe. At the same time, the awareness of the alienation led to a greater degree of conflict in their relationship with the alienating parent. For some this had occurred anyway because that parent had turned on them. Nonetheless, awareness of the alienation created a greater degree of separation and lack of shared reality with the alienating parent than had been present in their relationship up to that point. As Alice Miller argued, denying the truth allows one to avoid acknowledging a painful reality. Not knowing something that is true entails a loss of self as one closes off parts of one's own thoughts and feelings that—if conscious—would lead to the realization. Miller believed that the body holds onto the truth and that pain is incurred when the mind and the body are in conflict, "If your cognitive system asserts the opposite of what the cells in your body unerringly identify as the truth you will live in a permanent state of inner disorder" (1988, p. 5). For this reason, there was a palpable sigh of relief that could be felt as the participants described with candor the shortcomings of the alienating parent, including the reality that this person had put his or her own needs above the needs of his or her own children.

ADDITIONAL CONSIDERATIONS

Most of the adult children of PAS described the experience as a process, not as an epiphany or a single moment when the clouds parted and light shone down on them with a new clarity. However, three told of epiphanal moments worth describing. Alix likened the experience to "the big bang" when she suddenly realized that she would never be good enough for her mother. Elaine described a powerful moment in which she literally saw her father—whom she had learned to scorn—in a new light. She remembered driving through her hometown and pointing out to her friend the sad sight of a crippled man trying to make his way down the sidewalk, clutching a lamppost. As she approached the man, she realized, to her horror, that he was her own father, trying to get to the family home to see his wife and children. At that moment, she knew she had not truly seen her father for who he was. Edward, too, told of a specific moment when he was able to see his father in a new way. This occurred while standing on an airstrip waiting to board a plane for Vietnam.

A: I was getting on a plane, and it was the first time and only time that I had seen him cry, he cried.
Q: What did you think?
A: I was shocked. Because I was always told he didn't care.
Q: That was the first seed of doubt that what your mom said was wrong?
A: Yes.

In contrast, the majority of the adult children described coming to the realization as an unfolding process, not as a discrete event that could be pinpointed in time. This suggests that parents who are currently alienated from a child need to be patient with their children as they slowly work through this experience.

Although none of the adult children of PAS stated that a death of a parent was the primary catalyst, several commented that they did not believe that they could have come to the realization while the alienating parent was still alive. Because they had a reasonably satisfying relationship with the alienating parent, they did not allow themselves to realize that they also wished to have a relationship with the targeted parent until the alienating parent had passed away. As noted above in David's story, his mother had passed away three years before he contacted his father. "Only then was I beginning to feel comfortable talking to my dad. It still felt like I was betraying her. It took three years for her to be dead." Death was also a catalyst for Josh, who explained that he could not have been open to that exploration process while his mother was still alive. "My mother died in 2001 and it wasn't until she had died that I had begun to do the step work even though I had started with Co-dependent's Anonymous before that. I don't know how I could have done the step work and still related to her. It would have been very difficult because I was sort of seeing the truth about everything that had happened and I would have been very upset with her and I don't see how I could have hidden that from her and so it would have been a real challenge to try to relate to her in the present and go through all the step work about the past as it related to her and me. I have thought that looking back I couldn't do that work until she was gone."

Death was not always a catalyst, however. For Serita, the death of the alienating parent entrenched her further in the alienation. She felt that she had to carry the mantle of her mother's hatred of the father. Following her mother's death, Serita initiated legal proceedings for custody of her younger siblings because she knew that her mother would not want their father to raise them. "When my mom died and we had a funeral and he came, we as a family made a decision that we didn't want our father anywhere near her at the time of the funeral. That was relayed back to him. I think I blamed him for not making contact with us all that time. There were all these people telling us that he was sad and felt badly, but we never really had any contact with him, so I was 20 years old and the youngest was 8, and I think he should have been with us then, and I think he should have come back then. You know what I did? This is so stupid, but I went to the courts and I was trying for guardianship of the three youngest, who were under 16. So I carried the work of my mother on. I made a promise to her or to myself. After she died, I said to the youngest that I would be there for them in every way I possibly could and if that meant carrying on her legacy of keeping my father away then that was that. But I was only 20 and I was going to law school, and I was supporting myself, and I had a family to support at the same time, and it was very difficult for me, and I didn't have time to think about my father. And I didn't want him around." Serita did not realize that she had been alienated from her father until much later.

As noted at the beginning of this chapter, there are three ways to leave a cult: walking out, being thrown out, and being talked out (i.e., having an intervention). Most of the adult children of PAS can be considered as having walked out. That is, over time they came to understand that they were not having their needs met in the relationship with the alienating parent. Only a few could be considered as having been cast out (e.g. Ron, whose alienating mother moved away and left with his father, the targeted parent). Fewer still could be considered as leaving due to an intervention, although perhaps those who were influenced by a significant other (catalyst 8) could be considered having experienced an intervention of sorts.

In all cases, it is not clear what role readiness to know the truth played in the process. For example, it cannot be known if these catalysts had occurred at another point whether they would have led to the realization or did the individual have to be receptive (albeit unconsciously) to know the truth. Jonestown cult survivor, Layton's (1988) comment that "my inner voice screamed something at me, but I could not hear it" (p. 64) suggests that there needs to be a readiness to hear. The above stories show that at some point these adult children of PAS became ready to listen to their inner voices.

The long-term effects of the alienation—as experienced by the adult children—are explored in the next chapter.

Chapter 7

The Long-Term Impact
of Parental Alienation Syndrome

There is no escape when the past is endless
—Judith Alpert. *No Escape When the Past is Endless*

FROM THE OUTSET THREE ISSUES NEED TO BE ADDRESSED. FIRST, NOT all of the adult children experienced each of the negative outcomes described in this chapter. In fact, many of them perceived themselves as having positive life experiences and personal attributes and resilience in addition to the problems discussed below. There were many areas of strength in their lives despite the fact that they also experienced real hardship and difficulty. Second, it is also important to note that it was not possible to isolate these outcomes as directly resulting from the alienation, as opposed to the more general experience of divorce and the parental pathology that was probably underlying the alienation for at least some of the families. However, these outcomes are consistent with previous research on negative effects of intergenerational alliances, familial triangulation, and family system disruptions, which share certain features with PAS (Davis, Hops, Alpert, & Sheeber, 1998; Jacobvitz, & Bush, 1996). These outcomes are what the adult children themselves believed to have been the effects of the parental alienation syndrome and as such they offer insight into their felt experience. A final consideration is that these findings can only be thought to apply to people who identified themselves as having been alienated from a parent due to PAS. It is quite likely that there are individuals for whom the alienation was so subtle or successful that they never realized that they had been manipulated. It is not possible to determine whether the long-term outcomes of that group would resemble the outcomes presented below.

LOW SELF-ESTEEM (n = 26, 65%)

Consistent with the speculations of other researchers, including Waldron and Joanis (1996), self-esteem problems were prevalent. As Veronica explained, "My brother always thought he was ugly and I always thought I was, and I don't know if it was because thinking they didn't want us as babies you know. I did think I was bad, really nasty. I always had no confidence, nothing. Nobody likes me." Edward, too, reported low self-esteem. "I think it hurt my self-esteem. I have trouble taking any praise. No matter how much I accomplish it doesn't seem to be that much." This sentiment was echoed by many of the other adult children of PAS, including Bonnie:

I think part of me is missing as a person because you need to . . . as a child you need to have a safety feeling in your life and when you have somebody like my mother who is constantly sitting there telling you this person who is your dad and is part of you telling you he is such a bad person, and he's going to do all these terrible things, and it is like if he is so bad and I am part of him then doesn't that make me sort of like that too? I think part of me didn't develop the way it could have and that probably contributes to the self-esteem problems.

Josh reported similar experiences, "I had low self-esteem, low self-concept, no self-identity. Everything was based on what other people told me to do or how I should act. I had no thoughts or feelings of my own." The negative self-image experienced seemed to derive from at least three sources.

The first source of low self-esteem was the internalization of the hatred of the targeted parent. This process is consistent with object relations theory in which the "bad object" is taken as an "introject" into the child's understanding of him or herself (e.g., Greenberg & Mitchell, 1983). The children felt that the "bad" parent was part of them (genetically as well as through an early relationship), and that they must also be bad. The alienating parent's rejection of the targeted parent was experienced as a rejection of that part of them that was like the targeted parent. As Julia noted:

> Well I think when you turn a child against a parent that child feels . . . because you are from that parent, you take it internally and turn it against yourself. So it greatly lowered my self-esteem in the ways I knew I was like my father. I am more reserved and my father is reserved as an example. I am not a morning person. I don't jump out of bed and go good morning! Which my mother does and my father doesn't, so let's say I am like my father that way. And my mother would be like, "Oh you are just like your father. You are a grump in the morning." Any parts that I did feel were like my father made me feel bad about myself because she berated him so. So if I was like him how could that be good?

This phenomenon was particularly powerful for the adult children who were alienated from their same-sex parents and, as they matured, took on the physical likeness of that rejected parent. Divorce researchers such as Amato (1994) have also found that children experience difficulty when they physically resemble one of their parents in a high-conflict divorce.

Gretta's response was to glue her ears to the side of her head so that they looked less like the "sticking out ears" of her father. Betty said, "I started to wonder if because I looked so much like him whether she hated me too." In general, the children could not distinguish between the alienating parent's hatred of the targeted parent and that parent's hatred for those parts of themselves that were like the targeted parent. As children, they naturally concluded that the alienating parent hated them as well. Because the alienation campaign against the targeted parent started when they were relatively young (for many it went as far back as they could remember), the negative self-feelings seemed to be incorporated into the very core of their self-identity and sense of self-worth. This is consistent with Virginia Satir's (1967) observations that children who side with one parent against the other inevitably suffer from poor self-esteem later in life due to problems with identification.

Self-hatred also seemed to result from the alienating parents informing their children that the targeted parent did not love or want them. The following conversation with Amelia is illustrative of this:

Q: How did your mom telling you bad things about your dad make you feel insecure?
A: Well. Like I said, it made me feel like he . . . it made me worthless, like I didn't matter.
Q: Because she told you that he didn't love you?
A: Right. And that had a lot to do with me being insecure.

More than one adult child of PAS recalled an alienating parent claiming to have actually saved him or her from an intended abortion (one woman's father described the procedure in detail and provided graphic illustrations of aborted fetuses). Carl recalled his mother telling him that his father wanted to throw him in the river. These vivid and horrifying images planted themselves into the mind of the child as a fundamental truth (especially because the stories were repeated) about the targeted parent's feelings about the child. A particularly destructive form of this strategy is illustrated by Nicole's mother who returned letters that her father was sending to Nicole. She then challenged her daughter to explain how her father could love her if he could not even bother to write. Nicole eventually capitulated under the weight of the "evidence" and concluded that her father must not really love her.

Many others had memories of the alienating parent claiming, "Daddy doesn't love us anymore," conflating in the child's mind the end of the marriage with the parent's rejection of the child. In these cases, the children grew up assuming that the targeted parent had found them to be unworthy of love and concluded that they were in fact unlovable. In many instances they did not know at the time that the targeted parent had been trying to contact them and actually felt tremendous love and affection for them. They believed that the alienating parent was telling them the truth, exemplified in Robin's statement, "Of course I believed my mother. She was God." As Peck (1983) among others explained, when parental love is lacking, the child will naturally assume himself rather than the parent to be the cause, resulting in an unrealistically negative self-image. It is much too frightening to think that the parent, upon whom the child is dependent, is at fault. This self-blaming has also been borne out in the empirical research on parenting styles. Warm but consistent and strict parenting is related to positive child outcomes including self-esteem, while hostile parenting is related to self-esteem problems in children (Maccoby & Martin, 1983; Steinberg, Mounts, Lamborn, & Dornbusch, 1991). This is also consistent with the notion of internal working models of the world and self as described in attachment theory and research (Bowlby, 1969; Bretherton, Ridgeway, & Cassidy, 1990). What begins as the child's interaction with the outside world (being told the parent is rejecting him or her) becomes incorporated into the child's only known inner reality (he or she is not worthy of being loved).

Another source of self-hatred was the guilt the adult children of PAS experienced from betraying the targeted parent. Ron, who was made to verbally abuse his father on the telephone, worried about what impact that had on his father. He described his own feelings at the time as like "slicing his wrists." This suicidal imagery may indicate an unconscious wish to die, that is, to both escape the pain of the guilt and to be punished for the pain he caused his father. Elaine was encouraged to denigrate and belittle her father and only later did she realize that he was in fact a person worthy of respect and dignity. She was flooded with feelings of shame and self-loathing. "I was a horrible, horrible person to him. I joined in with my mom as far as saying he didn't do anything right. I was like a little copy of her when it came to him." Serita went so far as to fight her own father for custody of her younger siblings following the death of the alienating mother. She does not fully understand her own motivation, but she finds herself replaying in her mind the conversation she had with her father when she told him of her plan, "I can see his face in my mind's eye and he looked devastated and I feel really bad that I did that to him." After Sarah reconciled with her father, she was overcome with feelings of guilt. "When I started having a relationship with my father. I just discovered that in my interaction with him. I discovered the guilt. It was through frequent contact over the last several months that I realized I felt that way. I felt like I had to reach out to him and apologize because it was wrong for Mother to do that. And I felt like I owed that to him. I owed him an apology."

The adult children of PAS who left younger brothers and sisters behind when they finally escaped an abusive alienating parent also reported feeling tremendous guilt. Amelia had that experience. "And I felt a lot of guilt about moving out because I was leaving my sisters behind and I really didn't want them to have to deal with it, but it wasn't long after I moved out that they split up and then my sisters moved to Dallas." Although they recognized that they did the best they could under terrible circumstances and that they had been manipulated, many nonetheless suffered from feelings of guilt and shame at their own behavior, contributing to low self-esteem and a negative self-image.

DEPRESSION (n = 28, 70%)

Not surprisingly, the majority of the adult children of PAS also suffered from significant episodes of depression in their adult lives. They believed that their depression was rooted in early feelings of being unloved by the targeted parent and from the actual extended separation from that parent, both of which are psychosocial risk factors for depressive episodes (Bowlby, 1980). Nancy, an older woman whose mother died when she was just 2 months old, provided a particularly poignant example of this. At the time of the mother's death, her father was having difficulty caring for five children while holding down a full-time job that required him to be away from the home on alternating weeks. For this reason, he agreed to let his sister raise the baby. This aunt, whom Nancy called Mommy, subsequently alienated her from her father. She prevented visitation, denigrated him to her, and let it be known that any preference for the father would be disloyal, hurtful, and not tolerated. Consequently, Nancy only saw her father a few times a year despite the fact that he lived less than an hour away. Not only did she lose her mother from an early death but she lost her father as well. Because the loss of her father was unnecessary, she was particularly bitter. "You lose your mother and you lose your father and you're alone. I always felt alone."

Carl explained his experience with depression as having a hole in his soul. "And it is not something you can physically point to and say here it is but you know it is there." He claimed that it wasn't until he met his father 45 years later that he could feel the hole closing. Serita, whose mother pushed her father out of her life, said that not only did she lose her father because her mother made visitation impossible, but she also felt that she had lost her mother because of the conflict that ensued between them over Serita's relationship with her father. "I think I lost two parents. I think the way she handled it was incredibly naïve. She assumed that we would reject her for our father, especially me because I had such a strong bond with him. She was scared of that rejection. I don't know if I am depressed but there are times when I can't function. I can't get out of bed or I can't do work, and I am out for days and it is really difficult."

The impact of the loss of the targeted parent was exacerbated by the fact that as children they were denied the opportunity to mourn this loss. In fact, quite the opposite message was conveyed to them, that it was a positive event for the targeted parent to be out of their lives—essentially "good riddance to bad rubbish." The children were discouraged by the alienating parent from talking about or expressing interest in their relationship with the targeted parent. As noted earlier, Robin's mother introduced her new husband to him by saying, "Your father was a bad man. You can't have a bad man for a daddy. You deserve a good man to be your daddy. I have found a good man to be your daddy. This man will be your new daddy." From that point forward the word *daddy* was used to describe his stepfather and there was no language available to ask about the man who used to be his father. In this way it was conveyed to Robin that there was to be no discussion of that other person; and the little boy was left alone to manage his feelings of loss and rejection. Grief researchers and clinicians have outlined a series of stages individuals progress through when dealing with catastrophic change or loss, and it is generally believed that being able to process the loss and go through these stages is a necessary part of healing (Bowlby, 1980; Kübler-Ross, 1997). Conversely, inability to experience these stages of grieving is believed to be associated with subsequent relational problems and depression. This appeared to be the case for many of the adult children of PAS. The interview itself seemed to bring to the surface intense feelings of sadness for the child they had been and the traumatic loss they unnecessarily experienced at the hands of their own parent. Many wept quietly as they re-called their early histories of separation and loss.

DRUG AND ALCOHOL PROBLEMS
(n = 14, 35%)

Many of the adult children of PAS were drawn to substance abuse as a way to escape the feelings of pain and loss. The following type of comment, made by Elaine, was common throughout the interviews, "It was very painful and I started taking a lot of drugs at that time to try to block it out, not feel it." For Robin, "My drug abuse had gotten pretty bad and I had to get out of there or I was going to die and I knew it. I was slowly destroying myself." Many of the adult children of PAS were in substance abuse recovery and were aware that they had been consuming drugs and alcohol as a way to avoid the pain of the loss of the parent, the pain from low self-esteem, and the pain from the conflict that was part of the fabric of the relationship with the alienating parent. That is, in many but not all cases, the alienating parent's campaign to eliminate the targeted parent from the child's life took its toll on their relationship as well. The constant pressure to agree with the alienating parent that the targeted parent was of no value eventually backfired, and many of the adult children had a highly conflicted relationship with the alienating parent. In many, but again not all cases, the alienating parents were emotionally abusive in their attempts to subjugate the child's independent thoughts and feelings to their will. One response to this abuse was to escape into alcohol and drugs. For many of the adult children, the realization that the alienating parent had manipulated them also led to pain, anger, guilt, and resentment. The emergence of these intense negative feelings coincided with attainment of late adolescence or early adulthood, a time of increased access to and experimentation with drugs and alcohol. Walter reported that he had been drinking, "Since my early teens. I had an illustrious drinking career at the University of Tennessee." He connected his drinking to the parental alienation "How have I suffered? There is something that goes on when you are young; there is an emotional thing that goes on there that makes it extremely difficult for me to have stability. In AA it says there are those who suffer from grave emotional and mental disorders and there is no doubt in my mind after being in AA for 12 years, and especially where my life is right now, that I have suffered from that abandonment."

LACK OF TRUST (n = 16, 40%)

Lack of trust in themselves and others was a recurrent theme for the adult children of PAS. Some were women who were alienated from their fathers and reported not believing that a man would be able to love them. They assumed that if their father (their first male love) did not love them enough to stay involved in their lives how could any man find them worthy of love and commitment. Serita explained that she repeatedly created conflict in her romantic relationships, pushing her partners to see how much abuse they could take before they eventually rejected her. When a man finally did leave, she concluded that, of course, that would happen, all men would eventually abandon her as her father had done. "It all stems from my parents' separation and I think also because I wasn't allowed to have a fruitful relationship with my father after he left. That really scarred me in my relationships with men. I keep thinking they are going to leave and I have to test them until they do leave. As a result I am divorced and I find it really difficult to trust men."

Freud (1920/1955) termed this pattern of repeating the past, no matter how painful, the *repetition compulsion*, while others, including social psychologist Merton (1968), have referred to it as a *self-fulfilling prophesy*. Regardless of the term, the need to repeat the primal rejection of the parent in subsequent romantic relationships was apparent in many of the adult children of PAS. In this way, the individuals were re-creating the only experience they knew (rejection by a love object) and confirming their expectations of loss. According to object relations theory, as painful as it is to repeat the rejection, it is less painful than breaking with the past. For example, Greenberg and Mitchell explained Fairbairn's understanding of repetition this way, "Beneath the pain and self-defeating relations and organizations of experience lie ancient internal attachments and allegiances to early significant others" (1983, p. 173). To find new ways of relating entails losing the past and facing the terror of being alone.

Another version of the lack of trust expressed by the adult children of PAS was a sense of doubting their own perceptions of people because from a young age they were told by one parent that the other parent (whom most had positive memories of) was bad, dangerous, or in some other way worthy of fear or contempt. From this conflict between their own perception and what they were told to believe, they developed a lack of trust in people in general and in their own ability to make decisions and make their way in the world. Further, once they realized that they had been manipulated and that what they had been led to believe their whole lives about the targeted parent was not the truth (or at least not the whole truth), they became even more unsure of what to believe and whom to trust. "Everything you thought is not what you thought it was," said Nicole, and Oliver, a young man suffering from great emotional distress, explained, "I don't trust. You are supposed to trust your parents. They are supposed to give you love, care, and support. If one parent accuses the other parent it splits you. I was played off from one parent to the other and I learned I couldn't trust, and so it has made me so I can't trust people or be confident with people."

ALIENATED FROM THEIR OWN
CHILDREN (n = 14, 50%)

Another form of repetition was seen in a particularly tragic long-term outcome of parental alienation syndrome: many of the adult children of PAS were alienated from their own children. This was enacted in a few different ways, but in each scenario the individuals seemed to be repeating their early experience of loss and rejection. Not only were they unloved by a parent but they were unloved by their own child as well. One scenario entailed individuals with a narcissistic parent (who alienated them from the targeted parent) marrying a narcissistic person who alienated them from their own children. Several of the male participants remarked that they had married women very similar in personality structure to their mother (who was the alienating parent). To them, this is what love from a woman felt like and it was all they knew. When these marriages soured, the men became noncustodial parents who were subjected to the same alienation as their own fathers had been. Mark recalled taking a trip west to be with his dying father (whom he had been estranged from as a child) and returning home to find that his wife had moved away with his son. He did not see his son again for seven years.

These men reported that they had been devoted fathers trying to be involved in their children's lives in a way that their fathers could not be there for them. They were shocked and bitter that nonetheless they ended up in the same place: unwanted interlopers squeezed out of their children's hearts and lives. Because of their experience as alienated children, many were conscious of how important it was that their children know they cared, despite the alienation. They sent cards and letters on a regular basis even though they were probably not well received. David was particularly energetic in this regard. He told of creating several photo albums and scrapbooks commemorating the positive experiences that he and his daughter had shared as a reminder to her that they once had had a close and loving relationship. Another father, Mark, created a website in the event that his son wanted to contact him via the Internet. These men knew what alienation from a father felt like and were devastated that they were implicated in causing that same pain in their children's lives.

Two women who were alienated from their fathers subsequently lost their children to their own mothers. In both cases these mothers were domineering and narcissistic woman who cultivated their daughter's dependency. When the daughters were grown, these women set their sights on the grandchildren. As Veronica recounted, "My son kept running away to my mother and they were not bringing him back, and they were saying I was hitting him and all that, so they put in for residence for him and . . . I just didn't see that she was doing the same she did with me and my dad. I thought she had changed but. . . ." Veronica's mother convinced Veronica's two children to make abuse allegations against her, and based on that report, Veronica lost custody of her son and daughter. She understood parental alienation syndrome from both sides and looked forward to being able to help her children through the anger and guilt that she believed they will feel once they realize that they have been manipulated to hate their own mother.

A third scenario, represented by Peter, entailed a man purposefully withdrawing from a conflicted divorce and custody situation to "spare" his child.

> The reason I stopped all contact is because she said, "You know what I am going to do? I am going to file for abandonment." I said, "I didn't abandon her you won't let me. . . ." I didn't want to pull her [the daughter] from state to state just to see me. I want her to be happy. That is why I couldn't believe I am in the same situation I am in with my dad. I purposefully and intentionally cut off communication because I wanted her to be happy. I don't want her to have to think about visiting her dad, getting on a plane. It is only California and it is only Nevada but it was difficult for me here alone and so I guess I relate to my dad too.

It seems plausible that Peter felt compelled to withdraw from his daughter's life for reasons beyond those of which he is aware.

DIVORCE (n = 23, 57.5%)

High divorce rates plagued the adult children of PAS. This heightened rate of divorce is consistent with the general statistics on children of divorce (Wallerstein, Lewis, & Blakeslee, 2001) and also speaks to the relational and self-esteem issues already noted. Many of the adult children of PAS said that their marriages failed because of their lack of trust in their partner, their inability to be intimate, as well as their problems with depression and substance abuse. As noted above, there was also a tendency to select a life partner who was remarkably similar to the alienating parent. This typically meant a person who put his or her own needs first, lacked empathy for others, and desired an excessive degree of control over the children. Bonnie explained how she married a man who was quite similar to her narcissistic mother. "My ex-husband is a terrible person. The world revolves around him like he is a copy of my mother almost, and the funny thing is I didn't realize that until later on. Everything is about him even to the point where if I was spending time with my little boy he was getting angry because I wasn't spending that time with him." Carl also married a woman similar to his mother, a parent who did not understand his need to have a relationship with his father. He explained, "When my wife and I had disagreements she always yelled at me and I was always capitulating to her because she was the woman and we could not resolve things. I couldn't seem to get my point across or get any understanding of any kind."

OTHER AREAS OF IMPACT

Other, less prominent effects of the parental alienation syndrome noted in some of the adult children, include: problems with identity and not having a sense of belonging or roots; choosing not to have children to avoid being rejected by them; low academic and career achievement; anger and bitterness over the time lost with the alienated parent; and problems with memory. The latter is possibly due to the trauma of the emotional abuse (and other types of abuse, for some) as well as to the multiple losses (Alpert, 2001; van der Kolk, 1994).

SUMMARY

At least six major areas of functioning were identified as effects of parental alienation syndrome. Many of the adult children of PAS suffered from low self-esteem, lack of trust in themselves and others, depression, drug and alcohol problems, alienation from their own children, and divorce. These findings are not surprising in light of the multiple traumas associated with parental alienation syndrome. All of the adult children were aware that they had been manipulated to turn against the targeted parent. Although that was a painful realization, it was the beginning of reclaiming the parent they lost and the part of themselves that loved and cherished that parent.

Chapter 8

The Role of the Targeted Parent

If you can force your heart and nerve and sinew to serve your turn long after they have gone, and so hold on when there is nothing in you. Except the Will which says to them; "Hold on!"

—Rudyard Kipling, *If*

MANY PARENTS IN THIS STUDY CURRENTLY TARGETED FOR PAREN-
tal alienation ask what more they could be doing to facilitate the realization process in their children. This chapter presents the answers to that question from the perspective of the adult children of PAS. What did they remember the targeted parent doing that maintained the relationship and what else did they believe the targeted parent should have done? It is important to remember that there might have been efforts made that were helpful that they did not themselves recognize as helpful. What is presented is only from the perspective of the adult children. Below is a sampling of vignettes, several from each of the three parental alienation patterns (as described in Chapter 1), focusing on what they recalled that the targeted parent did and what they thought the targeted parent should have done. This is followed by a discussion of the major themes highlighted by these vignettes.

It is important to bear in mind that the alienating parent effectuated the alienation; the role of the targeted parent was secondary. Contrary to Johnston's (2003) conclusion that alienation is due to children's preference for the "better" parent, the experience of the adult children of PAS suggests that their alienation was a result of coercion, pressure, and manipulation to renounce the targeted parent. Thus, focusing on what the targeted parents did and did not do may appear to be a criticism of the targeted parents, or blaming the victim. It is not intended as such. Unless the targeted parent understands what role, if any, he or she plays in the alienation, he or she is doing less than everything possible to ameliorate the situation. Hearing the stories of the adult children of PAS, it is easy to imagine how shaming and frustrating being the target of parental alienation syndrome can be. Although the rage should rightly be directed at the alienating parent, it is easy to see how it could be directed at the messenger (the child). As Gardner (1998) has noted when he coined the term *independent thinker phenomenon*, the children affected by parental alienation syndrome are very convincing in their presentation of disaffection for the targeted parent. Thus, these parents may be tempted to respond to the messenger and say, "If you don't want to have a relationship with me, fine. I will remove myself from the picture and spare you all of the unpleasantness." However, such abandonment is the very fuel that alienating parents use to convince the children that the targeted parent did not love them. These alienating parents were very quick to point out to the children any lapses in the targeted parent's parenting, sowing the seed of doubt in their minds about the targeted parent's commitment to the relationship. As Nicole explained, "She'd bring up the lack of him writing me. She'd bring that up a lot. She'd say every once in a while, 'You were so misbehaved, such a bad child, look he doesn't even want to be around you. Look he doesn't write you.' That had some type of proof to it."

PATTERN 1: NARCISSISTIC MOTHERS
IN DIVORCED FAMILIES

Serita was a 30-year-old soft-spoken woman of Pakistani parentage, living in Birmingham, England. She was 13 years old when her parents separated. She was the oldest child and only daughter in a family of four children. After her parents separated, Serita's father lived nearby with relatives and he would come often to the family home to visit. However, Serita's mother used a variety of strategies to prevent visitation: not answering the door when he came to see the children, making him feel that he did not deserve to see the children (he was struggling financially), and inducing guilt in the children that they would be hurting her if they spent time with their father. In time all contact ended. Serita missed her father terribly and yet she turned against him and rejected his overtures. She went so far as to take her father to court to win custody of her younger siblings after her mother passed away. It was not until she matured and her brother became alienated from his children following an acrimonious divorce that Serita gained perspective on her own childhood. She shared that she was planning to reach out to her father in the near future but she had not yet done so. When asked what her father did to mitigate the alienation, Serita recalled that her father was able to let his children know (from a distance through a network of extended family and friends) that he was thinking about them.

> I think he did. I think he did fight. The reason I say this is because when he went back to Pakistan every time someone he knew came to this country he would send them to us so we would hear about our father. These people would say, "He misses you. He wants to see you. Here are some presents from him." He used to send cards and letters, which got torn up by my brothers and my mother. He would call and say he wanted to hear how I was doing and I would say, "Why the heck are you calling me now? Where the hell have you been all this time?" He would say, "I tried calling. I tried writing to you."

At the time Serita found his explanations weak and unconvincing, too little too late. She thought that he should have done more, especially in terms of explaining his side to her so that she would have a more balanced understanding of the situation.

*I think at the time he tried to explain to me that it was very diffi-
cult, and he was trying to do his best, and it hasn't been that easy
for him, and I didn't understand what he was talking about. I just
thought if there is a problem why don't you just say what the
problem is, say what the problem is instead of going around and
around in circles. He never hit the nail on the head and said,
"Your mother has done this" or "I am having problems with this
situation." He would just say, "There are problems and this is difficult and I am really doing my best and I always call your mom
and leave messages for you. Don't you get them?" and things like
that, which to me didn't sound like much of an explanation or
anything. It sounded like he was making excuses. I wish he had
tried to tell his side of the story, but I realize now with hindsight
that was his character. He has never been the kind of person to
try to tell things about himself or talk about himself.*

Serita believed that this would have lessened her feelings of
abandonment, at a critical time in her own development. "I was
missing him. I was grieving. I was being torn apart." However,
she also acknowledged that her mother would not have supported such efforts on her father's part. "But at least I would
have heard from him what he thought instead of just hearing
her side and then finally believing her side. Now looking back
I can see that his actions proved so much and her words proved
what she was doing. But at the time I couldn't see that at all."
She wished her father had done more, yet she recognized that
in part she was not able to hear what he was telling her because
her mother had already convinced her that he did not care for
her.

Carrie was 3 years old when her parents separated and her
father moved out of the home. Carrie had standard visitation
with her father for several years during which time her mother
denigrated him and tried to interfere with their relationship.
Visitation was initially difficult and became increasingly prob-
lematic after Carrie's father remarried. "He remarried and
when he lost the custody battle, he moved away." She vividly
recalled that day. "We pulled up to the house and there was a
sold sign in the yard. We were confused and we went up and
knocked on the door and there was no one there. We walked

across the yard to Grandma's house and Grandma told us 'Your dad is gone.'" Eventually Carrie's father notified her that he had moved to Florida. She and her brother were invited down for a visit and they arranged for a month-long summer vacation. However, soon after arriving Carrie's mother called and pressured her to return. Her mother told her that people whom Carrie considered to be unwholesome and unreliable were caring for her younger sister (from a different father) and Carrie felt a strong emotional pull to go home in order to protect her baby sister. In response to her early leave taking, her father refused to have any contact with her for several years.

> He called us and he got both of us on each end of the phone and he went through this tirade. He said, "I don't want you to say anything. I just want you to listen and once I am done with this conversation I am ripping the phone out of the wall. I don't want you to try to contact me. I don't want to see you." He basically told us, "I don't care what happens to you. I don't care if you ever have kids. I don't care if you graduate. I don't care if you live or die. Your mom has done this." That was when I was 10 and I never saw or heard from him again until I was 16.

Carrie reunited with her father at the age of 16 when he unexpectedly showed up for her wedding. Since then they have remained in touch. In recounting what her father did to try to prevent the alienation, Carrie explained, that he "fought for custody but then gave up and moved away without leaving word. He was angry because he was out of control in the situation with us. He had fought and lost and he thought the court system was highly skewed toward Mom that no matter all the evidence he presented that Mom was unfit, he wasn't going to get anywhere." She responded to the question concerning what more he should have done by saying:

> He could have stayed here in Ohio. I don't think that when there is a difference that people should live out of state. I think they need to get a job and pursue their interests in the same state so they can maintain frequent visitation with their kids. I think he screwed up because his way of dealing with his anger and frustra-

tion was to leave. I have forgiven him, but I will never forget it. It is ingrained in my memory the phone call that was made and the things that were said. You can't take those things away. He could have dealt with it in a different manner.

Mitch, 43, was a young boy of 5 when his parents divorced. According to Mitch, the alienation had already begun. "My mother always taught me, 'Oh don't trust him' and all of that for years even while they were still married during the estranged years." Following the divorce his father "eventually kind of fell out of the picture." At one point he recalled being asked by his mother to tell someone on the phone that he did not want anything to do with his father. "She was going on and on about he was so bad and to me sitting there and listening to the conversation and me being a good boy and wanting to do what Mom wanted, when she handed me the phone and said 'Tell them how you feel about your father.' I said 'I don't ever want to see him again and I have no interest in meeting with him.'" Mitch was 8 years old at the time. His father contacted him when Mitch was 18 years old but Mitch was not receptive.

Twelve years later, Mitch's brother passed away, and Mitch and his father spent time together. His father shared with Mitch how hurt he had been by Mitch's rejection and this brought a new understanding between father and son. When Mitch was asked what else, in addition to the periodic attempts to keep in touch, his father could have done, he responded:

While I was growing up? Nothing. Nothing. Oh she was very effective. Interesting question, but I don't think there was anything he could have done. I think she would have had the police right over there. Whatever she could do in terms of a restraining order she did. She was so involved with the newspaper and TV, she was very connected with politicians and judges and the chiefs and captains of the police department.

Amelia, 41, was born in Texas in the fourth year of her parent's marriage. There were two older sisters in the family. Her parents separated when she was 3 years old. There was minimal contact with her father and then a break until she was 9. At that time he remarried and visitation was reinstated for about one year but then stopped again until Amelia was 14, at which point she had some contact for a short period of time. Amelia did not see her father again until she was 25. Alienation strategies employed by her mother consisted primarily of denigration. Amelia recalled her mother saying, "That he did not want nothing to do with us and that basically he was a very bad person. It was all the time." Her mother also "fell to pieces" if the children brought up their father, indicating she was not emotionally strong enough for the children to love both their parents. "Well you'd have to know my mom. She'd start crying and say we didn't love her and that's just how she is."

Amelia believed all of the bad things her mother told her about her father. "All of it. I didn't really like him." What contact she did have with her father she described as, "kind of strange because we didn't know each other."

Amelia did not begin to realize that her mother was behind these negative attitudes until later, "Realizing that she wasn't always seeing things the way we were seeing them is when I really realized that she was not right. She would exaggerate things a lot of times. We (she and her sisters) would sit and listen to her talk to other people and realize that [what she was saying] is not really right, that is not really true." For Amelia, this was a painful realization. "It hurt. I had no way of getting into contact with him. I had no idea where he was. I didn't have my grandparents' phone number. I had no way." Several years later Amelia found her father and reestablished a relationship with him.

When asked what her father could have done differently, she responded that, "He could have tried to be around more. He could have tried to get to know us." She did ask him why he was not present in her life and he explained that he thought by removing himself he was preventing conflict with Amelia's mother. "He didn't want conflict with her. He thought it was better for us if him and her didn't see each other." Amelia, however, believed otherwise. "I think he was wrong. I think he was wrong." At present, Amelia has a strained relationship with her mother and almost no contact with her father. "I do believe he does love me but I am just not sure he knows how, and I believe he is really sorry for what happened but the anger in me makes it hard for me to have a relationship with him."

PATTERN 2: NARCISSISTIC MOTHERS
IN INTACT FAMILIES

Roberta, 44, explained that her father, who was a veteran, suffered from posttraumatic stress disorder. He was a quiet and unassuming man with simple desires. She described her mother as an emotionally needy woman who leaned on her children to gain support and sympathy for the difficult marriage in which she found herself. Through the constant emphasis on the flaws in his character, Roberta's mother induced negative feelings in her children toward their father. In addition, Roberta was made to feel that she would be betraying her mother if she had a meaningful relationship with father. However, she felt that what little relationship that she and her father were able to carve out for themselves, as limited as it was, made a significant impact on her life.

> *Just the time we did spend together meant so much to me. Even if we didn't talk about what was going on in the family. We did have times like that and they were very important to me. We'd go to the lake as a family outing sometime during the summer and we would go off and look for frogs or whatever or he would help me in my swimming instruction. We shared a love for nature. There were connections made and I wish there had been more.*

Roberta felt that her father could have spent more time with her and been less passive, but, "He was a busy man and he allowed this to go on to a certain degree."

Josh's parents remained married until his father died when Josh was 16 years old. His mother was the alienating parent, whose primary strategy was to confide in Josh about her disappointment with her marriage and to let him know that she was overwhelmed and discontented in her life. She told her young son that if she became too unhappy she would take him and leave his father and three stepsisters behind. This knowledge

drew Josh into his mother's world at the expense of a relationship with his father, a somewhat passive man and uninvolved
father. It was not until Josh entered a 12-step program for co-
dependency much later in life, after his mother had also passed
away, that he realized that his mother had alienated him from
his father. When asked what his father did to prevent or mitigate the alienation, he explained that his father took a stance of
bemused detachment.

> *In the novel* Pride and Prejudice *which was his favorite novel
> and he reread it often, there is a character who is the father of five
> daughters and the mother is sort of shrewish and not as bright
> and sort of unreasonable and he is very humorous and very philo-
> sophical about the situation of the troublesome wife and five
> daughters. He kind of escapes from it by his worldly wise humor
> and sort of a pose of sophistication. . . . . Detachment, that is a
> good word and it doesn't work out well in the novel for at least
> one of his daughters and he realizes later that his own approach to
> the whole situation has contributed, and I suspect that my father
> identified with the character.*

Despite this critique of his father, Josh did not think that there
was much else his father could have done.

> *It is hard to say what he should have done. What he did do is ev-
> erything he could do to maintain the status quo and opt for secu-
> rity and stability over change and risk. The fact that his first wife
> had taken his daughters from him (he later gained custody when
> their mother became ill) might have made him fear that if he re-
> ally rocked the boat my mother would take me away. I think my
> mother was a bit of an unsolvable problem and maybe my father
> did take the wisest approach. I am glad he took that approach. If
> he had become really healthy and gotten into recovery and set
> healthy limits with my mother and been honest, I think it proba-
> bly would have broken up the marriage and I think I would have
> lost him completely.*

Larissa described her mother as narcissistic and controlling, a
woman who did not want her to have a meaningful relation-

ship with her father. She denigrated him, told Larissa that her father did not love her, and manipulated her into hating him.

Just about all aspects of the alienation worked. I became my mother's puppet, her ally against my father. I suppose that must have been because I was gullible, and I didn't understand that she was trying to alienate anyone. I didn't see beneath her "victim veneer" to the reality, that she was in fact a practiced and unscrupulous liar who would say anything to get her own way. I genuinely believed that my father was as hateful as she said he was.

It was not until Larissa was an adult that she became aware of what her mother had done. Upon reflection she did not believe that there was anything her father could have done to prevent the alienation. Larissa saw her family as a finely balanced system in which any changes that her father might have made would have been countered by her mother.

He could certainly have been a more involved father, and taken a more obvious interest in his children. I'm not sure if he had any idea that his wife discussed their personal life and problems so freely. He probably had no idea of the sort of things she told me to cause alienation. His biggest mistake was in not understanding that my mother's intentions were not good.

Nonetheless, Larissa felt that any effort on her father's part would have been futile.

In the end I don't believe that anything he could have done would have made any difference to the outcome: given my mother's narcissistic personality, it seems inevitable that various family members would eventually become alienated from each other due to her behavior patterns. The best thing he could have done for himself was never to have married her, or failing that he should have divorced her. The best thing he could have done for my brother and me was to be a devoted father to us. That might not have saved his marriage though. Indeed, it may have driven my mother to such jealousy that she'd have divorced him and left him with no assets, and also tried to stop him from seeing us.

Elaine's parents never divorced, although they did spend a few years apart when she was an adult. Alienation strategies included constant bad-mouthing of her father and excluding him from family activities. "Almost like us against him kind of thing, treating me more like a peer or a friend rather than a child in the household. Dad doesn't do this right, Dad doesn't do that right." Eventually Elaine adopted the same attitude of mild disrespect and reproof toward her father. Her awakening came when she was 18 years old and saw how callously her mother was treating her father during his infirmity.

> I remember I was with a friend and my grandmom lived about a mile away from my sister's, and we were coming down main street, and we saw this older-looking man literally holding onto a light pole, and I remember saying to this person in the car, "Oh my god look at that poor old man," and as we got closer I said "Oh my god! That is my father. That is my dad." So we turned around and went back and got him and he said, "I have been trying and trying to see your mother and she won't pick me up and I want to see her," and that crushed me. That was really a crushing blow at that time and she was quite openly mean to him and had no use for him.

When Elaine was asked if there was anything else her father could have done to mitigate or prevent the alienation, she shared that she did not believe that there was anything her father could have done. "The deck was stacked against him. Whatever he did she would have found fault with. There always would have been something she was dissatisfied about."

Edward described his father as a simple man who worked hard as a butcher to support his wife and five children. Edward's mother was the alienating parent, constantly complaining about his father's shortcomings. "Oh, not providing enough money, not taking care of her enough, not being around enough, that was a big thing. He was kind of in a Catch-22 because he was always working to provide her with the money she wanted." Edward's mother convinced him that his father was a failure who was hurting her and not taking care of the family. "I became very angry at my father. I believed her that basically all of her unhappiness was due to him." Edward's mother was frequently depressed and she conveyed to her children that this was due in great measure to the inadequacies of their father. Edward recalled that as a young boy he became protective of his mother and resentful toward his father for hurting her. "It made me sad and angry at him. I exploded at him. I don't remember what touched it off but I do know I became so angry I attacked him. I was about 8." The result of the alienation was that Edward did not have the kind of closeness with his father that he felt he could have had. His mother, he believed, wanted her son entirely under her control, and he did not realize that his father had any feelings for him until he was leaving for Vietnam. Standing on the airstrip about to board a plane, he looked at his father and saw tears in his eyes. He was surprised to see any sign of his father's love for him. "I was shocked. Because I was always told he didn't care. That was the first time I started looking at him with unbiased eyes. Looking at the good qualities." From that point on Edward had a better relationship with his father, especially after his mother died and she no longer presented a barrier. When asked what, if anything, his father could have done, Edward explained that his father was intellectually limited and was probably not even aware that he was being dominated by his wife or that his children were being turned against him. Because of that, it was not clear what more his father could have done.

PATTERN 3: ABUSIVE/REJECTING PARENTS OF EITHER GENDER IN DIVORCED AND INTACT FAMILIES

Melinda was 3 years old when her parents separated and her father subsequently kidnapped her. She and her siblings had no contact with their mother for several years. Eventually, Melinda's mother won back her rights to have visitation with her daughter and they spent every other weekend together. In response, Melinda's father and stepmother began a campaign of alienation primarily through denigration of the mother. Melinda was not allowed to talk about her mother in her father's home and not allowed to bring home any presents given to her by her mother. Melinda absorbed these negative messages about her mother, believing her to be lazy and irresponsible, just as her father had portrayed her to be. "She and I didn't get along . . . we had a lot of problems." When Melinda was 13 years old, her mother discovered that Melinda had been sexually abused by her father; and custody reverted back to the mother. When asked what her mother did to protect the relationship in the face of the alienation campaign, Melinda offered that her mother fought for custody in the courts and she won the right for visitation. She recalled her mother never giving up on the relationship. "One time something happened and they said she wasn't allowed to see us that weekend. They decided no and I don't remember why but there was a lot of screaming going on and my mom came to the door and threatened the police and they got into a big fight." When asked what more her mother could have done, Melinda did not have anything to offer because she felt that her mother had been fighting for her all along.

Renee was just a toddler when her parents separated. She did not see her father again until she was 19. Renee recalled the last time she saw her father. "As far as I know we didn't see my dad after that. When I was 2 or 2½ he came and said he was leaving, and I sat there on his lap and cried and told him not to go, but I didn't really understand it and as far as I remember I don't ever remember seeing my dad until I was 19." Despite the absence from the family's life, Renee's mother still denigrated her father and worked hard to alienate Renee from him. "She never said anything good about him. She said he was worthless. He was an alcoholic. She never really said he beat on her but just that he didn't care about us; he didn't care enough to support us. We weren't really allowed to talk about him and if we did she would say he was worthless." One time when Renee brought up her father, her mother pushed her down a flight of stairs in a rage. Not surprisingly, she recalled being terrified of her mother. She was also sexually abused by her stepfather. Despite her father's physical absence, he tried to maintain a relationship by asking his friends and family to send her gifts from him. "I remember when I was probably about 13

I got a package from him at Christmas sent to my grandparents and I remember it was the most beautiful sweater, a very expensive wool sweater. I actually got the sweater because my grandmom brought it over and said, 'She is going to get this.' That is how he sent it, through my aunt (her father's sister)."

Around the same time Renee learned that her father had been trying to communicate with her. "I remember one time finding some letters that he sent us when we were kids and my mom would just keep them, and I remember I was playing in the car one time and opened the glove compartment and there were a whole bunch of letters there. I didn't get to read any of them because my mom found out and took them and I don't know what happened to them." She also recalled confrontations between her parents when her father was trying to visit, before he left. As a young adult Renee reestablished contact with her father but she struggled to overcome her deep-seated beliefs that he did not really care about her. "Well I think I was scared that if I said the wrong thing he was going to go out of my life again. You know. I don't know if that is exactly how I felt but thinking back on it I think that is why I didn't say anything for so many years . . . .I was thinking here is my dad now. If I make him mad . . . because I don't know what kind of subject it is with him because I didn't. I had been told all my life he is this worthless person. The question was posed to her what more her father could have done, and she responded, "It was easier for him to stay away from us knowing the kind of person my mom was, that it was going to be harder on us as kids if he was trying to be part of our lives, so he just decided to go and live his own life, and he knew that eventually we would have something to do with him which we all did."

When asked if there was anything he should have done, she exclaimed, "You would have to meet my mother! That is why as an adult I have come to understand why he did what he did. From the work I do I understand the decision he made. I grew up with my mom and I know the kind of person she was, and if she had half the energy then as she does now I can see why he realized it was easier to back off." She concluded, "When someone has that anger toward another person there is really not a lot that can be done." Renee still felt tremendous

resentment toward her mother and had only limited contact
with her.

Jason, 67, reported that his parents never divorced despite a
violent and unhappy marriage. He still had vivid memories of
a brutal childhood ruled by a domineering, aggressive father
who alienated him from his mother. "He would belittle her. He
had a whole bag of tricks to control us and one was the constant
belittling of people, of me, of my sister, and it was very effective
because there was no escaping it. You couldn't talk back or you
would be physically admonished or you would be mocked
even stronger. I am pretty bitter as you can guess." The result
of this relentless denigration and fear that he would lose his
father's approval was that Jason had a diminished relationship
with his mother. Looking back, Jason realized that without the
influence of his father, his relationship with his mother would
have been quite different.

*I would have a much more enduring relationship with my mother
if the idea hadn't been planted that there was something fundamentally wrong with her, that she didn't quite measure up. I
would have realized at the time that she was a pretty good person.
But I didn't want to spend any time with her because I bought
into some of his stuff that she was silly and mawkish or overly
sentimental and unreliable or whatever the sum total of the impressions that he tried to convey about her.*

With hindsight Jason realized his mother had both intelligence
as well as creative talent, which she could not fully develop
because of Jason's father's emotional abuse and domination of
the family. When Jason was asked if there was anything his
mother could have done to prevent the alienation, he could
think of nothing short of a divorce, but as he explained, "These
were Catholic people in the 1940s and 1950s. One of my father's
younger brothers got divorced and it was a scandal." Jason concluded that, in the end, the force of his father's personality
precluded any action on his mother's part, and there was
very little, if anything, that she could have done to lessen the
alienation.

Frank was 48, his parents divorced when he was about 12 years old. There was constant fighting in the household and the alienation took the form of his father demeaning and brutalizing the children and his mother. "She was always downgraded, called the worst things, slut, whore, no good, and so on. The times that he wasn't talking to us was pretty much either myself or my brother getting slapped around. I can remember one time in particular when we were told, 'You are going to stand right here and watch.' and he lined all four of us kids up in the living room and proceeded to literally beat the hell out of my mother and turned around and told us that is what a no good bitch is worth." Shortly after a trial separation of Frank's parents, they reunited and Frank ran away from home in order to avoid continued violence and abuse. From that point forward he had limited contact with both his parents. He understood that his father poisoned him against his mother but had not yet shared this insight with his mother. Nonetheless, he felt that she could have done more. "Oh yeah. She could have stood up for any one of us kids instead of standing there like he made her do and watching him rape my older sister, or instead of watching me be thrown into the TV with my back cut open, she could have called the police, all it would have taken was picking up the phone." At the same time he acknowledged, "Then again I look at the flip side and I remember her getting her head bashed open and there wasn't a whole lot she could do to protect us kids. So it is hard to know."

Iris was one of seven children of a volatile marriage. When she was 14 years old her mother packed up the children and drove several hundred miles away. Throughout the trip she told them that their father was a dangerous pedophile.

She said he was an alcoholic and a child molester and we weren't safe with him. My father was one of the kindest people. He wouldn't harm anyone, much less a child. But she kept telling us this for the whole three or four days in the car. When we got to Oklahoma my father was in the car right behind her. He followed us but we weren't allowed to talk to him. I remember her screaming at him in the front yard.

Iris had no contact with her father for several years and came to believe that he did not care for her. "Right after we left, my aunt and grandmother told me he was trying to get in touch with me and my brother but Mom had us so convinced that he wasn't, and being our mother of course we believed her. Oh I was heartbroken. I was so totally distraught that he didn't love me anymore." During the period in which there was no contact, her father sent gifts by way of an aunt, but Iris did not find out until later that they were actually from her father. As a teenager she ran away to her father's house for a short period of time and her father at that point had an opportunity to defend himself. "My father was very calm. My brother and I took this information to him and said, 'Look this is what she has told us all these years about you and the other kids and we want to know if it is true.' We just point blank asked him, 'Did you do these things?' and he very calmly told us 'No. I did not.' He said 'Why would I ever hurt one of my own children when I tried so hard to protect you all those years?"

Despite the newfound closeness she had with her father, Iris decided to return to her mother's home. She recalled her father saying to her, "You need to make the decision that is right for you and I will respect whatever decision you will make." However, during the interview she expressed the wish that he had been more persistent in trying to convince her to not return to her mother who was emotionally rejecting and physically abusive. "I think at the time if he had told me the truth about her I wouldn't have gone." Iris wished that he had told her, "Look your mom is really not normal and what she is doing to you is really not ok and I really don't want you to go back there." She believed that if he had said those words to her, she would have remained with him. "I would have stayed with him. If he had been honest with me then and told me what he thought. I would have stayed with him." When she asked him later why he did not try to prevent her from leaving, he said, "'I didn't want you to think badly of your mother. Regardless of what she does she is your mother and somewhere in there I think she does love you a little bit.' But I never believed that and I am totally against that now. No parent should let their children be treated that way." Iris ran away from her mother's home again and this time she stayed away until she attained adulthood. From that point forward she was able to develop a close relationship with her father up until the time that he passed away.

Nancy was 60 at the time of the interview. Her parents were teenagers when they met and they married soon after and had five girls. Nancy was the youngest. When she was 3 months old, Nancy's mother died and her father—being overwhelmed with the loss, having a job that required traveling, as well as having 4 older children—accepted his sister's offer to temporarily care for the baby (Nancy). This aunt and her husband (Nancy's uncle) became "Mommy" and "Daddy" to young Nancy. Although her father lived nearby and eventually was required to travel less for his job, Nancy remained with her "Mommy" and "Daddy" throughout her childhood. She saw her father infrequently and became alienated from him at the hands of her new family. She was told that her father (whom she called dad as compared to her uncle whom she called daddy) had a drinking problem and that he did not really care about her, and "that it was his choice to give me away." Alienation was also effectuated through guilt and manipulation, as illustrated by the fact that when she was in high school, Nancy asked to live with her father. "It was like, 'If you live with him you are going to hurt me. You're my daughter and it is just not going to be the same.'" She decided to stay with her mother. Visitation with her father was strictly controlled and limited, resulting in a strained relationship between father and daughter. "We really didn't bond." Nancy also absorbed the negative impressions of him created by her "Mother," "He was the daddy I didn't see very often. I felt that he was distant and cold."

Nancy did not realize that she had been alienated from her father until she was in her 40s and all of her parents had passed away. She began having flashbacks of being sexually abused by her "Mommy" and "Daddy." Once in therapy she began to understand that her new family needed to control her and prevent her from having a close and loving relationship with her father. "Oh it was horrendous. I just felt like a big part of me was there and I couldn't take advantage of it. He would have been so much a part of me. I missed that."

Throughout the interview Nancy recalled many ways her father tried to maintain the relationship, including continuing visitation and contact throughout the years. She admitted, though, that when she was a child she thought he could have done more, "But as an adult I saw how she manipulated the family and he was just part of that manipulation. She was bound and determined that it would always be her way and he followed. It was almost like she was laying down the ground rules and he had to follow those ground rules. She was in charge."

Carl was 45 years old at the time of the interview. His parents were in their 20s and neither had been married before when they met. They dated for two years and then married. Carl was born in the first year of their marriage, their only child. His parents separated when he was 4 years of age and he had no contact with his father until he was 45 years old. Shortly after the separation his father would come by for his visits, but his mother called the police and prevented contact, based on his being behind in child support. The alienation perpetrated by his mother consisted mostly of bad-mouthing. "For most of my adult life my impression over the years about my father was that he was alcoholic." Carl was also led to believe that his father was dangerous. Growing up, Carl did not have a close relationship with his mother. "I wouldn't say it was very close. I wouldn't say my mother was a very nurturing woman—I mean my mother became very bitter, she had been a single parent trying to raise a child on welfare. I think this created a lot of stress in her life which she took out on me as a child, her frustrations and her shortcomings." Although Carl grew up with a negative view of his father, he began to wonder about what kind of man he was, and as an adult he decided to find him. He described their first meeting after close to 41 years as a powerful experience. "It is difficult to describe. I can tell you it is quite a feeling to be able to look into your father's eyes for the first time in your life at the age of 45." Carl did not mention anything specific that he felt his father did to mitigate the alienation but he did have some ideas about what his father should have done. "Yes. Yes there are things he could have done. He could have tried to contact me, but like I said as time goes on it becomes more difficult, and there is a kind of guilt, the wall gets higher. I was the one who found him."

SUMMARY AND DISCUSSION

It is remarkable how consistent the stories were when viewed from the perspective of what the targeted parent did and should have done to prevent or mitigate the effects of the alienation. Across all stories, a few key points were made. The first was that many of the adult children of PAS felt that the targeted parents should have done more to fight for the relationship and prevent the alienation. This was true for those in divorced families, but especially for those in intact families in which the targeted parents had more frequent and easier access to the children. Many felt that the targeted parents were too naïve and trusting and generally unaware of the motivations of the alienating parents. There was also a sense that this was partly generational. Some of the adult children of PAS grew up during a period in western societies in which one parent was the primary caretaker (usually the mother) and the other was the breadwinner (usually the father) and the breadwinning parent was considerably less involved in childrearing than the caretaking parent. In these families, if the alienating parent was the caretaking parent, the opportunity for alienation was great, especially if the targeted parent tended to see himself as a hands off or secondary parent.

The adult children felt hurt and angry when the targeted parent finally gave up trying to have a relationship. No matter how adamant they had been that they wanted nothing to do with the targeted parent, they were still shocked when the parent respected that choice and walked away. It was usually experienced as rejection. When these parents did not call or write or send presents, this also hurt, especially because the alienating parents took full advantage of any lapse on the part of the targeted parent. The adult children had resented being put in the position of having to defend someone (the targeted parent) who provided ammunition to the alienating parent. Even though they understood that the alienating parent would probably belittle any cards or letters sent and would restrict all attempts at contact, they still wanted the targeted parent to continue to send cards and letters.

A corollary point is that the adult children did not feel that the targeted parent should have believed or responded to the child's rejection. Regardless of how adamant they had been that they wanted nothing to do with the targeted parent, they still did not want the targeted parent to accept that at face value. They expressed the belief that the targeted parent should have seen that the children were puppets, merely mouthing the words and performing the behaviors that they had learned in order to maintain the relationship with the alienating parent. In essence, they were asking the targeted parents to act as if there were two children: the alienating child going through the motions of the alienation and the child who loved the targeted parent and never wanted to lose that relationship. Because the targeted parents did not fully understand the extent to which their child was being manipulated, they responded rationally only to the content of the signals and messages being directed toward them (i.e., that the relationship was not valued or desired.)

At the same time, many of the adult children expressed the belief that no matter what the targeted parent did, the alienating parent would have been relentless in the alienation. Many felt that all efforts at maintaining the relationship would have been effectively countered. The alienating parents were perceived as ruthless and utterly determined to undermine the relationship between them and the targeted parent. Thus, many of the adult children felt that the targeted parents should have tried harder and should not have given up. But they did not believe that in the end the targeted parent would have been effective at mitigating or preventing the alienation. A few went so far as to say that if the targeted parent had tried harder, the alienating parent might have behaved even worse.

Many of the adult children found out after the fact that the targeted parent had tried harder than they had known. Some found out about court cases fought, that there had been letters and gifts that had been returned to the targeted parent unopened. In most cases learning about these attempts had meaning. Even many years later they were grateful to learn that the targeted parent did more than they had known.

Part III

CLINICAL CONSIDERATIONS

Chapter 9

Working with Adult Children of Parental Alienation Syndrome

Recovery can take place only within the context of relationships.

—Judith Herman, *Trauma and Recovery*

THIS CHAPTER EXPLORES SOME OF THE KEY ISSUES FOR THE ADULT children and can serve as a guide for clinicians working with this population. Of course, clinicians should use their own judgment and experience with individual clients when incorporating these suggestions into ongoing clinical work. Many of the suggestions offered below could also be of use to individuals outside the context of formal therapeutic work.

Parental alienation syndrome is a relatively new term, which has not permeated mainstream consciousness, and has certain myths associated with it (e.g., PAS is only caused by mothers in response to a divorce). Individuals in therapy may not be aware that what they experienced has a name and represents a particular syndrome. Naming an experience is the first step toward gaining power over it by giving it dimensions, containing it, and providing the individual with a framework for working with it (Peck, 1983). Naming also helps acknowledge that the experience is real and that it exists in the world as a specific entity. It also recognizes that there is a body of knowledge about it that can be accessed and that there are other people who have had a similar experience.

In order to determine whether a client has experienced parental alienation syndrome it is critical to determine whether the estrangement (physical or psychological) from one parent was induced (at least in great measure) by the other parent. It does not necessarily mean that the alienating parent was all bad or had purely malicious intentions, nor does it mean that the targeted parent was all good and was wholly a victim. It is important to bear in mind that not all estrangement should be classified as parental alienation syndrome. The term is reserved for situations in which one parent induces the estrangement of the child from the other parent when neither abuse nor neglect warranted such estrangement. Thus, the three critical questions are (1) Was the person estranged (physically or psychologically) from one parent? (2) Was that estrangement unwarranted? (3) Was the estrangement induced by the other parent? If the answer to all three questions is affirmative, it can be concluded that the person experienced parental alienation syndrome. Reviewing the eight manifestations of PAS identified by Gardner (1998) presented in the Introduction and the three familial patterns of parental alienation syndrome described in Chapter 1 should provide sufficient information for making a determination about the existence of PAS in a client's background. Once this has been accomplished, the therapist and client can proceed to utilize the information provided in this and other books in order to help the client understand more fully the meaning of PAS in her or his life.

One thing to bear in mind is that the client may be seeking therapy for reasons other than exploring his or her relationship with the alienating parent. In fact, the client may not be aware at all that there had been manipulation by one parent to turn him or her against the other parent. The client may still be actively involved with the PAS such that the alienating parent is viewed as all good and the targeted parent is viewed as all bad. This is not dissimilar to women who enter therapy for one set of reasons but eventually reveal to the therapist and to themselves that they are victims of emotional abuse in their adult romantic relationships (Loring, 1994). These women may be completely unaware that their symptoms (depression, somatic complaints, confusion, and so forth) are expressions of their emotional abuse. Thus, the therapist may develop a working hypothesis that a client is an adult child of parental alienation syndrome well before broaching that possibility to the client. If this is the case, it is likely that any criticism of the alienating parent may be met with intense resistance because the client is still involved in protecting that version of his or her childhood in which the alienating parent was the victim-hero and the targeted parent was the villain. The degree of enmeshment with the alienating parent will have to be determined and taken into consideration prior to the therapist raising the possibility that the client experienced PAS. Thus, acknowledging PAS may represent a significant paradigm shift for the client. As noted in Chapters 5 and 6, realizing that one has been alienated from a parent by the other parent entails several losses, including the loss of the idealized version of the alienating parent, the loss of time with the targeted parent (once that parent's worth has been acknowledged), the loss of innocence as the client recognizes the role he or she played in the alienation, and the loss of the possibility of winning the love and approval of the alienating parent.

Once a diagnosis of PAS has been made, the therapist and client should consider the presence of additional factors associated with PAS that may be relevant for the client's treatment. To begin with, the possibility that the client was also a victim of physical or sexual abuse should be explored. The prevalence of these other forms of maltreatment was higher in this sample of adult children of PAS than in the general population. However, it is not necessary to assume that such maltreatment was experienced, and that, if not recalled, was probably repressed. But, because the risk factors for PAS are similar to those of other forms of maltreatment (family stressors, poor impulse control, alcoholism, personality disorders), the likelihood that physical or sexual abuse was experienced in the PAS population should be considered.

To the extent that other forms of maltreatment were experienced, the therapist can draw on the literature for working with such populations. For example, difficulty with affect regulation, anger management, and interpersonal relationships, as well as posttraumatic stress disorder are common among adult victims of child abuse (van der Kolk, 1996). Practitioners have identified several critical treatment components for this population, including the development of a therapeutic rapport and a sense of safety and trust in the therapeutic process, confrontation of the traumatic events and material, and reintegration of self (Cloitre, Koenen, Cohen, & Han, 2002; Gold, 1997; Herman, 1997). Awareness of what Herman called traumatic transference is also advisable in cases of extreme child abuse (which describes the Pattern 3 families). Issues of trust and abuse of power experienced in childhood can get played out in the therapist's office, because the, "dynamics of domination and submission are reenacted in all subsequent relationships, including therapy" (Herman, 1997, p. 138).

There should also be a discussion of parental alcoholism because this was particularly prevalent in the sample of adult children of PAS. In light of the shame and secrecy surrounding familial alcoholism, it is quite possible that a client would not reveal this unless asked directly. Being able to draw on the study described in this book could help the therapist ameliorate the sense of shame typically associated with admitting alcoholism in the family of origin. If parental alcoholism has been identified it would be important for the therapist to consider the presence of alcohol or substance abuse issues in the client him- or herself in light of the elevated risk at which offspring of alcoholics are placed (Chassin, Pitts, DeLucia, & Todd, 1999). Regardless of the presence of alcohol and substance abuse in the client, the typical issues that affect the adult children of alcoholics certainly apply, including difficulty trusting, protection of the family secret, and an overdeveloped sense of responsibility (Wotitz, 1990). Therefore, therapy should involve an exploration of these issues and the value of addiction-specific treatment and peer support groups.

Therapy with clients who are adult children of parental alienation syndrome should also examine whether and how the client was emotionally abused by the alienating parent. A thorough discussion of the types of emotional abuse is warranted to determine which apply to the client's childhood experience (see Chapter 4). Creation of Loring's (1994) emotional abuse climate map may be a helpful exercise for the clients. This entails identifying the different types of emotional abuse experienced (ignoring, isolating, rejecting, and so forth), and describing exactly how each type was enacted. For example, a client might indicate that the alienating parent was rejecting and that rejection was expressed through verbal disparagements of the client's worth and a lack of physical closeness. The client might also indicate that he or she was isolated as a child when the alienating parent prohibited the child from socializing with peers and spending time with the extended family of the targeted parent. These actions are then linked to specific behaviors and responses on the part of the client such that when the parent isolated the client as a child, he or she felt more dependent on the parent; or when the parent was rejecting of the client as a child, he or she experienced an anxious need to please the parent. This map then serves as a guide for understanding the ways in which the emotional abuse resulted in an intensification of the tie between the child and that parent (furthering the alienation from the other parent).

Loring (1994) proposed that validation of the client's worth and ideas is critical for emotionally abused women because their very sense of self has been eroded and fragmented as a result of the abuse. It is likely that this model also applies to adult children of parental alienation syndrome because their worth has also been diminished through the PAS. Specifically, growing up with the belief that the targeted parent did not love the individual, that the alienating parent did not love the parts of him or her that were like the targeted parent, and that the alienating parent's love was conditional on meeting the parent's needs—especially the need for him or her to become alienated from the targeted parent—can diminish the client's sense of worth and value as an individual.

Whether the alienating parent had a personality disorder should also be discussed with the client who is an adult child of PAS. A review of the types of personality disorders most common in this sample, narcissism and antisocial personality disorder, can provide the client (and therapist) with a helpful heuristic for understanding the relational patterns the client experienced as a child. Common to all dramatic personality disorders is the parent's inability to recognize and respond appropriately to the needs of the child, especially if they are in conflict with the parent's own needs. There is an extant clinical knowledge base for working with adults from "narcissistic families." For example, Donaldson-Pressman and Pressman (1994) focused on helping the client (1) understand that the parents' needs were given precedence over the child's needs in such families, which resulted in the child assuming unrealistic responsibility for the parents' happiness; (2) accept that he or she was only a child and could not realistically be expected to solve the parent's problems; and (3) learn how to set appropriate limits and boundaries in his or her adult relationships. These key tasks are applicable for adult children of PAS to the extent that the alienating parent's relational style was narcissistic.

Comparing the alienating parent to a cult leader may also be a useful component of therapy with an adult child of PAS. That is, was the parent charismatic, controlling, demanding of loyalty, and able to use thought control and emotional manipulation to convince the child to renounce the targeted parent? The concept of cults is familiar to most people, thus providing an accessible framework for thinking about PAS. Most people accept that individuals who join cults were manipulated into their devotion and commitment, and clients can use the cult analogy to explain to themselves and others what they experienced as a child. The cult framework is also useful because the process of leaving a cult and recovering from cultic involvement may provide an analogy for understanding the process of recovering from PAS. Specifically, it has been found that leaving a cult represents merely a starting point for recovery. This was found to be true for former cult member Patrick Ryan: "Making the break from the movement was only the beginning. I had difficulties with reading, memory, concentration, focusing, body shaking, and dissociation" (1993, p. 136). Using the cult analogy, the client can accept that acknowledging PAS is the first step in a process of understanding and healing from his or her childhood. It may also be the case that how the client recognized PAS (i.e., which catalyst was involved, see Chapters 5 and 6) will affect how he or she will recover, just as walkaways and castaways from a cult have different recovery trajectories from those who leave as a result of counseling. According to exit counselor and cult expert Carol Giambalvo:

> Walkaways and castaways need the most help in understanding their recovery process. Former members who were cast out of a cult are especially vulnerable; often they feel inadequate, guilty, angry. Most cults respond to any criticism of the cult itself by turning the criticism around into the individual member. Whenever something is wrong, it is not the leadership or the organization, it is the individual. Thus, when someone is told to leave a cult, that person carries a double load of guilt and shame. (1993, p. 149)

Giambalvo suggests that providing information about mind control is vital in the recovery process for former cult members. When ex-cultists learn about thought reform and emotional manipulation techniques, they can begin to understand their cultic experience and how they came to subvert their own ideas and values in order to gain the acceptance of the cult leader. Consequently, discussing brainwashing techniques with an adult child of PAS may be warranted in order to help the client understand the degree of influence the alienating parent exercised over her or him and how submission to the alienation, as Jessica Benjamin (1988) described, became anchored in the client's heart.

Analysis of the relationship with the alienating parent from an attachment perspective is also suggested. It is likely that the client was anxiously attached to that parent if withdrawal of love was a strategy employed. Although two assessment procedures exist for reliably and validly determining an individual's attachment classification, neither is feasible within the context of therapy with an adult. One is appropriate for infants, the Mary Ainsworth (Ainsworth, Blehar, Waters, & Wall, 1978) Strange Situation, while the other requires a trained professional to implement and score, Mary Main's (Main, Kaplan, & Cassidy, 1985) Adult Attachment Interview. In the absence of a formal assessment, the therapist's classification of anxious attachment can only be a conjecture for adult clients who experienced PAS. Nonetheless, this formulation is grounded in theory and research, which has demonstrated that inconsistent parental warmth and availability is associated with anxious attachment in children. Thus, it can be surmised that the alienating parents who utilized withdrawal of love as an alienation strategy were in fact practicing the parenting style likely to result in an anxious attachment.

Attachment theory is useful in the context of PAS because it provides yet another way (in addition to the cult analogy) to understand why children "allowed" themselves to be so influenced by rejecting or manipulative parents. According to attachment theory, parental rejection and inconsistency produces anxiety in children who then seek to reduce the anxiety through reassurance and comfort from the caretaking adult. It is the very inconsistency of the parental warmth and availability that "hooks" the child into trying to win back the parental love. Children whose parents are consistently unavailable learn that their parents are not "there for them" and give up trying. Conversely, children whose parents are sometimes, but not always close and loving assume that when the parents withdraw their love that they, the child, did something to cause that withdrawal. Thus, they become trapped in the struggle to win back the love. This process is similar to what Loring (1994) described as the "traumatic bonding" of women with their emotionally abusive partners. Identifying this process of pursuing the unavailable parent allows clients to understand why they continued to seek love from the parent. If clients assumed that they were to blame for the parent's withdrawal of love, they felt compelled to win back the love so that they could feel good about themselves. Further, because they experienced intermittent reinforcement—that is, sometimes their behavior resulted in parental love and approval and sometimes it did not—they were essentially "taught" to be persistent and to keep trying. Intermittent reinforcement results in the most persistent learning behaviors because the individual never knows when the next attempt will result in success (Skinner, 1938). Only in recognizing the futility and cruelty of this struggle to win the "unwinable" parent can clients learn to separate their self-esteem from their parent's approval.

TASKS OF TREATMENT

In addition to understanding the various components of parental alienation syndrome, clients are faced with a number of tasks that they may want to engage in as part of the recovery and treatment process.

The first task for clients is to forgive themselves for having been manipulated by the alienating parent. Once clients understand the brainwashing and emotional manipulation techniques (alienation strategies), the emotional abuse components, and the anxious attachment, they should be able to recognize that there was no choice but to succumb to the parental alienation syndrome. One strategy that Donaldson-Pressman and Pressman (1994) utilized to dramatically convey this point with children raised in narcissistic families was to have clients bring in a picture of themselves as young children. This allowed clients to understand, to literally see, how vulnerable they were and how they could not possibly have acted in any other way. This strategy is also useful for victims of sexual abuse who cling to the distorted idea that in some way they asked for or deserved the abuse. Looking at a picture of an innocent young child challenges that distortion and allows clients to honor their youth and innocence. One clue that forgiveness is called for is the presence of guilt and shame, common experiences among the adult children of PAS (see Chapter 7). Because guilt and shame underlie depression, substance use, anxiety, eating disorders, and a host of other negative life choices, it is important that they be worked through so that clients can have a realistic understanding of what was expected of them as children. Self-forgiveness is the first step in that process.

Reuniting with the targeted parent should also be explored over the course of therapy, if that has not yet taken place. Prior to doing so, it will be important to address residual unrealistic negative feelings and attitudes toward that parent. That is, knowing one has been brainwashed against a parent does not result in an instantaneous evaporation of all of the programmed material. In their work with former cult members, Goldberg and Goldberg (1982) observed that ex-cultists continued to exhibit some of the character traits and ascribed to some of the attitudes of their cultic group. In cases of PAS this can be especially difficult because the content of some of the brainwashing material may actually have been true. It is harder to separate truth from distortion than truth from outright lies. Only when the client is psychologically separate from the alienating parent can he or she meet the targeted parent and begin to determine which thoughts and feelings about the targeted parent are based in reality and which are distortions and lies. For example, the facts, as described by the alienating parent, may be correct in some cases, but the motives ascribed to the targeted parent may have been distorted. Only through hearing the other side of the story can the client make an independent decision as to what to believe. The client should be cautious about fantasies that the targeted parent will be the idealized parent that the client recently "lost" through the awareness that the alienating parent had engineered the alienation. This can be quite painful, as Alix found out. She grew up with a narcissistic, physically abusive mother and the belief that her father must be a bad and dangerous person. Nonetheless, as a college student she hired a private detective to find her father. "I guess the reason why I defied all that, no matter what, I wanted to find out who my dad was, even if I could only talk to him by phone and I just had to know. I already had one abusive parent, why can't another one not be so bad? Do you see what I am saying?" Alix was searching for a good parent. Unfortunately, that was not what she found. "My dad is not any better than my mother, that's sad. In a way I raised myself." For many of the interviewees, the reunion with the targeted parent resulted in a positive relationship, but there is, of course, no guarantee that this will be the case. The client needs to have realistic expectations before meeting the targeted parent.

One topic of conversation between the client and the targeted parent could be what the targeted parent did and could have done to prevent or mitigate the effects of the alienation. As noted throughout this book, it is quite possible that the targeted parent wrote letters, made phone calls, sent presents, took the alienating parent to court without the client knowing about it at the time. Hearing about these efforts could be healing as the client learns that the targeted parent wanted a relationship, loved the client as a child, and valiantly tried to prevent the alienation. This was certainly true for Robin. When he reconnected with his father, he learned that his father had tried to stay in touch with him over the years. "Yes well. He had like 5–6 birthday cards that he actually had attempted to send me that were returned. Then he said he finally gave up because he didn't know where to send them anymore. That meant a lot to me, he gave them to me." Robin's father had kept the cards all those years and was able to finally give them to his son. From this Robin concluded that his father had been thinking of him all along. Also, hearing about what the rejection felt like from the targeted parent's view may help the client understand why he or she may eventually have stopped trying.

Another kind of reunion can also occur over the course of therapy for adult children of parental alienation syndrome: a reunion with the parts of themselves that they cut off in order to please the alienating parent. The client and therapist together can explore what aspects of the self had been cut off or buried. This may include positive feelings about aspects of the client that resembled the targeted parent, talents and interests that threatened the alienating parent, friendships that were not pursued in order to spend more time with the alienating parent, and relationships with the extended family of the targeted parent which were terminated as part of the "tribal warfare" as described by Gardner (1998) and Warshak (2001a). In this way, parental alienation syndrome entails alienation not just from the targeted parent, although that is the critical component, it also entails alienation from the self. As noted in Chapters 5 and 6, the child with PAS believes several lies: (1) the targeted parent is all bad and completely unworthy of having a relationship with; (2) the alienating parent is all good and deserves unquestioning loyalty; and (3) the alienating parent has the child's best interest at heart. The parts of the child that did not fully believe these lies had to be cut off from the child's conscious life. Because the alienating parent demanded total loyalty, the child had to bury any doubts about the alienating parent, any positive feelings toward the targeted parent, and any desire for independent judgment. The PAS child had to develop a PAS identity, much the way cult members develop a cult identity

(Hassan, 1988). In this way, there were parts of the client that were buried. But they can be found and reintegrated into the self so that the client can have a more authentic experience. This is not dissimilar to treatment of former cult members who need to examine what they gave up in exchange for acceptance into the cult. There is an admission fee into the relationship with the alienating parent. Because that love is conditional, and can be and was withdrawn periodically, the child learns what that price is and feels compelled to pay it. Through therapy the client can take back that admission charge and own all the parts of his or her self.

At some point in therapy the client may express interest in confronting the alienating parent about the experience of parental alienation syndrome. Many of the participants interviewed for this book had done so. Few claimed to have had a satisfying experience. Most described the alienating parent as incapable of hearing what was being said or admitting any wrongdoing. As Roberta said about her mother, "You can only go so far with her. It would mean making her look at herself as bad and that is hard to do to someone you love." Ron said, "I tried to have a meeting of the mind, a rational conversation, but I quickly figured out it just couldn't happen." Patricia, too, found little satisfaction in confronting her father, "He says it's not true to this day, and that she is the crazy one. He never has accepted any responsibility for his actions." These experiences are consistent with the personality structure of these alienating parents as well as Siegel and Langford's (1998) findings that alienating parents had elevated scores on personality tests indicative of defensiveness and inability to tolerate criticism. That does not mean that the confrontation was a bad idea for them or that it would be a mistake for a particular client. It depends on the client's intentions. If the expectation is to change the alienating parent or in some way undo the abuse, the client is probably not ready for the confrontation. On the other hand, if the purpose is to have the satisfaction of sharing with the alienating parent the client's version of his or her childhood, with no expectation of fixing or changing anything, then the client is probably ready. As Ron found, "It was still a good experience for me because I was able to walk away from that experience having the whole puzzle put together in my head." Having the client write a letter or practice the confrontation in a session (e.g., talking to the person in the empty chair [Perls, 1969]) may bring out any residual fantasy of changing that person that needs to be worked through prior to a confrontation.

The client needs to be prepared for the fact that the outcome of any meeting with the alienating parent is uncertain. Many of the adult children of PAS maintained a relationship with the alienating parent after the realization of the alienation, although most recognized that the relationship had been seriously compromised by the realization process. That is, once they recognized that they had been manipulated in order to satisfy the narcissistic needs of the parent, they no longer idealized that parent or felt obligated to meet the loyalty demands. Naturally, this altered the fundamental nature of the relationship with that parent because the adult children no longer endorsed the alienating parent's view that the targeted parent was all bad and the alienating parent was all good. Many had to learn how to set appropriate limits with these parents who did not necessarily respect typical parent–child boundaries. Again, this altered the relationship. Most reported not being as close to the alienating parent as they had once been, and quite a few had no contact whatsoever with that parent either because of continued abuse or because they felt so angry and resentful about the alienation that a relationship was simply not possible. Larissa found that writing a letter to her mother was the final act that allowed her to separate:

I wrote a couple of letters to my mother asking her why she'd done certain things when I was a teenager. The letter she wrote back would have made me fear for her sanity, if I hadn't just watched the psychopathy program. The letter reminded me how loutish I'd been, and how much I'd hated my father, but mostly it was filled with bizarre thoughts and irrelevancies. Mostly I didn't recognize the version of myself she was describing at all, but it was also laughable—she wrote something like, "Look how shaky my writing is, you've upset me so much I can hardly write." That really made me realize she lived in a land of complete fantasy, and that she didn't understand me at all and she never would. I felt

*great relief at that really, because I finally grasped that I didn't
need to waste any more time in trying to understand her and in
making her understand me—one more step in releasing my mind
from her influence.*

Another task for adult children of parental alienation syndrome
is to not become involved romantically with someone who has
the same personality disorder as the alienating parent. That is,
to not repeat the past by reenacting the same type of relationship. If the client is considering marrying someone who fits the
description of a narcissistic personality, she or he should be encouraged to rethink that choice. This person, no matter how
charming he or she is now, no matter how special the prospec-
tive partner makes the client feel, will probably turn on the client at some point. The client might already have experienced a
taste of the anger and vengefulness of crossing this person and
may believe that the withdrawal of love and anger that was
experienced was truly deserved. But the client needs to know
that no one deserves to be treated the way that narcissists tend
to treat people. Sharing a child with such a person would most
likely be a losing proposition. This person will need to be the
center of the child's attention and emotional life and may feel
jealous of the client's parental pride and joy. In addition, this
person may resent the child for favoring the client, also likely
to induce rage and vengeance. If the client should dare leave
this person, the client will then learn in no uncertain terms
what it means to be divorced from a narcissistic person. At that
point the client would be at risk for becoming alienated from
his or her own children, as the intergenerational cycle of PAS
continues.

Another way to repeat the past is to reenact the parental
alienation in one's own parenting relationship. Adult children
of parental alienation syndrome need to be cognizant about the
ways in which they are at heightened risk for becoming a targeted parent. (1) marrying someone likely to alienate them from
their children; (2) their own "pull" to walk away from their
children; and (3) having their own parents alienate their children from them. Being aware that these are traps that adult
children of PAS are susceptible to should help facilitate a more

conscious and considered approach to these issues. Perhaps in some cases the compulsion to repeat the past can be prevented.

SUMMARY

Working with adults who experienced PAS as children requires a thorough knowledge of the manifestations and patterns of PAS. The therapist should be familiar with assessing and treating childhood maltreatment, emotional abuse, children of alcoholics, and anxious attachments. Together the client and therapist can consider whether and how to reunite with the targeted parent and to confront the alienating parent. In all cases, the client should be helped to reunite with those parts of him- or herself that were cut off, denied, or buried in order to appease the alienating parent. Through this process the client can learn to be a more authentic person and, ideally, avoid the compulsion to repeat the past by becoming romantically involved with a person similar to the alienating parent and by becoming alienated from his or her own children.

Chapter 10

Working with Alienated Children

All great truths begin as blasphemies
　　　　　　　—George Bernard Shaw, *Annajanska*

IN THIS CHAPTER LESSONS LEARNED FROM THE STUDY ARE APPLIED
to working with children who are currently experiencing PAS.
In cases where PAS has been determined to be present and the
therapy is court ordered, Gardner's (1998) recommendations for
mental health professionals are applicable. That is, the therapist's primary role is to create opportunities for the child to
spend time with the targeted parent in order to experience firsthand that he or she is not a dangerous person as the child has
been led to believe. Gardner believed that PAS children need
an excuse to spend time with the targeted parent in order to
avoid the wrath of the alienating parent. If the therapist orders
visitation, which can be enforced with sanctions against the alienating parent, children will have such an excuse (to help the
alienating parent avoid the sanctions) and can, therefore, be
freed from the responsibility of appearing to choose or want
visitation with the targeted parent. Gardner's guidelines for
therapists were honed from years of clinical practice and
should be utilized when the situation approximates that for
which the guidelines were developed: court ordered therapy
for families in which PAS has been identified in the children of
divorced parents. This chapter was written for situations that

are *not* covered by Gardner's book; specifically, for therapists working with children outside the context of court-ordered postdivorce litigation, where PAS may be occurring.

IDENTIFYING/ASSESSING THE PRESENCE OF PAS

The first step for the therapist is to determine whether PAS is the underlying cause of a child's estrangement or negative feelings toward one parent. As Gardner (1998) noted, not all cases of children resisting visitation qualify as PAS. For example, if there is bona fide abuse or neglect then PAS is not an appropriate diagnosis. In addition, it is possible that as children mature they want to spend more time with friends in their home neighborhood and may resist visitation with a parent if it requires too many sacrifices of social activities. This too is not necessarily PAS. In order to determine that PAS is the causal factor underlying the child's attitudes and feelings toward one parent, the therapist ideally should see both parents. Based on extensive interviewing with the child and the parents, the therapist can conclude that PAS is present if the child's feelings and attitudes toward one parent appear to be a product of the feelings and attitudes of the other parent as opposed to being based in the child's reality. Gardner's eight manifestations of PAS can serve as a helpful checklist. Clawar and Rivlin (1991) also offer several signs that a child has been programmed, which may appear during treatment. These are described below along with examples, when applicable. These can be considered based on information obtained from joint or individual sessions.

Contradictory Statements

If the child makes contradictory statements about the targeted parent, this may indicate the presentation of a "programmed" message alongside a more genuine statement. For example, if a child states, "I hate my mommy" and then quickly adds that she misses her mother greatly, the therapist should consider that one of these sentiments is a programmed message while the other is a reflection of genuine feelings. As Veronica said, "I never could hate him, even though I had to say I did. The only reason I'd say it was to please my mum." As a child Veronica may have revealed both "hate" and "love" messages about her father, providing a clue that the negative statements were implanted from an outside source. Maria, even as an adult revealed such a contradictory statement about her father, the targeted parent, when she said, "I was very fearful of my father but I loved him very much and we had a close relationship."

Access to Inappropriate Information about the Targeted Parent

When children have access to information about the targeted parent that children do not usually have about their parents, someone, most likely the alienating parent, is providing the child with information in order to unduly influence him or her. Examples include children knowing or believing that the targeted parent had an affair, is an alcoholic, or is an inadequate lover or provider. This was common among the adult children of PAS interviewed, indicating that alienating parents did not exercise restraint in what kind of information they shared with their children about the targeted parent. For example, Robin commented, "What I was told was that he was very abusive and that he was an alcoholic, that he used to beat me and my brother and my mother, and he would come home drunk and take money and would go out drinking with it, that he was a womanizer." Oliver said, "She said he was an alcoholic, which I knew. I didn't know what alcoholism was." Alix explained, "My mom was very vocal about everything. She was like, 'Oh he beat me around and he was drunk and he drank a fifth of vodka and he held me down and I was crying and he wouldn't let me up.' My mom gave me details about everything." Iris said, "But she kept telling us how bad he was and he was no good and he was just going to hurt us and he was molesting these children. We didn't even understand what molest meant."

In all these statements the adult children of PAS are revealing access to knowledge when they were children that was beyond their capacity to understand. If children reveal during a therapy session that they have negative opinions about the targeted parent which appear to be based on information that children typically do not, and probably should not have, this is a clue that the child is being given information in order to influence his or her attitudes about the targeted parent.

Character Assaults

If the child assaults the character of the targeted parent with a blanket moral condemnation, this may be a sign of PAS. Children usually have a more generous view of parents than revealed by children with PAS, who can be vitriolic in their denigration of the targeted parent. In general, children tend not to make moral judgments about their parents (until they are teenagers), so such statements stand out as ideas placed there by an adult. Roberta shared that her mother, "Hated the way he thought. There were so many things over the years, he's dirty." As a child Melinda condemned her mother (the targeted parent) for being lazy and irresponsible, accusations she repeatedly heard from her father and stepmother. One indication of PAS is that the complaints are usually about characteristics that children do not normally think about. For example, children who complain that their parents are too permissive and should be harsher with them are revealing attitudes most likely programmed by the alienating parent. Even the most upstanding youth will not regularly seek punishment.

Alliance with the Alienating Parent

Children who use "us" and "we" to refer to themselves and the alienating parent are indicating an enmeshment that may be a component of PAS. Statements such as, "Why doesn't Daddy leave us alone," or "Mommy always bothers us," indicate that the child is aligned with one parent against the other. Alienating parents tend to talk in the us–them language of cult leaders, and children who repeat such statements are probably hearing them from the alienating parent. Amelia said of her father, the targeted parent, "He didn't love nobody but himself. He didn't care about us." In statements such as these, the child is confusing the targeted parent having left the marriage with leaving the children. Carrie's mother told her, "Dad left us, Dad abandoned us." This was said despite the fact that her father was visiting regularly.

Spying on the Targeted Parent

Children who reveal that they are spying on the targeted parent, are providing an important clue that they are involved with PAS. Children do not usually spy on their parents (or do so for their own curiosity not on behalf of the other parent), and doing so reveals the hidden influence of the alienating parent. When alienating parents ask their children to spy on the targeted parent, they are indicating that they think the targeted parent is dishonest (otherwise they would ask for the information outright) and malicious (purposefully withholding information that the alienating parent desires or needs). In this way the alienating parent garners the sympathy of the child and places the child in a position of working against the targeted parent. Mark told how his mother, "Would send me out on search and hunt missions where I would have to go and look for him and find him, and then when I would find him I had to come back and report and she would tell me what she thought he was doing." Patricia was instructed to call her mother's work number and listen to her voice mail in order to provide her father with evidence that her mother was involved in an extramarital affair.

Using Adult Phrases

Children who use language that is clearly outside their typical vocabulary and sophistication level are indicating that the thoughts are probably not their own. This clue is similar to the "borrowed scenarios" described by Gardner (1998). Children adopting wholesale the language and ideas of an adult are revealing PAS. Oliver explained that his mother refused visitation by saying, "Well, he wanted to see me but my mother wouldn't let him and she wanted to show him the price of business." Although he was an adult when he made the statement, it appears that he was remembering the language that was used at the time of the alienation. This would be an example of using an adult phrase because most children do not say "the price of business." Ron told, "When my dad oftentimes would call she would make me say to him that he was a fucking asshole, a fucking bastard." Again, language not typical for a young boy about 9 years of age. He went on to explain, "Sometimes she would make me say that he was a womanizer . . . I didn't know what that meant and here I was calling him one." Mitch told the story of how he had a telephone put to his ear and he said about his father, "I don't ever want to see him again and I have no interest in meeting with him." The phrase "no interest in meeting with him" is not a typical phrase for a young child. Such adult phrases spoken by children suggest the presence of programming.

Black–White/Good–Bad Language
to Describe Parents

When a child describes one parent as all good and the other as all bad, this is a sign that the child is aligned with one parent against the other. This is similar to Gardner's (1998) observation of the lack of ambivalence toward the alienating parent, one of the eight manifestations of PAS. Statements such as, "I believe everything my father says," may indicate PAS. One adult child of PAS described her (targeted parent) father as "evil." Jonah said he felt toward his mother, the targeted parent, "It was just pure hatred of her and pure trying to destroy her and get her out of my life. I believed that everyone else was wrong and that my father was right and that he was the one that actually cared about me and everyone else just wanted to do me harm." Larissa felt tremendous animosity toward her father, "I grew to detest him, with a truly visceral hate. I couldn't stand to be in the same room with him, or to even talk to him or have him talk to me." Patricia explained her feelings about her parents when she was a child in the following terms. "He was perfect, and she was a horrible person." After a certain age, children are able to see their parents as having both good and bad qualities, not as one being all good and the other as all bad. Thus, children who maintain a simplistic, polarized version of parents may be under the influence of PAS.

Seeing the Alienating Parent as a Victim of the Targeted Parent

When children are not involved in custody or parental disputes they are not inclined to develop opinions about who is harming whom (unless they witness firsthand the abuse of one parent by the other). It is only when alienating parents discuss such matters with the child or in some way indicate that the targeted parent is the cause of the alienating parent's problems, that children would develop such ideas. When they do express such strong statements that one parent "ruined the family" or is the cause of all the suffering of the other parent, it is likely that these ideas were induced by the alienating parent. Hannah had such a belief, "I did what I could do to make her life easier because her life was so hard because of my father. That was my mantra, Mom's life is hard. I have to try to help her." Edward, too, blamed his father for his mother's unhappiness, "She was depressed a lot and he got the blame for it. She didn't know so much what depression was but she knew she wasn't happy and she knew it was all his fault. It made me sad and angry at him." Larissa, "believed her, that she was totally and completely hard done and that my father was the source of all the troubles in her life, and in the family." This level of sympathy for one parent at the expense of positive feeling toward the other parent is a sign of PAS (unless the targeted parent is actually abusive).

Fear of Contact with the Targeted Parent

In the absence of abuse or neglect, fear of a parent is unwarranted. Several of the adult children of PAS shared that their alienating parents tried to create an impression that the targeted parent was dangerous, reckless, or in some way a person to be feared. David's experience is a case in point.

*We had a single car garage and we had windows on the garage
door, and then Mom had them taken out and replaced with solid
panels. The telephone number was changed to an unlisted number
and it just seemed like . . . like it was a secret where we lived and
the phone number, she told us not to give him the number. Then
we moved a second time and I hadn't seen my dad in several
years and it was a big secret and I wasn't supposed to tell anyone
where we lived. She just didn't want him to know. Something bad
might happen. She wouldn't even say that she was afraid of him,
just that she was afraid and not to let Dad know where we lived.
I wasn't supposed to talk to him.*

Mitch shared that when he was a little boy and his father came
to visit, his mother made him hide under the kitchen table. "I
woke up one morning and said that I didn't want to go to
school and she said, 'Your father is home. You better get under-
neath the kitchen table.' I just remember it was a thing where
she made me feel a little bit kind of scared about it or something." In the absence of abuse, children who express fear of
one parent have probably been programmed to do so.

Anxiety Arousal Concerning
the Targeted Parent

If a child expresses anxiety when discussing the targeted parent, for no apparent reason, then the alienating parent may be
influencing the child to believe that something bad will happen
to the alienating parent or to the child at the hands of the targeted parent. In either case, the child has an unrealistic view of
the targeted parent or is emotionally enmeshed with the alienating parent. Examples include telling the child that the targeted
parent will kidnap or harm the child when there is no history
of that kind of behavior or reason to believe that it is about to
occur. When the parent tells this to the child it induces anxiety
that can be observed in the session. Mitch was told, "To never
get in the car with him or anyone else no matter what they said,
even if they had some documentation to show that she was
dead and you have to come with me now, to not trust anyone
to get in the car because documentation can be falsified and

that he wanted to kidnap me. She always said he tried to take me away from her and that I had to always be careful and watch over my shoulder and that kind of thing."

Keeping Secrets from the Targeted Parent

Secret keeping is also an indication that the alienating parent and the child are colluding against the targeted parent. A child who has secrets with the alienating parent may feel remorse and shame. The child may then resist contact with the targeted parent in order to avoid feeling guilty. The child may also keep secrets because he or she has been led to believe that the targeted parent does not really love him or her or care enough to protect him or her. Melinda did not tell her mother that her father (the alienating parent) was molesting her. Her explanation of why she did not tell her mother was explored in the following exchange:

Q: How come you didn't tell your mom about it?
A: My *mom*????
Q: Yes.
A: I don't know. I just didn't want to bother her because she was very . . . she had her own life and I didn't want to upset her.

Melinda's father and stepmother reinforced in her the belief that her mother was too busy to really care about her. She seemed to have absorbed this message, indicated by the fact that she thought it would be a "bother" to her mother to find out that her daughter was being sexually abused.

Mirroring the Alienating Parent

Repeating beliefs wholesale from the alienating parent's point of view, or seeing the worst in the targeted parent, are also signs of PAS, as it was for Carl: "The impression was always that he was an alcoholic and he was probably living on skid row. I grew up with images of my father lying in a ditch." Another example would be if a child assumed the worst no matter what the targeted parent did. For example, a targeted parent who tried to maintain contact is accused of harassment, but when the attempts at contact stop that parent is accused of abandonment. When the child places the targeted parent in a no-win situation, PAS is at work.

Confusion Over Importance of the Targeted Parent

A child who makes a statement about not needing a father or mother (especially if there has been a stepparent to "replace" the targeted parent) may be signaling the presence of programmed ideas. Robin explained that his mother replaced his father with a new father and from that day on he was to refer to this person as daddy. He did not even have a word to refer to the person who used to be called daddy. Eventually Robin stopped referring to his father with the word daddy or father, and when asked about his father would talk about his stepfather. If he had been in therapy and asked about his father he probably would have indicated confusion about that person's role in his life, suggesting the presence of PAS.

Guilt Over Having Kept Secrets from and Hurting the Targeted Parent

Many of the adult children of PAS since rethinking their childhood have experienced guilt about how they treated their targeted parent. This was certainly the case for Patricia, "I also sometimes put her down to make him happy. This haunts me to this day. I never wanted to do anything to hurt her." Elaine felt that she was a "horrible, horrible person" for siding with her mother against her father. If such statements are made in the presence of a therapist, they are clear signs that the child is being asked to act against his or her own better judgment and conscience in order to please the alienating parent.

Disregard for the Targeted Parent's Authority

Blatant disregard for the authority of the targeted parent may indicate that the alienating parent is creating conflict or encouraging the child to not respect the targeted parent. Jonah went from joint visitation to living full-time with his father, the alienating parent, because he had become unmanageable for his mother. "I tortured her so much when I was there for the three days that she couldn't handle it. It was just too much for her." When Felicity returned from visitation with her father, the alienating parent, she would be difficult for her mother, "not on the same team," as she explained. "When I came home I would be angry at my mom and I felt like she was the bad guy and that came up in our arguments a lot. For a long time I guess I felt like I was opposed to her instead of living with her. Every time I came home from my dad's we would argue, with me feeling like she is this terrible person."

A therapist can keep an eye out for situations in which it appears as if the alienating parent is inciting conflict between the child and the targeted parent, although of course the child may not be aware of the invisible hand of the alienating parent working behind the scenes. Examples include scheduling desirable activities during the time the child is supposed to be with the targeted parent so that the child feels resentful of missing the activities, and demanding that the child do homework or other unpleasant activities while at the targeted parent's home in order to negatively influence the time the child and targeted parent spend together. Kate had that experience. "Like we'd [she and her father] be calm and happy but I'd be stewing about and thinking about it, turning over the thoughts in my head, tying to make sense. . . . One Halloween she [her mother] lost my candy. Instead of telling me she lost the candy she said that she would take it home and send it to my dad for me to enjoy there and a day later she said he lost it and then like four years later . . . years later . . . I was turning it over in my head and I asked him 'What did you do with my candy? Why did you lose my candy?'" When the alienating parent imposes rules about what the child can and cannot do while at the targeted parent's home, this undermines the authority of the targeted parent and keeps the child tied to the alienating parent. If the alienating parent tells outright lies about ways in which the targeted parent supposedly hurt the child, this, of course, also indicates that the alienating parent is trying to create problems between the child and the targeted parent.

Brain Twirling

Some children in therapy may reveal confusion over the messages the alienating parent is sending. For years, Edward had been given the message that his father was the source of all unhappiness in the family. However, when he became enraged at his father and attacked him, his mother then became angry with him. "I exploded at him. I don't remember what touched it off but I do know I became so angry I attacked him. I was about 8. What was really confusing was she started to defend him. 'How dare you talk to your father like that.'" When children in therapy express confusion over whether or not they are supposed to hate the targeted parent, PAS is probably an underlying factor.

Threatening the Targeted Parent with Court Battles and the Police

If a child reveals in therapy that she has threatened the targeted parent with going to court, it suggests that the alienating parent is discussing custody and legal issues with the child, something most experts agree is not appropriate. When it becomes clear that the statements made toward the targeted parent reveal hostility and a desire to manipulate or emotionally blackmail that parent, PAS is at work.

Reporting that the Alienating Parent is More a Friend than a Parent

When children feel that their parents are more like friends than parents, it may indicate that the alienating parent is sharing too much personal information with the child, is relying on the child for support and comfort, and may not be setting appropriate limits. These alone do not signify PAS but indicate a family system in which PAS is more likely to occur. Veronica said of her relationship with her (alienating parent) mother, "We were really good friends. It was brilliant. There was a lot of past abuse and she told me everything. I used to follow her. I was called her shadow by Stepdad because wherever she went I stayed with her. When I was little, when I was a teenager we'd do everything together." Alix explained that when she was growing up, "I felt she was in love with me. As sick as that may sound . . . I felt like she was in love with me. Her favorite saying was 'We are as close as twins.'" Hannah recalled her relationship with her mother, the alienating parent, "It was fabulous. I was her daughter. I didn't individuate from her. I did everything for her to make her life better. I felt very close to her. I told her everything. I made life decisions based on whether or not it would please my mother." This degree of enmeshment is a sign that the child and the alienating parent have an unhealthy relationship, which could lead to an alignment against the targeted parent.

Fear of the Alienating Parent

Children who express (verbal or nonverbal) fear of the alienating parent are providing a clue that some of their beliefs and actions may be motivated out of a desire to avoid the anger of that parent. When Jonah was asked how his father turned him against his mother, he explained, "It didn't necessarily have anything to do with what he said, it was just the fear because my father was an alcoholic. It was the fear that he instilled in me if I didn't comply with his demands that harm was going to come to either himself or the rest of my family." David said, "I was thinking this is crazy that it seems like every time I talk about my dad all hell breaks loose and it was easier to not broach the subject. At that point in my life to survive you just didn't talk about him at all." Although he probably did not mean survival in the literal sense, he did seem to feel that in order to manage his life he had to renounce his father.

In addition to these 19 signs of PAS described above, Clawar and Rivlan (1991) also offer several clues derived from statements the child makes in session about the alienating parent. Statements made by the child about the alienating parent are the most useful clues because there is less room for interpretation and bias on the part of the therapist. Children who inadvertently reveal that the alienating parent makes them feel bad for loving the targeted parent give the therapist a lot of information to work with in identifying the presence of PAS. Examples of statements the therapist should keep in mind include the alienating parent not wanting the child to have a good time with or love the targeted parent ("Daddy doesn't like it when I have fun at Mommy's house"); that the alienating parent gives nonverbal signals that the child should not love and value the targeted parent ("Mommy isn't as nice to me when I tell her that I want to be with Daddy"); and that the alienating parent directed the child to make certain statements to the therapist ("Mommy told me to tell you that Daddy is a bad man"). These are valuable statements also because the child has conscious access to the information and so the therapist can directly respond to the content.

It is important to note that these indicators are not organized by importance and that there are no empirical guidelines for determining how many have to be present, in what strength, and for what duration before a determination of PAS should be made.

Clinical Interventions with Alienated Children: Exit Counseling

Once it has been determined that PAS has occurred, the therapist's role changes from assessment to intervention. If the therapist is working within the legal system, then the necessary recommendations can be made to the court. Assuming that the therapist is working outside the legal system, the question becomes how can the therapist help a child who has been programmed against the targeted parent to have a more realistic assessment of that parent. It is important to note the choice of the word *realistic*. The goal of therapy should be to help the child client acknowledge and work within reality. The suggestions offered below are not a blueprint for therapy. Rather, they represent issues and ideas that the therapist should bear in mind over the course of the regular work with an alienated child, issues that can be integrated into individual sessions, regardless of the orientation or the goals of the therapeutic work.

From the outset, it is important to address the child's current relationship with each parent. If the child is living with the targeted parent and the alienating parent is the noncustodial parent with limited visitation, the implications for intervention and treatment of PAS are quite different from situations where the child is living with the alienating parent and has a minimal or highly conflicted relationship with the targeted parent. The therapist will need to bear in mind at all times the constellation of parental influence on the child and the likelihood that changes in custody could be made, if warranted. Further, as Ellis (2005) has pointed out. PAS is the solution for the child, not the problem. For the child, the problem is being caught in the middle of interparental conflict and the pressure to choose sides. PAS solves that problem for the child, and thus, like being in a cult, is not experienced as something that needs to be changed. The therapist needs to work with the child to help him or her understand first and foremost that alignment with one parent against the other is in fact a problem (because the child is losing out on the relationship with the other parent).

It is also important to note that individual therapy for PAS children is likely to be subject to third-party dynamics that undermine the endeavor (Garber, 2004). Specifically, Garber proposed that parents who are threatened by the therapist-child alliance can significantly and sometimes fatally interfere with that relationship. He offered some suggestions for therapists working with children in high-conflict families that may forestall or mitigate these undermining tactics.

Given that alienating parents function like cult leaders (see Chapter 2), an obvious avenue to explore is whether exit counseling techniques developed to help individuals involved with cults could be applied to children with PAS. Briefly, exit counseling is the strategy that is used to provide information to individuals currently involved in a cult in order to help them make an informed decision about their cult involvement. Although some exit counselors have a bias toward wanting the individual to decide to leave the cult, their stated goal is to provide education and information (Clark et al., 1993). An exit counselor meets with the concerned family to find out why they believe their child is involved with a cult. The counselors then educate themselves and the family about the particular cult in which the individual is involved and arrange for an intensive multiday intervention in which the information about the cult is provided to the cult member in order to help him or her make a more informed choice about participation in the group. The primary strategy of the exit counselor is to show to the individual that (1) he or she has been manipulated; (2) the cult actually victimizes others; and (3) the cult member has been adversely affected by involvement in the cult. As Giambalvo explained, "The interventions are based on an educational model. The cultist has been a victim of a sophisticated set of manipulations. Once she or he becomes aware of these manipulations, basic integrity usually will not allow a cultist to remain a part of a system that victimizes others—no matter how lofty the goals. An intervention, for the most part, is a discourse on ethics, values, and integrity" (1993, p. 149).

Unfortunately, the model of a short, intensive intervention may not apply wholesale to work with child victims of PAS. First, exit counselors work with adults while therapists are working with children. The ethical constraints of conducting mental health interventions with minors are different from those that apply when working with adults. For example, if the outcome of the PAS exit counseling session is for the child to "walk away" from the alienating parent, this needs to be carefully thought through. The loss of the parent, no matter how emotionally abusive, is still a significant event for the child, especially if the alienating parent is the primary caretaker and the child has minimal involvement with the targeted parent. Second, there is usually objective information about the cult available that can be revealed to the individual, which may spark a reconsideration of involvement in the cult. For example, exit counselors can gain access to internal organizational documents that reveal a darker side to the cult operations. The discrepancies between the stated purpose of the cult and this underside may be sufficiently disturbing to the cult member to awaken a desire to leave the cult. However, such information is typically not available about individuals (i.e., the alienating parent) and even if it were available, there may be no content to share with the child. Many parents who perpetrate PAS are probably law-abiding citizens with no criminal actions to hide (although the alienating parents who have an antisocial personality disorder may in fact have engaged in criminal activity). Third, walking away from a cult is not the same as walking away from a parent. As powerful as cult leaders are, in the end they are merely parent substitutes not actual parents. For all these reasons, working with PAS children is only partially comparable to working with cult members.

Despite these differences, there are several components of exit counseling that may be applicable. The first is to examine the negative impact of the alienating parent on the child's choices and well-being. Before taking on an exit counseling assignment, exit counselors try to determine the ways in which the cultist's life has changed due to cult involvement. "The most important question to discuss and answer is how the cultist has changed since joining the group, for concern about destructive changes is the family's ethical justification for considering an exit counseling" (Clark et al., 1993, p. 16). This is something that can and should be explored in therapy with a PAS child. Most likely, the concept of "joining" does not apply to PAS unless a child moved from the targeted parent's home to the alienating parent's home. Nonetheless, the therapist can explore with the child the values, hobbies, and friends that the child relinquished in order to please the alienating parent. Children who are readily willing to abandon friends, interests, and talents for the alienating parent can be encouraged to look at these choices, and then can be provided with a reality check that most parents do not and should not ask their children for such sacrifices.

Second, exit counselors try to remind cultists that it is normal and advisable to have relationships with their friends and family on the outside. In exit counseling, the family members are present in the room during the intervention in order to demonstrate their love and support. Cultists may have been told that their family no longer loves them, and the best way to counter this is to have the parents and family present during the intervention espousing their love and support for the cult member. This too applies to clinical interventions with PAS children who may have become convinced that the targeted parent does not really love them. The best way to challenge that notion is to schedule sessions with the child and targeted parent together to remind the child who that person is and the love they share, to provide the child with what Gardner (1993) referred to as "living examples" of the targeted parent. Joint sessions with the child and targeted parent might also be a valuable tool for providing them with time together. The therapist can help the child explain to the targeted parent the primary concerns about their relationship and afford the targeted parent an opportunity to explain his or her side and to show a willingness to improve. It is very important during these sessions to not let the child denigrate the targeted parent because this will only solidify the distorted negative feelings. The therapist must show respect for that parent and model to the child that this person is worthy of respect. Warshak (2001a) recounts a touching story of reuniting a child with her mother, which was accomplished primarily through his respecting and honoring the mother's talents as a lace maker and encouraging the mother to share these talents with her daughter. One thing to bear in mind when scheduling these sessions is that it will be important to ensure that the alienating parent is not in the waiting room during these visits. That parent's physical proximity may be enough to poison the child's ability to be open and positive toward the targeted parent. Educating the child to the fact that he or she needs both parents and that it is not in his or her best interest to relinquish one for the other can also be an important component of treatment.

Third, a portion of exit counseling is devoted to educating the cultist about mind control tactics in order to demonstrate how cult indoctrination works. Videos and written material are available to demonstrate how most people are susceptible to mind control techniques under certain situations. Educating the child client about mind control and brainwashing techniques can also be a component of therapy with a PAS child in order to provide him or her with the tools to combat it. Warshak (2001a) presents some creative ways that targeted parents can discuss mind control with their children, utilizing examples from marketing and advertising techniques, which most children have familiarity with via magazine and television commercials. Therapists, too, can demonstrate these techniques to explain to the child how it is possible to be tricked into believing something that is not completely true.

Exit counselor Steven Hassan found that encouraging the cult member to take the perspective of the friends and family members left behind is an effective intervention tool, "the way to unlock blind faith is to introduce new perspectives" (1988, p. 164). He explained:

> Each time the member is able to step out of his shoes and into the shoes of another—whether a member of a different group, or even his parents or his leader—he is weakening his psychological rigidity. Indeed, encouraging a cult member psychologically to take another perspective enables him to test his reality. In this process, the information he was programmed with takes on a new light." (1988, p. 164).

In his role as an exit counselor he asked clients to think about their cult involvement from the viewpoint of a respected older brother, a parent, anyone for whom the cult member has acknowledged and maintained respect. This technique could also be utilized by therapists working with PAS children. A related strategy offered by Hassan is to ask the cult member to remember the goals she or he used to have and then to imagine his or her life in the future. In this way, a discrepancy might be revealed to the individual regarding the impact of the cult experience. Again, PAS children who have made sacrifices for their alienating parent may be able to visualize the negative impact of those sacrifices in the future more easily than acknowledging them in the present.

Utilizing the model of exit counseling from cults can also be helpful for understanding the stages of working with a PAS child. In exit counseling these stages are experienced within a matter of days. Progressing through these stages in the treatment with PAS children—outside the context of an intensive exit counseling model—may take months if not longer.

Hostility, Denial, Dissociation

Initially, cult members are adamant that they are not in a harmful or detrimental environment and that their choice to be involved in the cult is made freely and with full knowledge of the consequences. They respond quite negatively to the motives of the family members who arranged the exit counseling session and are openly hostile toward the exit counselor. There appears to be no awareness of the mind control techniques used or the manipulations of the cult leader. There is complete loyalty to the cult and its leader.

Resistance

At some point the opposition to the message of the intervention turns to resistance, that is, conscious lack of interest in hearing anything negative. The statement might be something like, "Even if you knew bad things about the cult I do not want to know about it. I am committed to this choice and I do not want to hear anything that you think will change my mind." Although this may not appear to be progress, it is a step forward because the cult member is admitting that he or she is fighting against countervailing opinions rather than believing that there could be nothing negative to say about the cult.

Interest

Interest is defined as some curiosity as to what the exit counselor is saying. There is an acknowledgment that there might be some value to the exit counselor's opinions and information about the cult. The cult member expresses interest in hearing what the exit counselor has to say. He or she may still have no intention of leaving the cult but there is an acknowledgment that other people have opinions about the cult that are worth hearing.

Participation

During the participation phase, the cult member asks questions of the exit counselor and begins to actively participate in the intervention.

Making Connections

Making connections allows the cult member to apply to his or her own experiences the information about the cult and about thought reform. It is usually at this point that the cult member decides to separate from the cult.

These stages can be considered when a therapist is working with a child in PAS in order to gauge the child's readiness to progress through the process of wanting to acknowledge PAS and reestablish a relationship with the targeted parent.

WORKING WITH PAS CHILDREN: THERAPEUTIC CONSIDERATIONS

Children with PAS are currently involved in a relationship with an exploitive and coercive parent. It is quite possible that the child has developed some of these same interpersonal attributes as well (through modeling and through identification with the aggressor). This and related issues are discussed below.

Catching the Child when He or She is Coercive

One way to help the child learn that coercion is not an appropriate way for people to treat each other is for the therapist to confront the client about his or her own behavior. Thus, if a child client is manipulative in some fashion, it behooves the therapist to bring this to the child's attention and model for him or her how to stand up to someone who behaves that way. The therapist could say, "It makes me feel intimidated and worried that you are going to walk away from me, when you speak to me in that demanding and insistent tone. I am wondering if there is anyone in your life who talks to you this way." In this way the therapist is encouraging the child to question the alienating parent without actually criticizing that parent. The message is conveyed that anyone who interacts with the child in a coercive manner is doing something worth examining. This should give the child something to consider without putting the child in a position of having to defend the alienating parent to the therapist.

Sessions with the Child and the Alienating Parent

It is also suggested that the therapist schedule sessions with the client and the alienating parent together. This should allow the therapist to observe the child's comfort level, the degree to which the child speaks for him- or herself, and inconsistencies between what the child says and does when the alienating parent is and is not present. Inclusion of the alienating parent in the treatment session might have an added benefit of allowing the child to observe the alienating parent be disingenuous in what he or she says to the therapist (i.e., giving the "right" answer). This provides hard evidence to the child that the alienating parent is being dishonest and insincere. For example, it is unlikely that an alienating parent will denigrate the targeted parent or forbid the child to see that parent while in the presence of the therapist.

Family Systems Work

Joint sessions with the child and the alienating parent, as suggested above, are consistent with a family systems perspective. From this viewpoint, PAS represents a dysfunctional family system, which can best be addressed by working with various family subsystems (child and targeted parent, child and alienating parent, etc.). Many aspects of PAS such as the "parental child" or the "spousal child" and other forms of intergenerational alliances can be viewed as problems in the family system, even when that family is a postdivorce family system. According to Jean Goldsmith, when a child in a divorced family is symptomatic:

> it is apparent that when the noncustodial parent continues to be involved in child rearing, it is important to include all of the original family members as part of the treatment plan. This position is consistent with an understanding of the family members as comprising an ongoing post-divorce family system, for all the original family members will be expected to affect and be affected by the presenting problem. (1982, p. 307)

Needless to say, many aspects of PAS when present in intact families should also be addressed in a family system context.

Lack of Coercion

It is vital that the therapist of a child with PAS not be coercive or manipulative in any fashion. This will serve as a powerful counterpoint to the relationship between the child and the alienating parent. Opportunities for the child to experience healthy, noncoercive relationships may help him or her realize that the relationship with the alienating parent is not healthy. Validating the child's ideas and feelings, allowing the child to explore uncertainties and express needs and wishes should all be incorporated into therapy. Phrasing life goals, dreams, talents, and wishes as, "What do you want for yourself?" will be very important for PAS children who are used to thinking about their parent's needs, not their own. However, this does not mean that the therapist should never challenge the child's belief systems (e.g., about the alienating parent being all good and the targeted parent being all bad).

Helping the Child Manage Awareness of PAS While Living with the Alienating Parent

As noted above, it is probably easier for individuals to walk away from a cult than a parent. Unless there is an available targeted parent with whom the child has or could develop a close and loving relationship, the goal of therapy with a PAS child may not necessarily be to have the child leave the cult of the alienating parent. This needs to be considered from the very beginning of treatment. Is there a targeted parent in the child's life whom the child could live with or is the alienating parent the only viable parenting resource for this child. If the child is currently being physically or sexually abused or seriously emotionally abused, then child protective authorities need to be involved regardless of an alternative parenting resource. Absent abuse and absent a targeted parent, the therapist's goal should be to improve the child's self-esteem and support the child's pursuit of his or her own goals. Ideally the alienating parent can be included in treatment and the relationship between the child and the alienating parent can be improved as well.

Assessing Co-Occurring Maltreatment

As noted throughout this book, PAS children are at elevated risk for other forms of maltreatment as well as exposure to parental alcoholism. Children need to be assessed for physical and sexual abuse as well as exposure to parental alcoholism in order to ensure that the full range of familial issues are being addressed and that the child is currently in a safe environment (although it may be far from perfect).

Not Getting Caught in the Alienation

PAS children most likely experience two very different versions of the targeted parent: (the child's own memory or experience with that person and the alienating parent's version.) If the child has ongoing contact with both the alienating and the targeted parent, it is likely to be a very confusing experience that entails an ongoing shifting of reality. The therapist of a PAS child needs to be conscious of not replicating that experience in his or her dealings with the parents. For example, the therapist might meet with the targeted parent and experience that person as reasonable and primarily a victim of the PAS. When the therapist then next meets with the child client, he or she may be exposed to vitriolic denigration of the targeted parent. Most therapists are trained to feel empathy and compassion for their clients and will naturally feel negatively toward the targeted parent. Likewise, although the therapist may understand intellectually that the alienating parent is narcissistic and exploitive, he or she may be charmed or unconsciously intimidated by that parent. These tendencies to "buy into" the programmed message are very dangerous for children in PAS because the false "reality" of the PAS (the alienating parent is all good and the targeted parent is all bad) needs to be challenged in order for the child to embrace the true reality of the PAS. When the therapist endorses this false reality, recognition of PAS will be delayed.

Countertransference Toward the Targeted Parent

As noted above, the therapist might adopt some of the negative attitudes of the child toward the targeted parent as a result of the alliance with the alienated child. But the therapist might develop negative feelings toward the targeted parent for other reasons as well. For example, the therapist might feel guilty that he or she is not able to prevent the alienation and salvage the child's relationship with the targeted parent. Although the child is the client, the therapist may feel some obligation or desire to help the targeted parent (if the targeted parent is a sympathetic person in his or her own right). If the therapist feels bad that he or she is not able to assist the targeted parent, the therapist may turn these feelings into avoidance and anger (to ward off shame, guilt, and sadness over the loss experienced by the targeted parent). There may even be a tendency to blame the targeted parent and for the therapist to conclude, "That could never happen to me and my child, there really must be something wrong with that person for the child to reject his or her parent that way." Blaming the targeted parent allows the therapist to maintain an alliance with the child client, and allows the therapist to avoid dealing with the entrenched and seemingly unsolvable problem of PAS.

In light of the fact that the psychological literature lacks tested interventions, some therapists may not want to acknowledge that PAS is present. Further, the therapist may be concerned that if he or she confronts the child about the PAS, the child will terminate therapy. To some extent the therapist, like the child, is in a bind. If the therapist admits that PAS is occurring, the therapist may not join with, and so lose the client (in light of how defensive children with PAS can be). The therapist may also enrage the narcissistic manipulative alienating parent, and will be faced with admitting that there is a problem which clinicians know too little about. The alternative, to deny the PAS, allows the therapist to temporarily avoid the guilt and shame of failing the targeted parent, avoid the rage of the alienating parent and of the child, and allows the child and therapist to have a shared, albeit distorted, reality. In this sense, the therapist is replicating the child's experience. The child joins the alienating parent in order to have a shared reality with that parent. By not addressing PAS, the therapist joins the child for essentially the same reason, with a similar detrimental effect. Of course, countertransference related to the therapist's own history with divorce, visitation, narcissistic or manipulative parents, and abused, victimized children could all play into the therapist's response to PAS in a child client.

SUMMARY

The therapist working with a child who may be currently involved in a PAS situation can utilize the signs of PAS described above. Once PAS has been identified, the therapist can use aspects of exit counseling (developed from working with cult members) as a guide for working with such a client. Although the goal may not necessarily be for the child to leave the cult of the alienating parent, the therapist can help build the child's self-esteem and help the child acknowledge the reality of the coercion and abuse of power inherent in PAS. Awareness of the availability of the targeted parent will be crucial for such cases. When the targeted parent is still in the child's life, the child client can be helped to reestablish a positive relationship with that parent. At all times, the therapist must manage countertransference related to the dual experience of the targeted parent as both valued and reviled.

Chapter 11

Working with Targeted Parents

Grief fills the room up of my absent child, Lies in his bed,
walks up and down with me . . .

—William Shakespeare, *King John*

MENTAL HEALTH PROFESSIONALS WORKING WITH TARGETED PAR-
ents have many opportunities to provide education and support to people experiencing a tremendously painful time in
their lives. The loss of a child (be it complete or partial, physical
or emotional) is nothing short of devastating. Parents targeted
for parental alienation may feel helpless and overwhelmed by
the sudden change in their child and in the intensity of the
alienation campaign waged against them. Ideally an effective
intervention for parental alienation syndrome would exist,
which would then form the basis of working with targeted parents (in conjunction with the alienated child). In the absence of
tested, valid interventions, the following suggestions are offered to ease the burden of the alienation and provide whatever
insights can be gleaned as to how targeted parents can make
the most of the time they have with their child.

SELF-WORK

The adage that knowledge is power certainly applies to PAS.
Naming something makes it knowable and more accessible. It

seems quite plausible that many targeted parents do not know about parental alienation syndrome, and therefore are at a significant disadvantage in responding to the situation.

Education about Parental Alienation Syndrome

As Larissa commented about her father, "His biggest mistake was in not understanding that my mother's intentions were not good." Targeted parents who are not familiar with the concept of parental alienation syndrome could benefit from information and resources to help understand what is happening to their child. In this way they can determine whether court action is advisable either to change visitation and custody or to mandate treatment. Gardner's (1998) book is an excellent resource and a critical starting point for learning about the parental alienation syndrome. In the absence of such information, targeted parents may assume that the difficulties in their relationship with their child will resolve themselves naturally or that it is not really possible for a loving child to be turned against a parent. They may also assume that it is never advisable to speak negatively to a child about the other parent. Without understanding that parental alienation is at work, targeted parents may assume that the high road should always be taken and, therefore, may restrain themselves from countering the alienation when it appears. However, as both Gardner (1998) and Warshak (2001a) rightly pointed out, there are times when targeted parents must overcome the natural resistance to criticizing the other parent and address the alienation directly with their child.

As noted in Chapter 3, it may be advisable to approach the issue from a broad perspective. That is, rather than saying to the child that the other parent is engaging in a particular alienation strategy (which may or may not be true) it may make sense to discuss the concept generally with the child, by saying, for example, "Sometimes Daddy would rather we did not spend time together and feel close with each other. But that is not something you should have to think about. I know you love and need both your mommy and daddy." Depending on the age of the child, targeted parents and their child can develop strategies for countering the alienation; for example, by asking the child to make up his or her own mind about the targeted parent and not be influenced by others. In this way, targeted parents can try to limit the impact of the brainwashing and co-ercion. Gardner's (1984) *The Boys and Girls Book of Divorce* may be a useful teaching tool for PAS children, especially his recom-mendations regarding what children should do when their par-ents try to convince them to choose sides or speak badly of the other. He urges children to not heed the bad-mouthing and to make up their own mind about the other parent. For example, in situations of a mother denigrating the father, Gardner writes for children:

> At these times, it's better not to take what she says too seriously. You have to ask yourself at such times if your father really is the way she says he is. Have you seen him do these bad things she says he does? Have you heard him say the bad things she says he says? You also have to use your own opinions to help you decide whether she is right or wrong. (1984, p. 92)

Education about Personality Disorders

Parents targeted for parental alienation probably could benefit from a primer on personality disorders in order to help them determine whether such a designation is applicable to the other parent of their child. Knowing what they are dealing with may provide them with some clues as to how to interact more effec-tively with the alienating parent. However, it is not advisable to use labels such as *narcissist* or *psychopath* to the alienating parent or the child, as that may be considered inflammatory and derogatory.

Exploration of the Intergenerational Transmission of Parental Alienation

The discussion about personality disorders may lead to an ex-ploration of whether the targeted parents' own parents had a personality disorder and whether they experienced parental alienation syndrome in their family of origin. Perhaps there are intergenerational issues that can be addressed. The primary mechanism for the intergenerational transmission of parental alienation syndrome for the adult children was when an individual with a narcissistic parent (who alienated the child from the targeted parent) married someone who was also narcissistic. When that relationship ended, the narcissistic ex-spouse then utilized parental alienation strategies on the children of that relationship. Thus, targeted parents in therapy should probably explore the intergenerational dynamics that led them to marry a person like their own alienating parent and, thereby, repeat the pattern. For example, one dynamic could be that the low self-esteem that developed as a response to the parental alienation syndrome experienced as a child led to unconscious feelings of being unworthy of the love of one's own children.

Another fruitful avenue might be that targeted parents are in some way "honoring" the alienating parent by replicating the alienation. In other words, a young boy who was alienated from his father due to the alienation strategies of his mother, as a grown man may not be able to be close to his own children because that would activate his repressed rage at his mother for causing him to lose his father. Thus, he is preserving his relationship with his alienating mother by being alienated from his children. Alienation from his children may also protect him from the profound sense of loss he might feel if he were to be close to them and, thereby, realize what he had missed as a child. In this way, to be close to his children would awaken the unbearable longing for his own lost father. It is also possible that experiencing PAS as an adult is a way of honoring the targeted parent. Many of the adult children interviewed remarked that they only truly understood what their targeted parent experienced, when they became targets of PAS. As Veronica said, "I wrote a letter then saying I was sorry for what I put him through because I do understand he was in pain because I am feeling it."

Another lens through which to consider these intergenerational issues is that of the "obligation hierarchy" described by Boszormenyi-Nagy and Spark (1983). That is, targeted parents who were child victims of PAS may feel that they owe it to their own parents to replicate the PAS. For example, they may feel that they do not deserve to have a better outcome than their own targeted parents, and, therefore, are obligated to suffer PAS as adults in order to maintain a balanced psychological scorecard. This could be especially true for children who were particularly hostile and negative toward their targeted parent. This obligation to suffer PAS as an adult might also have been incurred in the relationship with the alienating parent who resented raising a child under tremendous hardship (the abandonment of the targeted parent, the inadequacy of the targeted parent, the unworthiness of the child). This too could cause such a child to feel that it is not his or her right to have a healthy functioning family in light of the unhappiness suffered by his or her own parents.

The intergenerational transmission of PAS may also be a version of the repetition compulsion described by Freud (1920/ 1955), in which individuals feel compelled to re-create the trauma of their childhood throughout their lives. Herman noted from her work with trauma survivors that, "traumatized people find themselves reenacting some aspect of the trauma scene in disguised form, without realizing what they are doing" (1997, p. 40). This phenomenon was borne out in discussion with the adult children of PAS, many of whom felt that because the targeted parent (appeared to have) abandoned them and found them unworthy, they deserved to have bad things happen to them throughout their lives. Rejection from the targeted parent or abuse by the alienating parent can combine to create a victim mentality in which adults replicate earlier feelings of helplessness and hopelessness in subsequent failed romantic relationships and loss of their own children. Walter, for example, commented that he behaved so badly in his relationships that, "It doesn't matter how strong they are, nobody is going to hang around my behavior," thereby increasing the likelihood that loved ones will abandon him.

Yet another way to think about the intergenerational transmission is lack of protection. That is, children who themselves are victims of parental alienation syndrome were not protected from the emotional manipulations and abuse of the alienating parent. Certainly the alienating parent did not protect them from the alienation strategies and the targeted parent did not successfully shield them and prevent the alienation. As adults, these adult children of parental alienation syndrome are not able to defend themselves from being the targets of alienation because they carry within them the belief that they cannot protect themselves. Josh's comment is particularly relevant to this, "It screwed me up in terms of boundaries with people . . . I didn't really learn fully to be assertive and stick up for myself and be an independent person." Such reasoning is consistent with van der Kolk, van der Hart, and Marmer's (1996) understanding that people need to be able to imagine some way of protecting themselves from harm and danger, and that the roots of this belief lie in children's experience of basic security from their caretakers. Thus, children who did not experience such basic safety and security from their caretakers are less able to secure protection for themselves as adults. This could explain comments such as Nancy's: "There is like an emptiness. You lose your mother and you lose your father and you're alone. I always felt alone. . . . I didn't know how to be a parent."

All of these lines of inquiry regarding the intergenerational transmission of PAS should be explored with targeted parents in therapy. It cannot be known whether or how this exploration and "self-work" will result in a successful resolution to the alienation. However, if targeted parents can be healthier and better adjusted, eventually they will be better parents to their alienated child, whenever that child is ready to have a relationship with them.

Education about Parenting

Along the same lines, most parents can benefit from parent education, be it formal or informal. This is especially true of parents who are being targeted for parental alienation. Targeted parents should consider taking a parenting class and working through whatever residual parenting issues that might be contributing to the conflict with their alienated child. The purpose is not to condemn or blame them but to help them improve parenting in whatever way it is possible to do so. Participation in a parent education program might also be looked upon favorably by judges or mediators involved in the case. Although no parenting program has been developed and validated specifically for targeted parents in cases of parental alienation syndrome, the principles of good parenting generally taught in any parenting program will be useful in this situation as well. Thus, the clients need to understand that the best defense is being the best possible parent. That means putting the child's needs first, being loving, warm, available, kind, fun, appropriate in limit setting, and creative. Parents should expose their children to art, literature, museums, nature, cooking, Yoga, the ocean, sports, music, current events, and all the joys and opportunities of life. All of these suggestions hold true regardless of whether they are divorced from or still living with the alienating parent. If targeted parents are still married to the alienating parent, encouraging the other parent to attend parenting classes as well is advised. Sometimes, hearing something from an expert is easier than hearing it from one's own spouse. It is also likely that in this context the alienating parent will have to endorse ideas that are directly opposed to alienation (supporting one's spouse, appropriate intergenerational boundaries, and so forth). In some cases verbally endorsing these ideas may influence the alienating parent's actual behavior, which could dramatically diminish the alienation.

Improving their Relationship
with the Alienating Parent

In many PAS situations it is probably not possible to improve relations with an "obsessed" alienator who seems completely focused on destroying the targeted parent's relationship with the child. On the other hand, it is worth exploring in therapy (and perhaps couples counseling as well) ways in which targeted parents could eliminate or avoid certain common problem areas. For example, if transition times are typically difficult because the alienating parent tends to raise sensitive issues in front of the children in "spur of the moment" confrontations, the targeted parents can recognize this trap and develop strategies for avoiding these scenarios. Targeted parents also need to ask themselves if there is anything they are doing that is making the situation worse, inflaming the hostility of the alienating parents. This exercise may be helpful in reducing their sense of helplessness and offer the satisfaction of knowing that they tried to the best of their ability to make interactions smoother with the other parent. Targeted parents still married to the alienating parent are in a better position to try to improve the relationship because there is some presumption of commitment from both parties to work together for the betterment of the family. Targeted parents could suggest couples counseling to work through unresolved and longstanding issues that are creating conflict and tension in the relationship. Perhaps, by having the marital relationship be more satisfying to the alienating parent, that parent will be less likely to try to have his or her needs (for revenge or comfort) met through alienating the children from the targeted parent.

Reading Stories about PAS

Powerlessness is a likely response to PAS (Vassiliou & Cartwright, 2001). One way to reduce some of the frustration and sense of being misunderstood and alone is for targeted parents to read fictional and nonfictional narratives about protracted custody battles. The use of narrative has a long tradition in the healing arts, including reading, writing, and listening to one's own as well as others' stories (Bettleheim, 1975; Brett, 1966; Burns, 2001; Giannini, 2001; Pennebaker, Colder, & Sharp, 1990). Nonfiction as well as fictional accounts of PAS abound (although often the term itself is not used) and there are several reasons why therapists and clients might want to read these stories as part of the therapeutic process. For example, reading stories about PAS offers the six "E's" of therapy: engagement, empowerment, education, enhancement, encouragement, enlightenment as described by Riordan, Mullis, and Nuchow (1996) and can begin to help targeted parents regain a sense of power and control. Therapists, as well, can enrich and deepen their own understanding of the parental alienation syndrome through such readings. Baker (2006) has provided a fully explicated analysis of the benefits of this effort and reviewed four particularly compelling true stories about targeted parents and alienated children.

RELATIONSHIP WITH THE PAS CHILD

Targeted parents need encouragement to stay involved in their children's lives. The more children have an independent and positive relationship with them, the harder it will be for the child to believe the negative ideas promulgated by the alienating parent. This mirrors Ellis's (2005) recommendation that targeted parents must erode the image of being the villain by offering experiences and information to the child about the parent that are incongruous with the information provided by the alienating parent.

Being an Involved Parent

If targeted parents behave as if the relationship with their child is not valued, their child will believe that and the seeds of parental alienation syndrome will grow even stronger. The job of targeted parents is to *not* provide fertile ground for the "seeds of alienation."

The alienating parent will take advantage of any lapses in judgment, and will certainly exploit such failings in subsequent legal confrontations. Being late for pickups, not showing up for visits, not attending major events in the child's life, endangering the child, not putting effort into making time spent together enjoyable and meaningful, will all be pointed out to the child (and to the court if applicable) by the alienating parent and will be used as part of the alienation campaign. These lapses will make the ground for alienation more fertile. In essence, targeted parents need to be aware of the consequences of their actions in the context of the alienation and possible legal proceedings, and hold themselves to a higher standard than other parents.

Although this may seem unfair, it is the reality of the situation. Targeted parents may have no control over what the alienating parent says about them but they do have control over how they behave with their child. They should avoid providing the alienating parent with ammunition that can be used against them. For example, Bonnie had a particularly difficult time when her mother pointed out that her father was not writing, "because that had some type of proof to it." It is especially important for targeted parents to provide safety and security to their child because these are the very areas that the alienating parent is undermining with the alienation strategies (see Chapter 3). Targeted parents should get up in the middle of the night with their child, if their child needs them. They should learn how to comfort their child; they should develop special routines and activities that just they and the child share together. The stronger the bond, the less able anyone will be to erode it. It is important, though, that these activities are performed out of love and not out of a need to be the most important person in the child's life. Parenting is not meant to be a competitive sport. The goal is to be the best parent possible, not to be the better of the two parents. These suggestions are particularly relevant for fathers who are targeted for alienation in traditional nuclear families where fathers are still less likely to be the caretaker. Thus, countering the alienation will require a greater degree of stretching in the parental role. Again, this is true regardless of the marital status of the targeted parent. In some Pattern 2 families, the fathers in intact marriages became alienated from their children due to a combination of maternal narcissism and paternal passivity.

Targeted parents who are still married to and living with the alienating parent should try as much as possible to be more actively involved in their child's life. Elaine recalled that her father did not join family activities, "If we took a ride in the car as a family he would close his eyes and rest and wouldn't really be a part of it and that stopped after a short time and he would just stay home."

Being "in the Moment"

Targeted parents should be encouraged to "be in the moment" with their child. What children remember is the feeling of the time spent together. As distracted as they might be, targeted parents should try to enjoy the time spent with their child. They will feel better afterwards. No time with one's children is unlimited; eventually children grow up. The last thing any parent wants is to feel that time with his or her child was squandered due to worrying about the future (fretting over upcoming court cases or other impending conflicts with the alienating parent), or ruing the past (reliving earlier frustrations and wounds). Doing so will result in losing the gift of the present. Being in the moment could also improve the relationship with the child. Children can sense if a parent is preoccupied and just going through the motions of being with them or whether there is genuine engagement in the relationship. Parents who are distracted by thoughts of the past or the future will convey that preoccupation to their child. This will taint the child's experience and weaken the relationship. Targeted parents need to develop a mantra that says, "This is *my* time with *my* child. All I have is right now. Right now my child is with me. I will be here now with my child." They may also need to develop inner language to help bring them back to the present when their focus shifts. Mindfulness techniques developed in Buddhism may offer a way to help targeted parents stay in the moment and enjoy the time with their child. Whitman's (2001) *Custody Chaos, Personal Peace* offers a Buddhist perspective on managing the frustrations and intense negative emotions aroused by difficult coparenting situations. Many of his suggestions apply to parental alienation syndrome, even in cases of intact families.

Not Talking the Child Out of His or Her Feelings

When a child says something that is untrue about the targeted parent, it may be tempting to respond with anger, frustration, and a desire to change the child's mind. However, like most people, children do not appreciate someone trying to change their mind or correct their thinking. Children usually find it insulting when told that they are not thinking for themselves. They experience their thoughts and feelings as their own. It may seem obvious to an observer that a child is being manipulated or brainwashed, but that is not the child's experience. Targeted parents' efforts to convince their children that they are not thinking for themselves may even backfire. That does not mean that targeted parents have to agree with everything their child is saying. They can agree to disagree. Together, targeted parents and therapists can work on strategies for dealing with the frustrations and humiliations incurred with PAS. For example, targeted parents could decide to say, "I see this situation differently from you but I do not want to spend our time together arguing about it." That way, they are "on the record" of not endorsing what the child is saying but are not trying to force the child to change his or her mind. As Warshak noted, targeted parents can "strike while the iron is cold" (2001a). At another time, when the child is not angry or agitated, targeted parents can introduce their perspective into the conversation. Of course, this technique should be used judiciously, to avoid the impression of being on a mission or having an agenda. Clawar and Rivlin also offer a compelling rationale for speaking directly about the alienating parent, "Protecting one's image and self-respect is just that—protection; and it is important for a child to have the truth" (1991, p. 35).

Holding onto Love for the Child

A particularly difficult aspect of parental alienation syndrome is not having a shared reality with one's child. Targeted parents have to learn to live with this frustration. Taking the frustration out on the child is very tempting in cases of PAS because the work of the alienating parent is insidious and virtually invisible. The child carries the message and the stance of the alienating parent inside and it is sometimes very hard to separate the child from the PAS. Targeted parents will need help in balancing their feelings of love for their child and the negativity they feel for the PAS message the child presents. In some respects it may be easier for targeted parents to devalue their child in order to be spared the pain of missing the child and yearning for a connection that is not currently possible. The impulse to depreciate the child is an understandable reaction, but it is not the message targeted parents want to convey to their child, because in doing so they would be modeling devaluation of loved ones (and, in that way, behaving like an alienating parent). The main task for the therapist is to help targeted parents hold onto their love for their child while mourning the loss of the relationship as it was or as it could have been if the other parent were not an alienator. Targeted parents should be encouraged to be consistent in their love and commitment to their child, to let their child know that they will *always* love them, be their parent, and want them in their life. This is particularly important because the alienating parent may be leading the child to believe that the targeted parent feels otherwise. However, it must be warned that there is a drawback to providing the child with unconditional love. In the short run, it is possible that the knowledge of the targeted parent's unconditional love will allow the child to be rejecting, knowing that the targeted parent will always love and forgive them, while the conditional love of the alienating parent will be more actively sought after. This is a trade-off targeted parents should be willing to make. Their child may eventually realize that the targeted parent's love, because it is unconditional, is a more valuable and meaningful love.

Reviving Positive Memories

Exit counselor Steve Hassan (1988) believed that one way to connect with a person's real self (as opposed to cult self) is by reviving positive memories. Targeted parents should be encouraged to draw on positive memories that their child has of their being together in order to reinforce the relationship and mitigate the alienation. Showing a child pictures of the two having a good time together may help the child remember that the targeted parent is not as uniformly bad and unworthy as the child is being led to believe by the alienating parent. The photographs stand as hard evidence of shared positive feelings and history. Another way to activate memories is to do things with the child that will remind him or her of these positive memories. For example, if the child and parent had a lovely time apple picking one fall, the targeted parent can arrange to do so again with the child. Fondly reminiscing about good experiences with the child (without overdoing it) can also be effective at undoing the alienation message that the targeted parent is all bad. Yet another way to activate positive memories is through the physical relationship with the child. If the targeted parent had a special way of stroking the child's head, or tickling her arm—and if the child will allow the targeted parent to perform those physical acts again—doing so may activate the memory traces of positive feelings and thoughts about the targeted parent. Hugging the child may serve the same function, because it will be likely to recall all the earlier hugs and shared loving moments between targeted parent and child. Of course, all of these physical connections can only have a positive effect if they are not forced on the child. If forced, they will create a new and negative memory of an insensitive or inappropriate parent. It is also important that the physical expressions convey "I love you" not "I'm upset, please take care of me." That is, they should be giving not clinging or grasping, which may frighten or disgust the child who does not want to feel guilty or responsible for the targeted parent's feelings.

HELPING TARGETED PARENTS
LIVE THEIR LIFE

The pain and loss of losing a child to PAS can be overwhelming and can overshadow all other aspects of a parent's life. Therefore, one task for the therapist will be to assist targeted parents in creating a meaningful life and experiencing some pleasure despite being alienated from their child. Several specific suggestions for doing so are offered below.

Managing the Shame of Being Alienated
from a Child

Another difficult aspect of PAS for targeted parents is the humiliation and embarrassment of being rejected by their child. Unless associates, friends, and family are aware of PAS they will likely conclude that the targeted parents somehow deserved the rejection of their child. This is a bitter pill. The therapist can help targeted parents understand that projection may be a factor. That is, the more targeted parents believe that the rejection was deserved, the easier it is to assume that others feel the same way. Thus, another task for the therapist is to educate targeted parents about parental alienation syndrome and to whatever extent it is possible, to normalize the situation for them. There are numerous websites, chat rooms, and discussion groups on the Internet devoted to this issue. Interacting with these groups may provide targeted parents with a community of support and the comfort of knowing that they are not alone in this painful experience.

A correlate of this problem is that targeted parents may feel tempted to try to disabuse others of the notion that the rejection by the child was deserved. Targeted parents may want to correct what they perceive to be another person's misunderstanding that the child rejected them for good reason. Because explaining the situation will most likely entail criticizing the alienating parent (i.e., saying to the person that the alienating parent turned the child against the targeted parent through a campaign of manipulation and lies) targeted parents need to be *very* careful about sharing this information. If an alienating parent discovers that the targeted parent was critical about him or her to others in the community, school, or neighborhood, then the targeted parent will rightly incur the wrath of the child and the alienating parent. Thus, targeted parents need to be discreet and develop some useful phrases that allow them to maintain pride without launching into a complicated diatribe against the alienating parent. Statements such as, "the situation is very complicated" Or "my child is really struggling right now with some personal issues" may hint to the listener that this is not a typical case of a child rejecting a "bad" parent, without risking being perceived as a person who recklessly denigrates the other parent.

Maintaining Hope

One task for the therapist is to encourage targeted parents to never give up hope. Targeted parents cannot know how much movement and work is going on under the surface of their alienated child. In fact, targeted parents may be the last to know that their child is beginning to question and rethink the alienating parent's behavior. Chapters 5, 6, and 8 may offer much-needed inspiration to parents currently targeted for alienation because the stories highlight two very important points. First, the accounts of realization in Chapters 5 and 6 demonstrate that a targeted parent can never tell when the child victim of PAS will become aware of the PAS. A seeming absence of realization does not necessarily mean that a realization will never occur. Second, no matter how rejecting the children were to their targeted parents, they did not actually want that parent to stop trying to have a relationship with them. The universal code, which they all seemed to follow, is that children can reject a parent but parents should never reject their child. Simply knowing that even the most rejecting child still wants the targeted parent to reach out may provide hope to a parent currently experiencing PAS.

Having a Meaningful Life

Another task for the therapist of targeted parents is to help them have a meaningful life while struggling with the shame, guilt, and loss due to parental alienation syndrome. At the same time, the therapist should be mindful not to suggest that they should "move on" or give up hope of having a more rewarding relationship with their alienated child. Targeted parents, however, may need "permission" to have any pleasure in their life in light of the fact that they are experiencing the trauma and pain associated with the parental alienation syndrome. Unlike typical grief situations in which there is a definitive endpoint to the trauma (i.e., death of a loved one, divorce, loss of a job, and so forth), the survivor eventually understands that after a certain point, life must resume. In parental alienation syndrome, however, there is no definitive end point. Even if the child says to the targeted parent something akin to, "Do not ever darken my doorway again," the targeted parent will (and should) continue to demonstrate love to the child (sending gifts at appropriate times, writing letters, sending e-mails and text messages, attending graduation ceremonies, inviting the child for holidays, and so forth). These points of contact, even if they are only symbolic, can keep alive in the targeted parents the hope for a reunion as well as the pain of the loss. In this way, targeted parents never progress through the stages of grief. The grief is never-ending. The only counterpoint to this is that targeted parents, too, deserve to share in life's pleasures and to not feel guilty for doing so. They need to understand that seeing a movie, enjoying the companionship of friends, sharing the love of their family does not diminish their love for the alienated child. Being "ok" in their life does not mean that they are "ok" with the alienation.

COUNTERTRANSFERENCE

Working with parents who have been targeted for parental alienation poses specific challenges for a therapist. First, these parents are experiencing a constant source of frustration and sadness in their life, which can be emotionally draining for the therapist to witness and share. The loss of a child, even if through PAS as opposed to death, is a very profound loss. The pain is keenly felt by these clients and, hence, vicariously by the therapist as well. Some therapists may want to reflexively avoid this pain and develop negative countertransferential feelings toward these clients. That is, if the therapist likes and values the clients less, the pain will be less real for the therapist.

The therapist may also find the concept of people losing their children through PAS very threatening (if it can happen to the targeted parents, it can happen to them as well). Perhaps they will devalue the targeted parents or unconsciously conclude that the targeted parents deserved the rejection in order to ward off the fear that this could happen to them. Blaming the targeted parents evens out the injustice of PAS and lessens the concern that the therapist is at risk for similarly losing his or her children.

Another complicated aspect of working with targeted parents is that these clients may be in therapy seeking solutions to the problem of PAS, rather than seeking personal growth and emotional support. To the extent that the clients wish and hope that their therapist will have a quick fix for or a magic solution to the PAS, they are bound to be perpetually frustrated with and disappointed in the therapist. This should be discussed in therapy and the clients should have the opportunity to mourn the fact that the therapist does not have an immediate and guaranteed solution to the problem. This is so because, unless the therapist is conducting couples or dyadic work he or she is at least one step removed. If the therapist is providing individual counseling to targeted parents it is unlikely he or she can directly have an impact on the child or the alienating parent. The therapist should encourage clients who are targeted parents to openly acknowledge the fantasy of the omnipotent therapist who can eradicate the PAS, and the therapist can join them in feeling the sadness and frustration. At the same time, the therapist and targeted parents can identify areas where improvements can be made (see first section of this chapter) and agree to work on them.

Acknowledgment of the fantasy that the therapist can solve the problem needs to be addressed before therapeutic work can progress. However, doing so will likely generate negative feelings in the therapist toward targeted parents who are forcing the therapist to accept the limitation of the therapeutic endeavor. It is also likely that at some point targeted parents will feel like attacking the therapist with a sentiment such as, "Why can't you just make this better?" and the therapist may resent the implication of failure or inadequacy.

Another aspect of the countertransference to bear in mind is the desire to promise more than can be delivered. Targeted parents tend to be very intense in their desire to reunite with their child and are likely to latch onto any shred of hope offered to them about how to do that. Therapists need to be careful not to offer false hope and to couch all suggestions in qualifying terms that make it clear that the therapist cannot know how changes in a targeted parent will ultimately get played out in the relationship with the child, especially because there is a third factor in all of this, the alienating parent.

The therapist should consider offering or recommending dyadic or family work in order to address the PAS family system more directly. Although targeted parents will probably continue to need the support and guidance provided by individual psychotherapy, real change in the family system may best come about through direct work with all the members of that system. This is more likely to be pursued in intact families, but it is worth exploring with all targeted parents the possibility that the alienating parent or the child will join them in family work.

SUMMARY

Therapists working with parents currently targeted for PAS can work with their clients to provide education, information, and emotional support. There are several avenues for exploration regarding the intergenerational transmission of PAS, which may prove fruitful for a client's personal growth and self-awareness. The therapist can also help targeted parents manage the shame, loss, and frustration associated with being a PAS targeted parent and can offer suggestions for engaging an alienated child. Like the therapist working with children currently affected by PAS, the therapist working with targeted parents needs to be mindful of countertransference, because it may be tempting to blame the parent as a way to avoid feelings of helplessness and vicarious traumatization.

Chapter 12

Final Thoughts

The woods are lovely, dark and deep.
But I have promises to keep,
And miles to go before I sleep
And miles to go before I sleep
—Robert Frost, *Stopping by the Woods on a Snowy Evening*

WHEN I SET OUT TO STUDY ADULT CHILDREN OF PARENTAL ALIEN-
ation I was unprepared for the intensity of the journey I was
about to embark upon. Within weeks of posting my invitation
on the Internet I was bombarded with e-mails from targeted
parents wanting to know when and how their children would
come home to them. I explained that I wanted to know the very
same thing, and that was the purpose of the study. I gently but
firmly explained that I simply did not know the answer to "the
question." I offered to include their name on a mailing list of
people to notify if and when my book would be published. The
urgency of their request and their frustration at my inability to
provide the knowledge they sought was palpable.

In planning this project I was concerned that it would be difficult to find people who were adult children of parental alienation, not because they weren't "out there" but because they
may not know who they are. The term *adult children of parental
alienation* did not exist at the time I launched the study. When I
asked on the Internet to speak to people who were turned

against one parent by the other, I was quickly inundated with requests for information by people who felt that this experience was applicable to them. In no time at all I had scheduled and completed 40 in-depth interviews.

The interviews themselves were intense experiences. The participants openly shared their stories with me, a complete stranger. Many wept during the interview, and all reported that the interview was difficult yet rewarding. The difficult part was sharing their painful and shameful experiences. The rewarding part was twofold. First, many expressed gratitude that I was interested in their experience, that I had a name for it, and that I wanted to learn what it meant to them. In addition, many appreciated the opportunity to help others like themselves who are child victims of PAS. At the end of each interview, I humbly thanked the person for sharing his or life story with me. I felt both drained from hearing about their trauma and at the same exhilarated that maybe I could play a role in helping alienated children and families. The data collected in this study, I believe, powerfully portray the experiences of individuals who were alienated from one parent due in large measure to the actions, attitudes, and behaviors of the other parent.

Like all studies, this one had its share of methodological limitations. First, a retrospective design was utilized which did not allow for a determination of causality. For example, although the participants described the outcomes of the alienation from their perspective, it cannot be known whether in fact such associations exist. In particular, many of the outcomes described (low self-esteem, lack of trust) may be due to the divorce or marital discord rather than more specifically to the alienation. Without a comparison group of adult children of divorce who did not experience parental alienation, it is not possible to determine the alienation-specific outcomes. However, to the extent that the aim was to describe and understand the participants' felt experience, the findings can be considered valid. Another limitation is that the participants varied in their age at the time of the interview. Thus, some had not had a chance yet to experience all of the possible negative outcomes. For example, a 19-year-old participant had less time to experience depression or guilt than a 60-year-old participant. In that respect, the findings may underrepresent the negative outcomes of parental alienation syndrome. Additionally, it is quite likely that there are many adults who were alienated from a parent and were not aware of the fact that they had been manipulated by their other parent. There is no way to ascertain the patterns of alienation and outcomes for these adults. And, finally, the motivations and experiences of the alienating parents were not directly assessed. The only source of data was the perceptions, beliefs, and memories of the adult children. For example, it is possible that the alienating parents suffered as well and that there may have been some justification for the negative statements made about the targeted parent.

Another important limitation is the lack of data on how PAS is experienced in other cultures and ethnic groups. With a few exceptions, the empirical work on PAS has been conducted on white, middle-class samples residing in the United States. Whether PAS is experienced at the same rate and in the same configuration in U.S. Black and Hispanic families needs to be studied. Further, in light of the existence of PAS advocacy groups throughout the Western countries (i.e., United Kingdom, Australia, and Canada) there is clearly a need to more fully document this phenomenon around the world. Important questions about how variation in familial and cultural contexts impacts the prevalence and process of PAS can only be answered with such international perspectives. The forthcoming *International Handbook on Parental Alienation* (Sauber, Lorandos, & Rand, in press) and recent work by Spruijt and colleagues are positive steps in that direction (Spruijit, Eikelenboom, Harmeling, Stokkers, & Kormos, 2005).

There are many areas in the field of PAS that urgently require empirical exploration. In particular, future research should identify the individual, family, and community level factors that help support or resist the development of the parental alienation syndrome. The ecological-transactional model of child maltreatment developed by Cicchetti and Lynch (1993; Cicchetti, 2004) offers a framework for developing and testing theory regarding the ways in which PAS occurs within children, families, and communities. In this model, "The balance among risk and protective factors and processes both determines the likelihood of maltreatment occurring and influences the course of subsequent development" (2004, p. 733).

At the individual level, there is a need for a general developmental perspective on PAS and a need for greater understanding of the child's role in the alienation. For example, in multi-sibling families do all children succumb to PAS or is there variation among the children in their degree of alienation from the targeted parent? Perhaps some children are more resistant to thought control and emotional manipulation than other children.

Cognitive level, emotional maturity, level of autonomy, and nature of self-esteem are all individual-level factors that might mediate the effectiveness of alienation strategies at different developmental points. For example, there are likely to be developmental periods when children are more susceptible to influence—especially about a parent—than other times. In infancy and toddlerhood belief systems (or in attachment theory, internal working models) about one's parents are first developed. Early research on children's cognitive development has established the ways in which cognitive schemata, such as Daddy is dangerous or Mommy is sick, once formed, are resistant to change (Ginsberg & Opper, 1969). New information, even if inconsistent with the schemata, is assimilated into and, hence, supports the existing framework rather than revises it.

Adolescence, as well, presents a likely window for influence and change, as children are able to emotionally and cognitively distance themselves from the beliefs and values of their family of origin. Children not yet alienated may become so during this stage of development for a number of reasons. First, the courts allow teens greater involvement in their own custody arrangements, a fact probably known to alienating parents who may intensify their campaign at this time. Second, as adolescents struggle to separate from their primary parent, they may be more open to the influence of the other parent, especially if that parent is willing to lure the teen with visions of enhanced autonomy and freedom (which most teens believe they want and can handle, even when that is not necessarily the case). At the same time, it is possible that teens are better able to withstand the pressure to become alienated due to stronger egos and more firmly developed boundaries between themselves and their parents. The intersection of the skills and strategies of the alienating parent and the strengths and vulnerabilities of the child needs further exploration.

As suggested above, another aspect of the child's contribution that also requires further clarification is the secondary gains—psychological and material—which accompany the alienation. Put another way, in addition to preventing the loss of the alienating parent, PAS might offer the child additional benefits. For example, it is possible that alienating parents are able to seduce the child through a system of material and psychological rewards, such as enhanced acceptance by the extended family of the alienating parent or greater freedom and autonomy (perhaps inappropriate and beyond the child's developmental capacity) as further inducement for the alienation. Understanding the full set of benefits and gains associated with PAS will be necessary for the development of effective treatment and prevention.

Within the same family, there might be variation in degree of alienation of the children. It is possible that some children are less sought after than others such that they experience a lower degree of pressure to become alienated. There might be typical father-daughter and mother-son dyads that are more prone to coalesce around PAS than other parent-child configurations. The oedipal triangle might serve as an ideal platform for PAS, especially with pre-school and adolescent children for whom acceptance by the opposite sex parent is particularly salient.

Another important within-family factor might be the role that siblings play in helping each other resist or succumb to alienation efforts. Although only one person from each family was interviewed for this book, most participants were members of sibling groups. Undoubtedly, the alienation was in some way filtered through that experience. It is plausible that in some families siblings function as surrogate alienators (alienating parent collaborators) while the not-yet-alienated child is with the targeted parent. In this scenario, the fear of losing sibling favor or being reported to the alienating parent may solidify the alienation. Alternatively, in some families the children might discuss the alienation strategies and work together to develop counter-alienation techniques. Perhaps validation of the reality of the alienation by a sibling may help a child recognize, and hence, withstand the manipulation and distortions (Iris and her brother seemed to have helped each other in this way).

Family-level belief systems might also play a role in PAS. Some families might be matriarchal with marginalized or absent fathers. In such an extended family context, it is probable that a child would become alienated from a father but not from a mother. Another scenario might be a child living in a neighborhood in which one parent's extended family also reside (such as Joanne's mother's family), lending a natural buffer to alienation from that parent or an ally in that parent's campaign to alienate the child from the other parent.

Community and cultural beliefs about the value of each parent also warrant understanding. For example, children growing up in a neighborhood where most children live in mother-headed households might be more likely to become alienated from a father than children for whom two-parent families is the community norm. Parents who ascribe to culturally-bound beliefs about parent-child relationships (e.g., children should make the effort to reach out to their parents, children must always treat their parents with respect or else they will be cut off), such as Maria's father, might be at a disadvantage in flexibly responding to a child's alienation. These cultural and community-level risk and protective factors require further elucidation and empirical investigation.

Also worthy of exploration is an empirical investigation into the relationship among the three levels of PAS (mild, moderate, and severe) and the 8 components of PAS as outlined by Gardner (1998) and described in the Introduction to this book. Currently, it is not known how much variation exists in the manifestation of these 8 components within the three levels of PAS. Such knowledge will lay the groundwork for the development of a reliable and valid PAS assessment tool, which is critically needed by child custody evaluators. Further, it is possible that the catalysts for the realization are specific to the level of alienation or degree of the 8 components. It was not possible to assess that in the current study but this is also important for the development of prevention and intervention programs.

I also believe that there are several areas for immediate improvement in the clinical and legal communities that intersect with PAS families. To begin with, children likely to be targeted for PAS need access to information and support in withstanding the pressure to collude with one parent against the other. This could come in the form of a series of books tied to the developmental level of the child that are widely available in schools and public libraries, and that teachers and school guidance counselors can use in a targeted and timely fashion. Schools and community centers could also offer support groups for children of divorced families that focus extensively on alienation strategies and techniques for coping with and responding to them. Such information could perhaps help children acknowledge the reality of their own situation and understand the importance of engaging unbiased helping adults to intervene in the family system.

Targeted parents are also in dire need of support and assistance in preventing PAS and intervening when the first signs of alienation reveal themselves. They need access to materials for children, emotional support, on-the-spot guidance, and access to PAS experts to prevent the early stages of PAS from burgeoning into full-blown alienation. Currently, too few mental health professionals are even aware of PAS let alone knowledgeable about how to intervene. Different intervention strategies should be developed and tested so that families have access to the most effective methods possible.

Therapists, too, need additional knowledge and training as well as clinical supervision and support in order to identify cases of PAS (even in the absence of familial awareness of it) and to prevent their own collusion in the alienation against the targeted parent. Ideally therapists would have access to materials to share with targeted parents and their children, as well as a roster of experts who can provide guidance for effective therapeutic interventions.

The legal system is in need of evidence of the validity of the construct of PAS and tools for developing timely and effective interventions in order to prevent alienating parents from exploiting lack of such knowledge in the service of the alienation. Professionals throughout the legal system should be educated about the existence of PAS, including mediators, lawyers, and judges. They should be aware of the common signs of PAS—as manifested in the legal context—in order to evaluate the context and meaning of a child's estrangement from a parent.

Clearly, there are many areas where continued research and clinical expertise are seriously needed. It is my sincere hope that the findings from this study will spur the development of knowledge about all of these and related issues in order to guide and inspire clinicians working with targeted parents and their children. They need—and deserve—all the help and care they can get. So let me end, where I began, with the words of an adult child of parental alienation syndrome.

PATRICIA'S STORY

Patricia, 32, was born in St. Louis, Missouri. Her parents were in their teens when they met. They dated a few years before marrying, and Patricia was born within the first year of their marriage. Patricia's parents were married during her entire childhood and her father was the alienating parent. His alienation strategies included alluding to her mother having an affair as well as ongoing denigration and ridicule of her worth and character. "He used to always put my mother down, on a daily basis. Anything good that my siblings or myself did was because 'we had the good genes from him.' Anything we did wrong was my mom's fault because she had 'a crazy insane mother and an alcoholic father, and when his alcoholic sperm met her insane egg, they made her and her crazy family.'" Patricia shared that her father was physically abusive to both her and her mother, who at one point tried to leave the marriage. "After he bruised her pretty badly, he told her that she would ruin everyone's life if she left him. She didn't leave and he stopped abusing her physically, but it turned to mental abuse for all of us."

When Patricia became a teenager her father claimed complete control over her social life, dominating her out-of-school time by overseeing her involvement in several sports, in all of which he demanded excellence from Patricia. These activities cemented Patricia to her father even further and excluded her mother completely. "I was brainwashed by him, made to feel as if he was perfect, and she was a horrible person." Patricia did not realize the extent of the alienation until she was well into her 20s and she discovered that her father had been lying to her about her mother having an affair. That opened her eyes to the fact that her father was being dishonest about other aspects of the family dynamics as well. "Finally, some things made sense. Fortunately my mother's love for me was unconditional, and she accepted me back into her life, without any questions."

Patricia was asked what her mother did to prevent or mitigate the alienation, and she responded that her mother was unaware of what was happening. Everyone in the family followed along with whatever her father said, and used to joke about "not upsetting the apple cart," or "leave a lying dog to sleep." "We did whatever we could to not upset him." It wasn't until Patricia's mother went to see a counselor, that she finally understood that she had a choice. Until then, "Her best mitigation was just picking herself up and carrying on as if everything was going to be ok." Patricia was also asked what more her mother could have done and she shared that partly she wished her mother could have received counseling earlier, "But then part of me is ok with what happened, because then I would not have my sister or brother. I just wish he could have respected her so that she did not have to suffer so much." Patricia also shared that since her parents' divorce her mother's life had become much harder. The costly and emotionally draining litigation over the younger children had taken its toll, exacerbated by the fact that Patricia's younger siblings were becoming increasingly alienated from their mother. In the end, Patricia could not say whether things would have been better if her mother had gotten a divorce earlier and, short of that, she could not think of anything else her mother could have done. She was simply grateful that she had finally come to appreciate and value her mother and was able to have an independent and loving relationship with her outside the control and manipulation of her father.

Appendix

The Sample of Interviewees

Pattern	Pseudonym	Gender	Age at interview	Age at separation	Custodial parent	Alienating parent
1	Alix	Female	30	Birth	Mother	Mother
1	Amelia	Female	41	3	Mother	Mother
3	Betty	Female	26	2	Mother	Mother
3	Bonnie	Female	28	3	Mother	Mother
1	Carrie	Female	33	3	Mother	Mother
3	Carl	Male	46	2	Mother	Mother
1	David	Male	48	5	Mother	Mother
2	Elaine	Female	51	NA	NA	Mother
2	Edward	Male	63	NA	NA	Mother
Mixed	Felicity	Female	19	1	Mother	Father
3	Frank	Male	48	NA	NA	Father
1	Gretta	Female	35	12	Mother	Mother
1	Hannah	Female	50	5	Mother	Mother
3	Ira	Male	32	Birth	Mother	Mother
3	Iris	Female	43	12	Mother	Mother
3	Jason	Male	67	NA	NA	Father
2	Joanne	Female	47	NA	NA	Mother
3	Jonah	Male	28	11	Father	Father
2	Josh	Male	43	NA	NA	Mother
1	Julia	Female	37	Birth	Mother	Mother
3	Kate	Female	21	2	Mother	Mother
2	Larissa	Female	50	NA	NA	Mother
1	Maria	Female	50	11	Mother	Mother
2	Mark	Male	39	NA	NA	Mother
3	Melinda	Female	32	2	Father	Father
1	Mitch	Male	43	5	Mother	Mother
3	Nancy	Female	60	Birth	Mother	Mother
2	Nicole	Female	19	8	Mother	Mother
3	Oliver	Male	52	8	Mother	Mother

Pattern	Pseudonym	Gender	Age at interview	Age at separation	Custodial parent	Alienating parent
2	Patricia	Female	32	NA	NA	Father
Mixed	Peter	Male	57	2	Mother	Mother
3	Renee	Female	36	2	Mother	Mother
2	Roberta	Female	44	NA	NA	Mother
3	Robin[1]	Male	39	4	Mother	Mother
1	Ron	Male	40	9	Mother	Mother
1	Sarah	Female	44	12	Mother	Mother
1	Serita	Female	30	13	Mother	Mother
2	Tracey	Female	33	NA	NA	Mother
1	Veronica	Female	40	3	Mother	Mother
1	Walter	Male	39	2	Mother	Mother

Note: [1]Robin is not a pseudonym

References

Ainsworth, M., Blehar, M., Waters, E., & Wall, S. (1978). *Patterns of attachment: A psychological study of the strange situation*. Hillsdale, NJ: Lawrence Erlbaum.

Alpert, J. (2001). No escape when the past is endless. *Psychoanalytic Psychology, 18* (4), 729–736.

Amato, P. (1994). Life-span adjustment of children to their parents' divorce. *The Future of Children, 4*, 143–164.

American Psychiatric Association. (2000). *Diagnostic and statistical manual IV-TR*. Washington, DC: Author.

American Psychological Association. (2001). *Publication manual (5th ed.)*. Washington, DC: Author.

Baker, A. J. L. (2006). The power of stories/stories about power: Why therapists and clients should read stories about the parental alienation syndrome. *American Journal of Family Therapy, 34*(3), 191–204.

Baker, A. J. L., Curtis, P., & Papa-Lentini, C. (in press). Sexual abuse histories of youth in child welfare residential treatment centers: Analysis of the Odyssey project population. *Journal of Child Sexual Abuse*.

Baker, A. J. L., & Darnall, D. (2006). Behaviors and strategies employed in parental alienation: A survey of parental experiences. *Journal of Divorce and Remarriage, 45*, 97–124.

Benjamin, J. (1988). *The bonds of love: Psychoanalysis, feminism, and the problem of domination*. New York: Pantheon.

Berg, B. L. (2003). *Qualitative research methods for the social sciences*. Boston: Allyn & Bacon.

Bettleheim, B. (1975). *Uses of enchantment*. New York: Knopf.

Boszormenyi, N. I., & Spark, G. (1983). *Invisible loyalties*. New York: Bruner/Mazel.

Bowlby, J. (1969). *Attachment*. New York: Basic Books.

Bowlby, J. (1980). *Loss*. New York: Basic Books.

Bretherton, I. (1985). Attachment theory retrospect and prospect. *Monographs of the Society for Research in Child Development, 50*(1–2), 3–35.

Bretherton, I., Ridgeway, D., & Cassidy. J. (1990). Assessing internal working models of the attachment relationship. In M. Greenberg, D. Cicchetti, &

E. M. Cummings (Eds.), *Attachment in the preschool years* (pp. 273–310). Chicago: University of Chicago Press.

Brett, D. (1986). *Annie stories*. New York: Workman Press.

Burns, G. (2001). *101 healing stories: Using metaphors in therapy*. New York: Wiley.

Cartwright, G. F. (1993). Expanding the parameters of parental alienation syndrome. *American Journal of Family Therapy, 21* (3), 205–215.

Chassin, L. Pitts, S. C., DeLucia, C., & Todd, M. (1999). A longitudinal study of children of alcoholics: Predicting young adult substance use disorders, anxiety, and depression. *Journal of Abnormal Psychology, 108* (1), 106–119.

Cicchetti, D. (2004). An odyssey of discovery: Lessons learned through three decades of research on child maltreatment. *American Psychologist, 59* (8), 731–741.

Cicchetti, D., Cummings, E. M., Greenberg, M. T., & Marvin, R. (1990). An organizational perspective on attachment beyond infancy: Implications for theory, measurement, and research. In M. T. Greenberg, D., Cicchetti, & E. M. Cummings (Eds.), *Attachment in the preschool years: Theory, research and intervention* (pp. 3–50). Chicago: University of Chicago Press.

Cicchetti, D., & Lynch, M. (1993). Toward an ecological/transactional model of community violence and child maltreatment: Consequences for children's development. *Psychiatry, 56,* 96–118.

Clark, D., Giambalvo, C., Giambalvo, N., Garvey, K., & Langone, M. (1993). Exit counseling: A practical overview. In M. Langone (Ed.), *Recovery from cults* (pp. 155–180). New York: W.W. Norton.

Clawar, S., & Rivlin, B. V. (1991). *Children held hostage*. Chicago: American Bar Association.

Cloitre, M., Koenen, K., Cohen, L. R., & Han, H. (2002). Skills training in affective and interpersonal regulation followed by exposure: A phase-based treatment for PTSD related to childhood abuse. *Journal of Consulting and Clinical Psychology, 70* (5), 1067–1074.

Courtois, C. A. (2004). Complex trauma, complex reactions: Assessment and treatment. *Psychotherapy: Theory, Research, Practice, Training, 41* (4), 412–425.

Darnall, D. (1998). *Divorce casualties: Protecting your children from parental alienation*. Dallas, TX: Taylor.

David, B. Y., Hops, H., Alpert, A., & Sheeber, L. (1998). Child responses to parental conflict and their effect on adjustment: A study of triadic relations. *Journal of Family Psychology, 12* (2), 163–177.

Donaldson-Pressman, S., & Pressman, R. (1994). *The narcissistic family: Diagnosis and treatment*. New York: Lexington Books.

Ellis, E. M. (2005). Help for the alienated parent. *American Journal of Family Therapy, 33,* 415–426.

Erikson, E. (1964). *Childhood and society*. New York: W.W. Norton.

Fairbairn, R. W. (1952). *Psychoanalytic studies of the personality*. London: Routledge.

Festinger, L. (1957). *Theory of cognitive dissonance*. Stanford, CA: Stanford University Press.

Forward, S. (1997). *Emotional blackmail*. New York: Quill.

Frankl, V. (1959). *Man's search for meaning*. Boston: Beacon Press.

Freud, A. (1966). *The ego and the mechanisms of defense*. New York: International Universities Press. (Original work published 1936)

Freud, S. (1955). Beyond the pleasure principle. In J. Strachey (Ed. & Trans.), *The standard edition of the complete psychological works of Sigmund Freud* (Vol. 18, pp. 1–64). London: Hogarth Press. (Original work published 1920)

Freud, S. (1961). Civilization and its discontents. In J. Strachey (Ed. & Trans.), *The standard edition of the complete psychological works of Sigmund Freud* (Vol. 21, pp. 57–145). London: Hogarth Press. (Original work published 1930)

Garbarino, J., Guttman, E., & Seeley, J. W. (1986). *The psychologically battered child*. San Francisco: Jossey-Bass.

Garber, B. (2004). Therapist alienation: Foreseeing and forestalling third-party dynamics undermining psychotherapy with children of conflicted caregivers. *Professional Psychology: Research and Practice, 35* (4), 357–363.

Gardner, R. A. (1984). *The boys and girls book about divorce*. Northvale, NJ: Jason Aronson.

Gardner, R. A. (1991). *The parents book about divorce*. Cresskill, NJ: Creative Therapeutics.

Gardner, R. A. (1993). *Psychotherapy with children*. Northvale, NJ: Jason Aronson.

Gardner, R. A. (1998). *The parental alienation syndrome: A guide for mental health and legal professionals*. Cresskill, NJ: Creative Therapeutics.

Garrity, C., & Baris, M. A. (1994). *Caught in the middle: Protecting the children from high conflict divorce*. New York: Lexington Books.

Giambalvo, C. (1993). Post-cult problems: An exit counselor's perspective. In M. Langone (Ed.), *Recovery from cults* (pp. 148–154). New York: W.W. Norton.

Giannini, A. J. (2001). Use of fiction in therapy. *Psychiatric Times, 18*(7), np.

Ginsberg, H., & Opper, S. (1969). *Piaget's theory of intellectual development*. New York: Prentice Hall.

Gold, S. (1997). Training professional psychologists to treat survivors of childhood sexual abuse. *Psychotherapy, 34* (4), 365–375.

Goldberg, L. (1997). A psychoanalytic look at recovered memories, therapists, cult leaders, and undue influence. *Clinical Social Work Journal, 25* (1), 71–86.

Goldberg, L., & Goldberg, W. (1982). Group work with former cultists. *Social Work, 27*, 165–170.

Goldberg, L., & Goldberg, W. (1988). Psychotherapy with ex-cultists: Four case studies and commentary. *Cultic Studies Journal 52* (2), 93–210.

Goldsmith, J. (1982). The post-divorce family system. In F. Walsh (Ed.), *Normal family processes* (pp. 297–330). New York: Guilford Press.

Goleman, D. (1985). *Vital lies, simple truths*. New York: Simon & Schuster.

Golomb, E. (1992). *Trapped in the mirror*. New York: William Morrow.

Greenberg, J. R., & Mitchell, S. A. (1983). *Object relations in psychoanalytic theory*. Cambridge, MA: Harvard University Press.

Hamarman, S., & Bernet, W. (2000). Evaluating and reporting emotional abuse of children. *Journal of the American Academy of Child and Adolescent Psychiatry, 39* (7), 928–930.

Hassan, S. (1988). *Combating cult mind control*. Rochester, VT: Park Street Press.

Herman, J. (1992). *Trauma and recovery*. New York: Basic Books.

Hotchkiss, S. (2002). *Why is it always about you?* New York: Free Press.

Howes, P. W, Cicchetti, D., Toth, S., & Rogosch, F. A. (2000). Affective, organizational, and relational characteristics of maltreating families: A systems perspective. *Journal of Family Psychology, 14* (1), 95–110.

Inglis, R. (1978). *Sins of the fathers*. New York: St. Martin's Press.

Jacobvitz, J., & Bush, N.F. (1996). Reconstructions of family relationships: Parent-child alliances, personal distress, and self-esteem. *Developmental Psychology, 32* (4), 732–743.

Johnston, J. (2003). Parental alignments and rejection: An empirical study of alienation in children in divorce. *Journal of the American Academy of Psychiatry & the Law, 31*, 158–170.

Johnston, J. R. (1994). High conflict divorce. *Future of Children, 4* (1), 165–182.

Johnston, J. R., & Kelly, J. B. (2004). Rejoinder to Gardner's "Commentary on Kelly and Johnston's 'The alienated child: A reformulation of parental alienation syndrome.'" *Family Court Review, 42* (4), 622–628.

Kelly, J. B., & Johnston, J. R. (2001). The alienated child: A reformulation of parental alienation syndrome. *Family Court Review, 39* (3), 249–266.

Kent, S. A. (2004). Generational revolt by the adult children of first-generation members of the children of God/family. *Cultic Studies Review, 3* (1), np.

Kernberg, O. (1975). *Borderline conditions and psychological narcissism*. Northvale, NJ: Jason Aronson.

Kübler-Ross, E. (1997). *On death and dying*. New York: Scribner.

Kvale, S. (1996). *InterViews: An introduction to qualitative research interviewing*. Thousand Oaks, CA: Sage.

Langone, M. (1993). Introduction. In M. Langone (Ed.), *Recovery from cults* (pp. 1–21). New York: W.W. Norton.

Langone, M. (2004). The definitional ambiguity of the "cult" and AFF's mission. Available at http://www.cultinfobooks.com/infoserve_aff/aff_term defambiguity.htm.

Lawrence, D. H. (1991). *Sons and lovers*. Everyman's Library Edition. New York: Alfred A. Knopf. (Original work published 1913)

Layton, D. (1998). *Seductive poison*. New York: Doubleday.

Lifton, R. J. (1969). *Thought reform and the psychology of totalism*. New York: W. W. Norton.

Loring, M. T. (1994). *Emotional abuse*. San Francisco: Jossey-Bass.

Maccoby, E., & Martin, J. A. (1983). Socialization in the context of the family: Parent–child interaction. In P. H. Mussen & E. M. Hetherington (Eds.),

Handbook of child psychology: Vol. 4. Socialization, personality, and social development (4th ed., pp. 1–101). New York: Wiley.

Maccoby, E., Mnookin, R. H., Depner, C. E., & Peters, E. H. (1992). *Dividing the child: Social and legal dilemmas of custody.* Cambridge, MA: Harvard University Press.

Main, M., Kaplan, N., & Cassidy, J. (1985). Security in infancy, childhood and adulthood: A move to the level of representation. *Monographs of the Society for Research in Child Development, 50* (1–2), 66–104.

Masterson, J. F. (1981). *The narcissistic and borderline disorders.* New York: Brunner/Mazal Publishers.

Merton, R. K. (1968). *Social theory and social structure.* New York: Free Press.

McKibben, J. A., Lynn, S. J., & Malinoski, P. (2002). Are cultic environments psychologically harmful? *Cultic Studies Review, 1* (3), np.

Miller, A. (1988). *Thou shall not be aware: Society's betrayal of children.* New York: Farrar, Straus & Giroux.

Minuchin, S. (1974). *Families and family therapy.* Cambridge, MA: Harvard University Press.

Minuchin, S. (1993). *Family healing: Strategies for hope and understanding.* New York: Touchstone.

Muster, N. J. (2004). Authoritarian culture and child abuse in ISKCON. *Cultic Studies Review, 3* (1), np.

National Clearinghouse on Child Abuse and Neglect. (2003). *Substance abuse and maltreatment.* Washington, DC: Author.

Ofshe, R. J. (1992). Coercive persuasion and attitude change. In E. F. Borgatta (Ed.), *Encyclopedia of Sociology* (Vol. 1, pp. 212–224). New York: Macmillan.

Opperman, J. (2004). What to do when your parent stops seeing you as mom or dad. *The Children's Voice, Summer,* np.

Peck, M. (1983). *The people of the lie.* New York: Simon and Schuster.

Pennebaker, J. W., Colder, M., & Sharp, L. K. (1990) Accelerating the coping process. *Journal of Personality and Social Psychology, 58* (3), 528–537.

Perls, F. (1969). *Gestalt therapy verbatim.* Highland, NY: Gestalt Journal Press.

Rand, D. C. (1997a). The spectrum of parental alienation syndrome, Part I. *American Journal of Forensic Psychology, 15* (3), 23–52.

Rand, D. C. (1997b). The spectrum of parental alienation syndrome, Part II. *American Journal of Forensic Psychology, 15* (4), 39–92.

Rand, D. C., Rand, R., & Kopetski, L. (2005). The spectrum of parental alienation syndrome, Part III: The Kopetski follow-up study. *American Journal of Forensic Psychology, 23* (1), 15–43.

Riordan, R. J., Mullis, F., & Nuchow, L. (1996). Organizing for bibliotherapy: The science of the art. *Individual Psychology, 52* (2), 169–180.

Rohner, R. P. (2004). The parental acceptance–rejection syndrome: Universal correlates of perceived rejection. *American Psychologist, 59,* 830–840.

Ryan, P. L. (1993). Eastern meditation group. In M. Langone (Ed.), *Recovery from cults* (pp. 129–147). New York: W.W. Norton.

Satir, V. (1967). *Conjoint family therapy.* Palo Alto, CA: Science & Behavior Books.

Sauber, S. R., Lorandos, D., & Rand, D. (in press). International handbook on parental alienation syndrome. Springfield, IL: Charles C. Thomas.

Sedlack, A., & Broadhurst, D. D. (1996). *Third national incidence study of child abuse and neglect.* Washington, DC: U.S. Department of Health and Human Services. (Administration for Children and Families, Administration on Children, Youth and Families, National Center on Child Abuse and Neglect)

Shaw, D. (2003). Traumatic abuse in cults: A psychoanalytic perspective. *Cultic Studies Review, 2* (2), 101–129.

Siegel, J. C., & Langford, J. S. (1998). MMPI-2 validity scales and suspected parental alienation syndrome. *American Journal of Forensic Psychology, 16* (4), 5–14.

Singer, M. (1966). *Cults in our midst.* New York: Jossey-Bass.

Skinner, B. F. (1938). *The behavior of organisms.* New York: Appleton Press.

Smullens, S. (2002). *Setting yourself free.* Far Hills, NJ: New Horizon Press.

Spruijit, E., Eikelenboom, B., Harmeling, J., Stokkers, R., & Kormos, H. (2005). Parental alienation syndrome (PAS) in the Netherlands. *American Journal of Family Therapy, 33* (4), 303–318.

Steinberg, L., Mounts, N. S., Lamborn, S. D., & Dornbusch, S. M. (1991). Authoritative parenting and adolescent adjustment across varied ecological niches. *Journal of Research on Adolescence, 1* (1), 19–36.

Straus, A. L. (1987). *Qualitative analysis for social scientists.* New York: Cambridge University Press.

Teachman, J. S., & Paasch, K. (1994). Financial impact of divorce on children and their families. *The Future or Children, 4,* 44–62.

Thompson, R. (2000). The legacy of early attachments. *Child Development, 71* (1), 145–152.

Tobias, M., & Lalich, J. (1994). *Captive minds, captive hearts.* Alameda, CA: Hunter House.

Trull, T. Waudby, C. J., & Sher, K. J. (2004). Alcohol, tobacco, and drug use disorders and personality disorder symptoms. *Experimental & Clinical Psychopharmacology, 12* (1), 65–75.

Turkat, I. (2002). Parental alienation syndrome: A review of critical issues. *Journal of the American Academy of Matrimonial Lawyers, 13,* 131–176.

van der Kolk, B. A. (1994). The body keeps scores: Memory and the emerging psychobiology of posttraumatic stress. *Harvard Review of Psychiatry, 1,* 253–265.

van der Kolk, B. A. (1996). The complexity of adaptation to trauma: Self regulation, stimulus, discrimination, and characterological development. In B. A. van der Kolk, A. C. MacFarlane, & L. Weisaeth (Eds.), *Traumatic stress: The effects of overwhelming experience on mind, body, and society* (pp. 182–213). New York: Guilford Press.

van der Kolk, B. A., & Fisler, R. (1995). Dissociation and the fragmentary nature of traumatic memories: Overview and exploratory study. *Journal of Traumatic Stress, 8,* 505–525.

van der Kolk, B. A., van der Hart, O., Marmer, C. R. (1996). Dissociation and information processing in posttraumatic stress disorder. In B. A. van der Kolk, A. C. MacFarlane, & L. Weisaeth (Eds.), *Traumatic stress: The effects of overwhelming experience on mind, body, and society* (pp. 303–327). New York: Guilford Press.

Vassiliou, D., & Cartwright, G. (2001). The lost parents' perspective on parental alienation syndrome. *American Journal of Family Therapy, 29*, 181–191.

Waldron, K. H, & Joanis, D. E. (1996). Understanding and collaboratively treating parental alienation syndrome. *American Journal of Family Law, 10*, 121–33.

Wallerstein, J., & Blakeslee, S. (1996). *Second chances: Men, women, and children a decade after divorce.* New York: Mariner Books.

Wallerstein, J., Lewis, J., Blakeslee, S. (2001). *The unexpected legacy of divorce: The 25-year landmark study.* New York: Hyperion.

Warshak, R. (2001a) *Divorce poison.* New York: Regan Books.

Warshak, R. (2001b) Current controversies regarding the parental alienation syndrome. *American Journal of Forensic Psychology, 19* (3), 29–59.

Weitzman, J. (2004). Use of the one-way mirror in child custody reunification cases. *Journal of Child Custody, 1* (3), 27–48.

Weldon, M. (1999). *I closed my eyes.* Center City, MN: Hazeldon Press.

West, L. J., & Langone, M. (1986). Cultism: A conference for scholars and policy makers. *Cultic Studies Journal, 3* (1), 117–134.

Whittman, J. (2001). *Custody chaos, personal peace: Sharing custody with an ex who's driving you crazy.* New York: Perigee Books.

Winnicott, D. W. (1960). *Maturational processes and the facilitating environment.* New York: International Universities Press.

Wotitz, J. (1990). *Adult children of alcoholics.* Deerfield Beach, FL: Health Communications, Inc.

Zimbardo, P., & Anderson, S. (1993). Understanding mind control: Exotic and mundane mental manipulations. In M. Langone (Ed.), *Recovery from cults* (pp. 104–125). New York: W.W. Norton.

Index